D1030347

THE SWEATED TRADES

Outwork In Nineteenth-century Britain

For
DAVID and ALISON

who will grow up in a world where,
I hope, outworkers do not exist

THE SWEATED TRADES

Outwork in Nineteenth-century Britain

DUNCAN BYTHELL

Department of Economic History
University of Durham

BATSFORD ACADEMIC
LONDON

First published 1978
© Duncan Bythell 1978
ISBN 0 7134 1259 3

Printed and bound in
Great Britain by
Billing & Son Ltd
Guildford and Worcester
for the publishers
B. T. Batsford Ltd
4 Fitzhardinge Street
London W1H 0AH

Contents

Preface

Readers of this book are entitled to two words of apology. First, although it has grown laboriously and in piecemeal fashion over a period of nearly ten years, it can claim to be no more than a superficial introduction to a large and complex, but rather neglected, subject. I am well aware that, as a synthesis, it rests largely on printed and secondary sources, and that it is heavily dependent on the writings of other scholars, both past and present; accordingly, I shall be quite happy if, in due course, its shortcomings, rather than its merits, stimulate others to dig deep into local archives in order to explore the many interesting and important areas where I have merely scratched the surface.

Second, although the title refers to 'Britain', the reader will find few references to outwork and outworkers in Scotland, Wales, or Ireland: limitations of time and space have prevented me from expanding my study to deal adequately with the rather special problems of the outworkers in these countries, with the result that – apart from the occasional glance outside – the book concentrates very definitely on England.

The ideas in this book have been gradually modified and developed over the years as a result of conversations with friends, colleagues, and pupils who have now become too numerous to mention. But in revising the completed typescript more recently, I have been especially grateful for the helpful criticisms provided by two of my Durham colleagues, Richard Britnell and Martin Daunton, and by my friends Michael Rose and Gordon Phillips, of the Universities of Manchester and Lancaster, respectively. All four of them kindly read my original draft in its entirety, and offered many useful comments: they are in no way to blame for the faults which remain.

For their help in transforming typescript into print, it is a pleasure to thank: Professor G. E. Mingay, the series editor, and John Day, of B. T. Batsford Ltd; Christopher Foster, who assisted in making the index; and Elizabeth Rainey and Robert Ryder, who greatly lightened the burden of proof-reading.

Finally, I am indebted to the University of Durham for a term of sabbatical leave and for a grant from its research fund: without these, the task of collecting the materials which have gone into this book would have been even more protracted.

Duncan Bythell
Department of Economic History
University of Durham

— *Introduction* —
Definitions and Difficulties

We are periodically reminded that the Victorians believed in a 'gospel of hard work' and that they expected this message to be acted upon with zeal by all who were under the unfortunate obligation of having to sell their labour for a wage in order to make a living.[1] According to Samuel Smiles, the chief evangelist of this gospel, 'Labour is not only a necessity, but it is also a pleasure'; and he went on to quote without disapproval the words of another evangelist, St Paul, – 'He that will not work, neither shall he eat'. The corollary of such a belief was, or at any rate ought to have been, the notion that an individual's hard work would bring him a certain minimum of material comfort and an infinite amount of non-material satisfaction: as Charles Booth put it, 'where there is industry there ought to be no poverty'; or as Smiles himself said, 'industry enables the poorest man to achieve honour, if not distinction'.[2] Yet even the industrious among Victorian wage-earners were often poverty-stricken. Why was this? Smiles had a ready answer: material comfort could only be permanently guaranteed if the industrious man also took precautions against future misfortune by saving something from his present income – 'if some can do this, all may do it under similar circumstances, without depriving themselves of any genuine pleasure or any real enjoyment'.[3] There was thus a simple explanation for what Booth called 'the anomalous combination of poverty and industry': 'Habitual improvidence', thundered Smiles, 'is the real cause of the social degradation of the artisan. This too is the prolific source of social misery. But the misery is entirely the result of human ignorance and self-indulgence . . .'[4] In other words, every individual had the keys to both prosperity and penury in his own hands. From such a belief, one final conclusion followed: 'everything that is wrong in Society results from that which is wrong in the individual'.[5]

Needless to say, this reassuringly simple view of contemporary problems raised more than passing doubts in the minds of some Victorian social observers, for it contradicted the evidence of their

9

eyes. Some of them came to appreciate that whole groups in society *could* be at once poor and hard-working, without being obviously intemperate, ignorant, or self-indulgent; and they learned that, for many wage-earners, protracted bouts of overworking – which served to produce a mere pittance out of which saving was impossible – alternated with long spells when employment and income were almost impossible to come by. Among others, Friedrich Engels found this to be the case with the cotton handloom weavers of Lancashire in the 1840s:

> They consider themselves fortunate if on the average they can earn between 6s and 7s a week for fourteen to eighteen hours a day spent behind the loom . . . I have visited many of these weavers' workshops, which are usually in cellars, situated down obscure, foul courts and alleys . . . They live almost entirely upon potatoes, supplemented perhaps with a little porridge. They seldom drink milk, and they hardly ever eat meat . . . These poor wretches are the first to be thrown out of work when there is a commercial crisis, and last to be taken on again when trade improves.[6]

Similarly, Henry Mayhew recounted numerous instances of industry and sobriety still accompanied by destitution in the letters on the trades of London which he wrote for the *Morning Chronicle* in 1849-50. His description of one waistcoat-maker whom he visited provides a typically horrifying specimen:

> Everything in the place evinced the greatest order and clean-liness. Nor was the suffering self-evident. On the contrary, a stranger, at first sight, would have believed the occupant to have been rather well-to-do in the world . . . [Yet] her story was the most pathetic of all I had yet heard:

> 'I work for a slop house – waistcoat work', she said. 'The general price for the waistcoats I have now is 6d, 8d, and 10d. I can make one a day sometimes, and sometimes three in two days, just as it happens, for my health is very bad . . . I must work very close from about nine in the morning to eleven at night to earn that. Prices have come down very much indeed since I first worked for the warehouse – *very much*. The prices when I was first employed there were as much as 1s 9d for what I now get

1s 1d for . . . I find it very difficult to get sufficient to nourish me out of my work . . . I generally average about 3s [a week]'.[7]

Later Victorians continued to be reminded that many who were 'morally' worthy still did not secure a fair day's pay for a hard day's work, and they were driven to conclude that some general failure in social and economic organization must be at least partly to blame. They began to employ the useful term 'sweating' to describe this phenomenon, and a large number of different industries came to be lumped together as 'the sweated trades'. In these trades, according to Charles Booth, were to be found 'overcrowding, irregular hours, low pay; periods of terrible strain, overtaxing the powers and exhausting the vital forces; periods of slack employment or absolute want of work, discouraging and slowly undermining the persistent energies and bread-winning determination of the worker not possessed of heroic elevation of character'.[8] And this – it must be stressed – was not the experience simply of a few feckless or unfortunate individuals: it was the common lot of tens of thousands of workers.

This pattern of unremitting but ill-rewarded toil followed by unemployment and total destitution was particularly marked where wage-earners still worked at home in 'domestic' workshops. Throughout the nineteenth century, observers of the industrial worker's condition and prospects usually found their most heart-rending examples among the survivors of the once-typical 'out-workers' of the 'cottage industries' whom men like Engels idealized when they looked back to England's immediately pre-industrial past.[9] Handloom weavers, framework knitters, nailers, needle-women, cobblers, and matchbox-makers – these were, *par excellence*, the groups of workers for whom life had apparently resolved itself into two grim alternatives: sweat, or starve.

The fate of such workers – rightly regarded as the principal casualties of a century of industrial 'progress' carried through by the largely unrestrained workings of a competitive, capitalist, market economy – attracted the intermittent attention of contemporaries, and still receives a perfunctory mention in textbooks of economic history. Yet many aspects of their story are still unexplored, and even its broad significance is often misunderstood. Why did such workers survive so long into the nineteenth century? Why were they so poor? What did they try to do about their lot? Could

society at large have done more to help them in their plight? Why
did they eventually disappear when they did? These are among the
problems which this book seeks to explore, and for which it will try
to suggest tentative answers.

Definitions

Our first problem must be the deceptively simple one of defining
exactly what types of industry and what forms of industrial
organization we will be considering.

In the older textbooks of economic history, the various forms of
industrial organization for the production of goods (especially consumer goods) for the market are often reduced to two contrasting
types, one labelled 'the domestic system', and the other 'the factory
system'; and the displacement of the former by the latter is usually
held out as one of the principal features of the experience called
'the industrial revolution'.[10] Most historians admit that the transformation was completed only slowly, but most give the impression
that the triumph of the 'factory system' was 'inevitable' after the
great crop of inventions in the late eighteenth century which
'revolutionized' textiles, metallurgy, and energy utilization. Yet in
spite of the simplicity of this broad overview, our whole concept of
what the older 'domestic system' of industry actually involved is
often uncertain and ambiguous.

This confusion arises because historians employ a variety of other
terms – the most common being 'the outwork system' or 'the
putting-out system' – as if they were synonymous with it. Undoubtedly, the 'domestic system' has been a picturesque concept for
generations of students and teachers because it suggests vividly the
physical environment in which work was done: it conjures up
visions of contented craftsmen, cheerfully carving cuckoo clocks in
the comfort of their kitchens. Unfortunately, it fails to indicate at
whose behest or for whose use the work was being done. Thus
work done at home purely for family or household use – the
knitting of stockings, the running-up of shirts and dresses, and the
making of shoes or even furniture – can obviously be said to be
done 'domestically'. We know, of course, that in poor agrarian
economies with large subsistence sectors many manufactured goods
are made in this way. However, we are not here concerned with
such an economy, but with Britain during the period when she

became the world's wealthiest society, when she devoted herself increasingly to the production of manufactured goods (many of them designed for international markets), and when the scale and form of her industrial organization were being transformed dramatically by important changes in technology. Yet paradoxically, for much of this period of industrialization in the nineteenth century, many processes of industrial production continued to be carried on in essentially domestic circumstances in garrets, cellars, and bedrooms. This remarkably persistent type of organization, far from being confined to some subsistence sector, remained an integral part of the large-scale manufacturing, under the auspices of private capitalists, of many goods destined for mass markets at home and abroad.

The term 'the outwork (or putting-out) system' – although in A. P. Usher's words it is 'neither euphonious nor elegant' – carries these further connotations in a way which 'the domestic system' does not, and will consequently be used in this study.[11] For it reminds us that much of the work done domestically was first 'put-out' by capitalists from their central workshops and warehouses to be completed by dispersed workers, and afterwards 'taken-in' by the same capitalists, who were then responsible for marketing the finished product. The capitalist, in other words, owned the materials in the make, and the worker supplied the labour and received a wage in return. Sir John Clapham regarded outwork of this kind as 'still the predominant form' of industrial organization in the 1820s: in the basic textile processes of spinning and weaving, in the making of clothes, shoes and knitwear, and in several miscellaneous manufactures including metal trades like nail- and chain-making, capitalist outwork was the norm, and was to survive in some cases until the end of the nineteenth century.[12]

Even the term 'outwork' is open to objection, and its indiscriminate use can lead to confusion. It may be true that not all domestic work was outwork, but it is equally true that not all outwork was done under domestic conditions. For the notion of outwork in a capitalist economy can easily be stretched to cover any work done under subcontract agreements. Such systems, whereby a major job of work is undertaken by a chief contractor, who then sublets part of it to any number of others on such terms as are mutually agreeable were, and still are, common not only in consumer goods industries, but also in the making of large and complex producers' goods which rely on highly sophisticated technology, and in building and construction. Subcontractors can vary enormously in the scale of their operations, and in the circumstances under which they work: some operate in large factories and workshops and employ hundreds of workmen, whereas others carry on in purely domestic surroundings. In a sense, the individual outworker is the smallest of subcontractors, and 'outwork' and 'subcontract' are merely points on a continuum. The boundaries between small-scale subcontracting and outwork are especially indefinite in the case of the metal trades of Birmingham and Sheffield – which are (perhaps arbitrarily) largely excluded from this study – and in the case of clothing, which is included. Perhaps the chief differences between the subcontractor and the true outworker are to be found in the former's greater economic independence of the persons from whom he takes work, in his more substantial fixed capital, and in his propensity to be an employer of labour in his own right.

The unclear distinction between subcontract and outwork serves as a reminder that not all small units of production were necessarily domestic in environment, or co-extensive with the family. The fact is that much unsophisticated outwork, which produced simple goods by uncomplicated processes and used inexpensive and primitive tools, was well suited to a variety of sizes of units, of which the household was only one. The master weaver, with his journeymen and apprentices, as well as the sweater in his tailor's den, was involved in outwork just as much as a starving seamstress in her garret, or the Irish weaver in his cellar. Outwork could, therefore, be done in various forms of 'small workshop', and not just in genuinely domestic surroundings.

Not all small workshop manufacture was necessarily either outwork or subcontract, however, and here yet another complication arises. In the towns of nineteenth-century England there was a vast array of small, self-employed producers of a wide range of goods and services for an essentially captive clientele of local customers. Enjoying, especially in the pre-railway age, a large measure of protection by distance from the competition of their more enterprising fellows in the big industrial centres, these artisans and handicraftsmen carried on their business in small workshops or domestic workplaces using old skills and simple tools, and they only gradually lost their monopoly of local custom in the second half of the nineteenth century, as better transport and new retailing and marketing methods came to affect the home market. In life-style and outlook, these self-employed craftsmen and small masters may appear to have much in common with the outworkers; the essential difference, however, lay in the fact that outworkers were producing at the behest of capitalists for a mass market, not for individual customers in a highly localized one.

One additional complication needs to be considered. It is customary to talk of outwork or domestic *industries*, but it would be more accurate to speak of the outwork or domestic *processes*. For within the various stages in the production of a finished article by a particular firm at any given moment of time, some processes might be done centrally under factory or large workshop conditions, whilst others were done domestically under the outwork system. The essential point is that, within a given industry, there was no necessary antithesis between outwork and factory systems; the two could, and did, co-exist for long periods, complementing one another in perfect harmony.

Indeed, the problem of the co-existence of different forms of organization within the same industry goes beyond this. Even where no part or process in an industry had yet passed into factory conditions, it was still very possible at the same date to find all the different forms of organization - small subcontracting, genuine outwork, independent handicraft, and subsistence production for household use - co-existing in the making of particular goods. In the manufacture of any of the items of clothing considered in this study, and even in the basic textile manufactures, specimens of each type might be found in the nineteenth century. None of the industries considered here was carried on *exclusively* under the outwork system, and the only justification for treating these in-dustries as a group is that, in the early part of the century at any rate, they relied heavily on outwork, and that this 'system' was chiefly responsible for the *mass*-production of a particular good. Within each industry, the proportion of the total product which was made under outwork conditions changed over time, and these changes did not necessarily involve a diminishing share: as Clapham said of the 'early railway age', although outwork was 'losing ground on one side to great works and factories, it was always gaining on the other at the expense of household production and handicraft'.[13]

What then, were the distinguishing features of industrial out-work, which was so widespread in so many industries during the nineteenth century? For us to describe an industry as an outwork industry, it would seem that the following criteria have to be satisfied:

1 The basic unit of production in one or more of the key processes was often co-extensive with a domestic household, and the workers in that unit were, as a rule, members of the conjugal family.
2 The goods made, or the processes undertaken, in the domestic workshop were normally of small value individually, and the skills and equipment used in making or performing them were usually simple.
3 The objects which were wholly or partly made under these circumstances were consumer goods destined for the mass market, and the supplying of this market was almost invariably in the hands of large capitalists. The workers did not produce on their own account or make direct for customers, but were strictly wage labourers earning a piece-rate for work done on materials which belonged to these capitalists.

At the beginning of the nineteenth century, it is clear that several industries were to a large extent organized on these lines: the spinning and weaving of basic textiles, much of the manufacture of personal consumer goods such as clothes, boots, and stockings, and the making of certain common items of hardware, of which nails were the most important. Taken as a group, they can be called the 'outwork industries', for their common features presented many common problems to those involved in them – problems, that is, both for the entrepreneurs who tried to make the system viable as a form of industrial organization, and also for the workers to whom this kind of work implied a distinctive way of life. Taken as a group, these industries also present certain common difficulties of methodology and approach to the historian. Both these problems now demand consideration.

The sheer number of the outwork industries listed above suggests that the 'system' was hardly likely to be some rigid monolith. Indeed, A. P. Usher was at pains to stress that it was

. . . highly elastic . . . the variety of detail possible in this system enables us to appreciate clearly all the phases of the long transition from craftwork to the factory, and the minuteness of the changes affords interesting illustrations of the continuity of industrial development.[14]

Subsequent chapters will show just how diverse some of these variants could be: but before examining the wide range of diversity, it is perhaps desirable first to establish an 'ideal type' of outwork. By referring back to this ideal, the reader should more readily appreciate the special features which the 'system' actually developed in any particular industry.

A simple description provides the best starting-point. In the eighteenth century, outwork formed the basis for England's principal manufacturing industry - woollen textiles: and Daniel Defoe's famous account of its organization in the West Country at the beginning of the century offers a succinct statement of the salient features:

> . . . [the] towns are interspersed with a very great number of villages, . . . hamlets, and scattered houses, in which . . . the spinning work of all this manufacture is performed by the poor people; the master clothiers, who generally live in the greater towns, sending out the wool weekly to their houses by their servants and horses, and at the same time bringing back the yarn that they have spun and finished, which then is fitted for the loom.[15]

In these few words, all the key features of 'pure' outwork are enumerated. We have a great industry controlled by urban merchant-manufacturers who, through the medium of agents, 'put out' the most labour-intensive parts of the process of manufacture to the poor of the surrounding countryside.

Our simple model thus suggests that outwork depended upon a partnership of three fairly distinct groups. At the top of each trade were a small number of merchant-manufacturers who gauged the market for their particular product and purchased the materials from which that product was made: at the bottom were the mass of 'independent', undisciplined wage-earners who, with their own tools in their own workshops, completed the various processes of making up these materials; and in between, acting as essential links in the complex chain of putting out materials and taking in finished or semi-finished work, were the assorted middlemen under their various local names. In this 'pure' form, the provision of capital would reflect a clear differentiation of functions between the partners: the merchant-manufacturer or entrepreneur would furnish the working or circulating capital in the form of materials in the make and goods in stock; whilst the wage-earners would themselves supply the fixed capital in the shape of workshops and tools. As we shall see, however, the reality of most outwork industries in the nineteenth century was far more complex than this simple ideal suggests.

It is easy to see that, even in a simplified model, this kind of partnership would be liable to strain and tension. Most obviously, the interests of wage-earners and wage-payers would often conflict: to a manufacturer facing keenly competitive markets, lower wages simply meant lower costs, but to the worker they meant a spell of belt-tightening. Likewise, the losses arising from under-employed machinery and workspace during depressed trade were insignificant to the manufacturer, but crucial to the outworker: whereas conversely the problem of delivery dates or embezzled materials was a constant nightmare for the urban capitalist, but was of lesser concern to the 'independent' wage-earner in his home-workshop. With such distinct interests, conflict was never far away. But so long as any particular industry remained confined to a particular town, the outwork system rested on a personalized basis, and latent conflict could be minimized, or at least resolved along well-developed lines. The more widely an industry overflowed over a whole region, however, the more it was shared between a number of different centres with extensive rural hinterlands; or the more its markets came to be ultimately controlled by the great merchants of London (or Manchester), then the more obvious would both the impersonality of relationships and the clash of economic interests become.

Large-scale outwork inevitably weakened contact and undermined the community of experience and interest between merchant-manufacturer and outworker. Equally, however, it enhanced the importance of the third 'partner' – the agent, putter-out, 'fogger', 'bagman', or whatever. To the distant urban merchant, he became a manager-figure who took care of labour recruitment and discipline, who did a good deal of the basic book-keeping, and who solved many of the irksome problems of transport and carriage: to the worker, he was the essential source of employment and income, and dependence on his services created further scope for tense and suspicious relations. Ubiquitous but elusive, the middleman will be encountered under a variety of local names and performing a range of functions which differed from one industry to another. More than anything else, the ambiguous role of the middleman demonstrates the flexibility of the outwork system. For it is precisely because he can merge imperceptibly at one extreme into the ranks of the genuine entrepreneurs and, at the other, become almost indistinguishable from the real wage-earners, that any attempt to construct a simple model of outwork requires continuous qualification as the actual mechanics of industrial organization come to be examined in the separate trades.

Difficulties

Many of the outwork industries to be discussed in this book still await the close attention of historians and, indeed, one of the objects of this preliminary survey is to encourage further detailed exploration of the surviving local records. However, any would-be student of the history of the poor and humble - even in a relatively recent period - will quickly become aware of the limitations of his evidence and of the unsatisfying answers which he is bound to give in consequence to questions of real importance to the understanding of social and economic change. The study of a vanished industry, a defunct form of economic organization, or an archaic social institution will be hampered by these difficulties at an early stage. Because outwork had become only marginal to the mature economy of the early twentieth century, and because the outworker's distinctive way of life ceased to be common several generations ago, some of its features can no longer be traced in detail. Given imagination and sympathy, a qualitative, impressionistic general picture can be built up: but deficient data make it especially difficult to speak precisely about certain crucial *quantitative* aspects of the subject. Two fundamental areas of uncertainty stand out clearly in almost every industry: it is impossible to make more than tentative and qualified statements about the course of *wages* and earnings; and it is equally difficult to speak other than approximately of the *numbers* employed in the country as a whole at any particular date. For there was no Ministry of Labour to collect the former information: and although census-takers developed an increasingly sophisticated occupational breakdown of the total population in the mid-nineteenth century, their efforts still do not make it possible to say what proportion of a given industry's employees were outworkers, especially in trades like shoemaking, where self-employed craftsmen, outworkers, and factory-hands co-existed for much of the century.

Other reasons for our inevitable uncertainty about these two key problems will become readily apparent as the fortunes of different groups of outworkers are considered in subsequent chapters. It is sufficient here to state that *some* of the data which would have been necessary to enable us to speak definitively about these two matters probably *never* existed, and, indeed, it is impossible to conceive that they ever could have existed. A form of capitalist industrial organiz-ation where many firms competed over many years and which relied on much casual, part-time, and unorganized labour was likely to be characterized by sharp and sudden fluctuations in the numbers employed and by variations in the wages offered and earned, and it is unlikely that all the shifts and variants would have been fully documented.

These problems are further compounded, of course, by the fact that, no matter what documentation may once have existed about outwork, only a small proportion of it survives today. The business records of merchants and manufacturers engaged in it are par-ticularly difficult to come by, since many of the firms were small and ephemeral, and most went out of business long ago. Thus it is difficult to trace the changing profitability of outwork operations, and to assess an industry's capacity for economic survival on an outwork basis. Similarly, although it is possible to discover the earnings of individual workers from a firm's wage books, these seldom survive in an unbroken series, and in any case, in a highly competitive system where few standard rates of pay existed, it will not be clear whether one firm's record in this or other respects was typical of the industry at large. Furthermore, the success of outwork depended on the role of the putter-out, agent, or factor, who linked merchant and workman: it was in *his* records (or more likely in his head) that many of the humbler details of the system's operations would be carried - yet the chances of their surviving are even more remote. In these circumstances, the business history of outwork must inevitably be patchy and unsatisfying.

If employers' papers are thin on the ground, so too are the personal records of the experiences and attitudes of the outworkers themselves. Among the small body of well-known working-class autobiographies, there are, of course, such works as Samuel Bam-ford's *Early Days* and *Passages in the Life of a Radical*, which provide a fascinating picture of the Lancashire weaving communities in the early years of the nineteenth century, and Joseph Gutteridge's *Lights and Shadows in the Life of an Artisan*, which demonstrates the rich cultural life of a materially impoverished urban weaver in mid-nineteenth-century Coventry.[16] In addition, a few less substantial diaries and memoirs of outworkers are available in print: the diary of William Varley, a Lancashire country weaver in the depressed 1820s, and the brief autobiography of Lucy Luck, a Luton straw-hat maker in the later nineteenth century, are good examples.[17] But few private letters or household accounts of humble origin survive to cast light on the everyday lives and personal problems of weavers, knitters, nailers, and the like: we depend instead on reports of their statements and acts in the local press, and on their revelations as witnesses before the various Parliamentary enquiries which looked at the problems of outworkers at various points in the course of the nineteenth century.

Much of the surviving material which provides details about the outworker's life was, in fact, generated by his social superiors, and represents *their* analysis and judgement of *his* problems and behaviour. Indeed, middle-class perspectives colour the outworker's fictional appearances – in Kingsley's *Alton Locke* or Disraeli's *Sybil*, for instance – as well as the records of his real-life existence. The historian of the outworker must always be conscious of his dependence on the magistrate, the Poor-law official, the journalist, and the philanthropist for information: for the elusive worker is most likely to emerge from his hidden world when he threatens public order and commits crime, when he is destitute, or when the sudden discovery and revelation of his condition provokes shocked, and often exaggerated, reactions in polite society. However sympathetic these contemporary observers might be, one suspects that there were features of the outworker's lot which they wilfully or absent-mindedly ignored or misunderstood, and elements in his behaviour and attitude of which they disapproved. These shortcomings must always be borne in mind when sifting through the miscellaneous mass of local evidence which can help to illuminate the history of the various outwork industries.

The present study makes no claim to be based on such local archive material for the trades and districts discussed below: it results rather from an attempt to generalize about topics which the author explored in his work on the cotton handloom weavers, and its object is to present problems and offer hypotheses which will only be resolved and upheld (or rejected) if and when other students are encouraged to look more closely at the relevant records. Nevertheless, there is one basic source, fundamental as a starting point in the study of much British economic and social history in the nineteenth century, which has been extensively used in the chapters which follow. British historians are fortunate in the wealth of printed material unearthed over the years by the succession of Royal Commissions and Parliamentary Select Committees which looked at a wide range of the social problems produced or exacerbated by industrialization and by urban development. However, even this vast quarry has its problems and it is perhaps worth spelling them out in some detail.

In the first place, there are significant differences in origin and procedure between Royal Commissions and Select Committees of the Lords or Commons. The latter type of inquiry is initiated and pursued directly by members of Parliament meeting as a group to summon and cross-examine witnesses: the evidence thus gained is published verbatim, together with any resultant recommendations which the Committee may decide to make. Both the membership of the Committee and the body of witnesses can easily become unrepresentative, and in certain notorious cases there is a strong bias towards pre-selected evidence and pre-determined conclusions. The Commons' Committee which examined the state of the handloom weavers in 1834-5 suffered from these shortcomings, and half a century later the Lords' Committee on 'sweating' was similarly unsatisfactory.[18] Much of the evidence heard by the latter inquiry was cooked up in somewhat unscrupulous ways by Arnold H. White, a sensational radical journalist with a fatal weakness for overstating his case.[19] With clear evidence that the protagonists at these inquiries were inclined to exaggerate to this extent, it is not surprising that contemporaries were sometimes unimpressed by the findings of Select Committees, and that non-partisan MPs often refused to support their zealous colleagues' more eccentric proposals.

Royal Commissions, on the other hand, were made up of a small number of appointed 'experts' who were generally not themselves Parliamentarians, who were less obviously partisan, and who usually looked at the problem under consideration in greater depth and in a less hurried atmosphere: they often sent out assistant commissioners to gather comprehensive information on the spot. Yet even commissioners had preconceived ideas, and might accept only those parts of the evidence which supported their prejudices. This was notoriously the case with.the Commission which preceeded the reform of the Poor Law in the early 1830s, and it was equally true of the Commission on the handloom weavers at the end of the decade.[20] Both were dominated by the formidable figure of Nassau Senior, the leading orthodox economist of the day, who used the final report of the latter inquiry to parade his favourite panaceas of free trade and universal education and to take a quite unnecessary side-swipe at trade unions, of which he had a morbid dread.

Likewise, although Parliamentary Committees might be guilty of pre-selecting suitable testimony, it was sometimes argued that Royal Commissions suffered from boycotting by possible witnesses out of fear of recriminations. Richard Muggeridge, who painstakingly conducted the 1844-5 Commission on the Midland framework knitters single-handed, was warned by one witness that 'most of the hands object to coming to give evidence, because they are afraid that at one time or other it may injure them when the demand for work is slack'.[21] But since Muggeridge toured all the leading towns, met deputations from surrounding villages, and took evidence from some 600 persons, it seems unlikely that any major problems failed to be discussed in his hearing. Indeed, one great advantage of an inquiry like Muggeridge's, where all the evidence of every deputation was printed verbatim, is that the actual phrases and sentiments of the outworkers themselves survive in a way that is unparalleled in any other comparable form of evidence.

Reports in Parliamentary Papers, therefore, still have great importance and value, in that they give us the views – often at considerable length – of a variety of generally well-informed and well-intentioned contemporaries. But what happens when two apparently equally credible witnesses produce contradictory evidence at one of these enquiries? Whom should one believe? An example of such a disagreement can be found in the report of the 1838 Commons' Committee on the working of the new Poor Law. At one point, this Committee considered the position and prospects of the distressed handloom weavers of north-east Lancashire: a witness, Alfred Power, recently appointed commissioner for the area, stated that there had lately been a sharp decrease in the number of weavers; but John Fielden, a member of the Committee and a leading local manufacturer who had been concerned with the weavers' plight for years, refused to believe him.[22] Which of the two was the more *likely* to know the truth of the matter – the government official with a relatively recent but quite close acquaintance with the district and its problems, or the veteran local manufacturer whose public life on the national political scene in late years had probably reduced his immediate contact with day-to-day developments back home? It is impossible now to guess.

Thus, although Parliamentary Papers tell us something of the truth, it is unlikely that they tell us the whole truth. They can direct attention to the main problems and provide an invaluable starting point for research, but they need to be supported and modified at every turn by the various local materials which still survive in public libraries, in record offices, and occasionally in private hands. Since what follows in the present study rests largely on the Parliamentary Papers and on the existing body of published secondary writings, it is obvious that many of its 'conclusions' must be regarded rather as tentative hypotheses, which future detailed work by other hands may well undermine. The aim, therefore, is to furnish a basic framework within which students of those industries and areas where outwork existed until well into the nineteenth century may develop their own discoveries: in the light of their findings, the framework will have to be modified and, in the end, superseded and discarded.

To produce such a framework, the book is divided into three sections. The first and longest of these, in three chapters, describes the key features of the main industries in turn, and tries to establish a broad chronology of their rise and fall over the course of the nineteenth century. Secondly, a tentative attempt is made to produce an elementary analysis of the economic basis of outwork, in order to establish why this form of industrial organization persisted longer in some sectors than in others. Finally, we shall consider how the problems arising from outwork's persistence (or, in some cases, its decline) impinged upon the political life of nineteenth-century Britain.

Part One
DESCRIPTION

—1—
Outwork in Textiles

Introduction

It is fitting that a study of the changing role of the outworker in English industry should begin by looking at his place in the spinning and weaving of various textile fabrics. In no other group of large-scale industries had outwork become so firmly entrenched by the late eighteenth century; and in most accounts of industrialization since that time, no development has received such consistent mention as the replacement of outwork in this sector by new machines and by factory organization. Since textiles formed much the biggest segment of our industrial economy until well into the nineteenth century, it is not surprising that the transformation of this group of manufactures should have tended to be seen as the key feature of our 'industrial revolution'.

Traditionally, the production of various sorts of woollen cloth formed much the biggest branch of the English textile industry, and Daniel Defoe listed several major regions where it was carried on in the early eighteenth century on an essentially outwork basis, though with many local variants. In the east of England, there was the baize trade of Essex, centred on Colchester, and the great East Anglian worsted industry whose chief seat was Norwich. In the south-west there was the old-established Devonshire industry around Exeter, and the great centre of the broadcloth industry in Somerset, Wiltshire and Gloucestershire, which provided our 'ideal type' of outwork quoted in the Introduction. Further north again, Shrewsbury and Wrexham served as marts for the flannel industry of mid-Wales, and there were smaller centres in the Midlands around Banbury and in the far north-west around Kendal. But the other major home of both the woollen and the worsted manufactures, of which Defoe also provided a classic description, was the West Riding of Yorkshire, with its five great markets at Wakefield, Huddersfield, Halifax, Bradford, and Leeds, and with its outliers across the

Pennines around Rochdale and Colne. In this last area, Defoe emphasized that the master clothiers were more numerous, and the scale of their operations generally much smaller, than else-where; but they too were essentially employers of wage labour, providing carding, spinning, and weaving work for their own and their neighbours' families. All these areas in part competed with one another, but each also had its own specialities and its own particular markets; the responsiveness of each to new opportunities varied; and thus the relative importance of the different regions tended to change over time. Undoubtedly, over the course of the eighteenth century the chief development in this respect was the more rapid growth of the industry in Yorkshire which, as Defoe himself noted, went in for 'clothing the ordinary people, who cannot go to the price of the fine medley cloths made ... in the western counties of England'.[1]

The production of cloth for the market, under the organization of master clothiers great and small, provided outwork of various kinds, as each successive process saw the work passing through the hands of different men and women. But the two most important processes entrusted to outworkers were spinning and weaving, and until the end of the eighteenth century the former undoubtedly employed much the larger numbers. Contemporary estimates varied consider-ably, but it is clear that several spinners were needed to supply the yarn for one weaver – a situation exacerbated by the fact that spinners were women and children, many of whom were only part-time, casual workers seeking to supplement the family income in a modest way. As a result, country folk in remote spots could often be found spinning for the clothiers of the urban centres of the industry. Thus although Defoe found no 'settled manufacture' at Ipswich, he noted that 'the poor people are however employed, as they are all over these counties, in spinning wool for the towns where manufactures are settled'; whilst at Norwich, not only did the town weavers employ 'all the country round in spinning yarn for them', but even imported it from as far afield as Yorkshire and Westmorland.[2] The expanding Yorkshire industry was ranging equally widely in its search for spinners by the late eighteenth century: the Akroyds of Halifax were sending work as far away as the villages of the Forest of Bowland and the northern parts of Craven, whilst other manufacturers were putting out spinning in the Scottish border counties.[3] Young and Eden bear testimony to the ubiquity of spinning outwork in the Midlands and the north by the late eighteenth century. Apart from the obvious centres of textile manufacture, Young in the 1770s found spinners for the Warrington sailcloth and sacking industry in Cheshire, for example, and Eden twenty years later discovered farm labourers' wives in Rutland and Cumberland, and lead miners' wives in the north Pennine dales, all supplementing their husbands' incomes by spinning at home.[4] The far northern counties, in particular, furnished a large number of spinners, some on the older woollens, and some on the newer linens; Young noted, for instance, that at Guisborough 'the employment of the poor women is spinning of flax', that around Richmond 'the employment of the poor women and children is spinning of worsted', and that in some parts of south Durham both occupations were followed.[5]

It would be quite wrong, however, to imagine that the long existence and near-universality of outwork in textiles, and in wool in particular, had made the 'system' rigid or static until it was rudely disrupted by the famous spinning inventions of the second half of the eighteenth century. The hundred years after the Cromwellian interregnum saw important developments which altered the distribution of outwork over the face of the country and added to the complexity of its character. Outwork, by its very nature, implied at this period the employment of an essentially *rural* population in *non-agricultural* pursuits, and throughout the hundred years 1660-1760 there is abundant evidence of its expansion in several parts of the country. In an ingenious argument, Dr Eric Jones has tried to relate the tendency of some regions to specialize in rural outwork to the remarkable increase in overall agricultural productivity in this period:[6] he notes that in the first half of the eighteenth century new techniques in arable farming, which were of particular value to farmers on the light soils in parts of the south and east of England, helped to produce grain surpluses in the country as a whole, at a time when the pressure of population on food resources seems to have been relaxed. This situation, Jones claims, worked to the disadvantage of farmers in g'less favoured situations, such as the wetter, more elevated parts of the north and west and on the heavy midland clays'[7] who were increasingly obliged to concentrate instead on dairying and on supplementary earnings from industrial outwork.

In support of this argument, Dr Jones cites the growth in the few decades around 1700 of the Honiton lace industry in a wide area of

the south Devon countryside; of lace-making and straw-plaiting in
the south Midland counties of Bedfordshire, Buckinghamshire, and
Northamptonshire; of nail-making in the west Midlands; and of
framework knitting in the hosiery industry around Leicester, Nottingham, and Derby.[8] He might equally well have pointed to
several comparable developments in textile outwork in the first
seventy years of the eighteenth century. For within the woollen
and worsted industries these years saw the particularly rapid
growth of output in the West Riding of Yorkshire and its satellite
areas in Lancashire – a process chronicled in the works of Heaton
and Crump and (more recently and tentatively) measured by
Deane and Cole – a development which was shifting the centre of
gravity of this great industry away from the former centres in the
south-west and East Anglia. The same period saw the remarkable
growth of both the linen and silk industries – the former especially in west Lancashire and north-eastern England, and the latter
around Coventry and in Cheshire – both of them being essentially new industries in England and enjoying a considerable measure
of government encouragement and support.[9] And the same years
also witnessed the growing importance of the textile area around
Manchester, which specialized in cheaper fabrics where cotton,
wool, and linen were all employed – a development which has
been chronicled so meticulously by Wadsworth and Mann. Thus
the outwork 'system' in the eighteenth century was far from
static; new fabrics were coming into use, new areas were being
drawn into the network of textile production, and older regions
were adapting to new needs and products. But the weaknesses of
the system were also becoming increasingly obvious: the hundreds
of thousands of domestic spinners – widely scattered and capable
of only low levels of output – represented a technology which
had to be superseded if the textile industries were to go on expanding. Fearing a shortage of cheap labour at a time when overall population growth seems to have been negligible, entrepreneurs
and inventors were increasingly from the 1730s seeking ways to
speed up and cheapen the spinning process; they were becoming
aware, as manufacturers in other industries who relied on outwork were to do later, of one of the chief constraints in the
system. As soon as their search for a solution was successful, the
continued existence of large-scale outwork in textiles was bound
to be affected.

The Decline of Outwork in Spinning, 1780–1820

It is traditionally assumed that the biggest single blow ever inflicted on outwork as a whole came with the spinning inventions of the late eighteenth century. Beginning with James Hargreaves' spinning jenny, a series of new machines rapidly and dramatically broke through the productivity bottleneck which had long been apparent in the highly labour-intensive hand-spinning process. One of the new techniques, Richard Arkwright's water-frame, was from the beginning designed to rely on water power, and required large workshops or 'factories' in which to be carried on; and by the late 1790s the third of the great machines, Samuel Crompton's mule, was being driven by steam power, also on a factory basis.

Initially, the jenny, which could be used on wool as well as cotton, was not incompatible with the outwork system of manufacture, for it was 'a domestic machine little larger than an armchair'.[10] It is true that the use of the jenny provoked the wrath of the outworkers of east Lancashire when it was first introduced and that many were destroyed in riots in March 1768; but indignation seems to have been directed, not against the jenny's potential as a factory machine, but rather against the introduction of a labour-saving device at a time of particularly low wages and high food prices in the district. Increasingly, the larger jennies did come to be housed in special workshops, but Aspin and Chapman have clearly shown that small jennies were accepted as an adjunct to domestic textile work in many families, and that, especially in some areas of the woollen industry, they showed remarkable powers of survival into the nineteenth century.[11]

Nevertheless, the implications of the new spinning machines for this major branch of outwork were serious; and although the production of cotton was the earliest affected, it is worth remembering that some of the machines were readily adaptable to other fibres, and that in other cases corresponding spinning 'revolutions' had either already taken place – as in the case of silk-throwing, imported from Italy by the Lombe brothers of Derby about 1720 – or were to happen almost immediately afterwards, as with Kendrew and Porthouse's patent for flax-spinning of 1787, which was to make the fortune of the Marshalls of Leeds.[12] Thus all areas and all varieties of textiles were affected by the new spinning techniques.

The new machines had two obvious consequences. The first was the total disappearance, in the early years of the nineteenth century, of outwork in spinning from some of the more marginal textile areas, especially in the south and east of England: the second was the transformation between 1770 and 1830 of spinning in most of the more specialized textile regions of the north from a domestic into a factory occupation. Neither of these developments has received much attention from historians, and both, indeed, are difficult to trace, in spite of the fact that the number of family economies seriously disrupted as their womenfolk ceased to spin at home must have been enormous. In the case of the more specialized areas, the general response of the spinners is fairly clear: those women and children who remained in the labour market either became involved in factory spinning, or switched in substantial numbers to handloom weaving, which remained a labour-intensive outwork industry, and which, especially with the dramatic expansion of the cotton industry, needed a vast influx of new workers.

But in the case of the more marginal areas, where cotton never caught on and where demand for the local product may have been failing for some time, the evidence is more sketchy. When the local textile industry withered away, no response short of migration seems to have been open to the casual female and infant outworkers; and this was a solution which, in a pre-railway age, these dependent members of a farm-labourer's family were hardly likely to consider. Unless alternative forms of outwork were also available locally, the disappearance of the supplementary income which spinning had formerly brought had simply to be accepted. Comments on the lamentable consequences of the decline of outwork in spinning can be found in some of the replies submitted by various overseers of the poor to the 1824 Select Committee of the House of Commons on the poor rate. The overseers at Acton in Suffolk, for example, complained that 'want of employment, no spinning going on, is one great cause of the rates being so enormously high', whilst at Framlingham in the same county it was alleged that 'the women and children here have little or nothing to do, as here is no manufactory; the spinning of wool by hand, which used to employ so many, is now done away, it being transferred to Yorkshire and done by machinery'.[13] In his more robust way, William Cobbett, too, lamented that the mechanization of spinning for the Witney blanket industry had destroyed domestic spinning in many Cotswold villages and had caused 'decay and misery': 'This work is all now gone', he complained, 'and so the women and the girls are a "surplus *popalashun*, mon"', and are, of course, to be dealt with by the "Emigration Committee" of the "Collective Wisdom".'[14] As a contributory factor in the growing problem of rural poverty, which was to be exposed so dramatically in the 'Swing' riots of 1830, the disappearance of textile outwork from various parts of the south and east was not insignificant.

When Eden, in the early 1790s, described the prevalence of outwork in spinning throughout the country, therefore, he was depicting a state of affairs the end of which was very close at hand. Of course, the existence of a state of war between 1793 and 1815 distorted the process of economic change which the new machines had set in motion. Markets for certain fabrics were suddenly reduced, either because of periodic difficulties in overseas trade or because of changes in fashion and taste at home, so that output from the more marginal areas was bound to suffer: Eden himself ascribed the 'declining state' of both the Colchester baize manufacture and the Norwich worsted trade in part to the loss of foreign markets because of the war.[15] Conversely in many rural districts more women and children seem readily to have found employment in the greatly extended agricultural sector, as husbands, fathers, and brothers left their ordinary occupations to join the army or navy.[16] Both these developments undoubtedly accelerated the disappearance of spinning from some districts. The process was not entirely one-sided, however, being counterbalanced in some places by the heavy military demand for such fabrics as sailcloth and heavy woollens; by the massive, albeit irregular, growth in the international and domestic markets for the new cotton cloths; and by the growth under wartime stimulus of the demand for various non-textile products which sometimes merely saw the substitution of one kind of outwork for another at a local level.

A good illustration of this last process can be found at Kettering. When Eden reported on the state of the woollen industry there in the 1790s, he found that 'since the war, business has considerably declined', and large numbers of men had joined the militia and the army; but, stimulated by government contracts, a large-scale boot and shoe manufactory quickly grew up there on an outwork basis.[17] The restoration of peace, of course, created its own further dislocations, as some extended sectors found themselves saddled with over-capacity and as the labour markets were flooded with returning soldiers and sailors. Once the long period of re-adjustment (which lasted until at least 1820) was over, however, it is clear that many country workers whose districts 'lost' textile outwork either during or just after the war never got it back. Thus the combined influences of technological development and the chances of war served to intensify the growing regionalization of the textile industries in the forty years after 1780.

Apart from the impetus they gave to the local concentration of the major textile industries, both through the beginnings of the factory system and as a result of the decline of the more marginal producing areas, the great spinning inventions of the late eighteenth century had a further significance which historians have not always fully recognized. Historically, the textile industry has come to use an increasing range of raw materials and to manufacture an ever-widening variety of fabrics. 'New draperies' have constantly come into fashion and competed with the old, and whereas in some areas traditional producers have shown remarkable fondness for their old ways, there have been many examples of entrepreneurs and workers in other places who have shown an equally remarkable capacity to switch their attention from one branch of the industry to another. What the machines of Hargreaves, Arkwright, and Crompton made possible above all was the amazing growth of cotton goods as the latest form of 'new drapery', which took away markets from rival fabrics such as wool and especially linen, which changed south Lancashire into the world's most advanced industrial region, and which offered the prospect of rich rewards to textile producers both old and new.

Although there was a dramatic expansion of the cotton industry in the last two decades of the eighteenth century into areas previously associated with other textiles, it is not difficult to explain. Cotton goods came in a very wide variety, ranging from heavy calicoes, corduroys, and velvets at one extreme down to the finest muslins at the other; their versatility for both clothing and household purposes greatly exceeded that of any other fabric; but above all the combined effect of the new spinning machines and of other technical developments such as the Witney cotton gin and the new processes of bleaching and dyeing quickly rendered them cheap and accessible to mass markets at home and abroad.[18] The apparently slower growth of the woollen industry – by mid-eighteenth century standards – and the possible absolute decline in the total output of linen in the last years of the century are witnesses to the inroads being made into their markets by the new products.[19]

Geographically, therefore, the cotton industry spread rapidly over the north of England, the lowlands of Scotland, and parts of northern Ireland, replacing or reducing the woollen or linen industries in many places. Within England, the Manchester region and the hosiery area around Nottingham and Derby provided the original bases for this expansion, for these were the areas which had long been using some raw cotton as one of the inputs in the various goods which they traditionally made. From south Lancashire there was a great surge forward in the 1790s into Rossendale and beyond, as towns like Burnley and Colne ceased to maintain their traditional trans-Pennine links with the Halifax worsted industry, and began instead to look southward to Manchester and to cotton. Indeed, even places on the Yorkshire side of the watershed, such as Todmorden and Skipton, came to be cotton towns. Further north, the woollen and linen districts along the Cumberland coast, from Whitehaven to Carlisle, likewise switched to the new fabric; whilst in remoter spots in the Lake district and the Yorkshire dales, and even in County Durham, isolated cotton mills made their appearance. Areas which did not take up cotton at all suffered accordingly; the depressed state of the Norwich cloth trade in the 1790s was partly blamed by Eden on 'the prevalent taste for wearing cottons, which has necessarily lessened the consumption of stuffs'.[20]

The process of physical expansion was, in part, the obvious response of some local entrepreneurs to the latest 'new drapery'; but there were other elements in the story. To some extent, the new industry spread itself widely because many of the early mills in which the new spinning machines were housed relied on waterpower for their motive force, and their location was determined by the availability of suitable streams. But the growth of the cotton industry had further implications for industrial outwork, because its geographical expansion was partly dictated by its search for additional labour, and especially for weavers. A vast amount of extra weaving capacity was required to meet the demands of the market for the new fabrics and to work up the vast quantities of machine-spun yarn now being turned out; and it might have been logical to expect that the obvious solution to this problem was for weaving rapidly to follow spinning into the factory. The remarkable fact is, however, that this did not happen on any significant scale until the mid-1820s. Instead, the increase in weaving capacity was supplied by an enormous expansion along traditional outwork lines, as a whole new army of men, women, and children was recruited to the handloom; many of them were either former domestic spinners, or had previously been occupied in weaving other fabrics, but former agricultural labourers were also prominent among the many recruits.

Traditional concern with the *survival* of handloom weaving and with the poverty associated with it *after* the 1820s has in the past deflected the attention of historians from the great *growth* of handloom weaving in cotton which took place between 1780 and 1820. Yet in this particular consequence of the great spinning revolution we see a lesson of fundamental importance to the whole question of industrial outwork in the nineteenth century. Far from killing outwork, the spinning factories merely led to a shift in its centre of gravity from spinning to weaving; and far from being antithetical or competing forms of industrial organization, in a very important sense the two could co-exist within a major industry and could complement one another. Indeed, the two could even *grow* side by side, as the entry of one stage in the long chain of processes in a particular manufacture into the factory merely created *more* work for *more* outworkers in the subsequent stages. More than any other, it is this last aspect of outwork which makes its study a subject of importance to the real understanding of British industrialization during the nineteenth century. Only when we can accept that, under the circumstances of the time, outwork was not some dying pre-industrial dinosaur, but was rather a perfectly rational, viable, and adaptable form of organization in many industries, as capable of expansion as of contraction, can we hope to understand its long survival and its ultimate disappearance.

The Handloom Weavers: Cotton*

It cannot too often be emphasized that the cotton handloom weavers, whose plight in the 1830s has aroused sympathy and concern ever since, were not really the 'survivors' of some traditional or long-established group of 'craft' workers. Their particular division of the great army of outworkers was rather the recent and short-lived product of the spectacular developments in the late eighteenth century, and their numbers continued to be swollen by

* This section is largely drawn from the author's *The Handloom Weavers* (Cambridge, 1969), to which further reference should be made.

new recruits for only a few decades before the powerloom came into widespread use in the early 1820s. Unfortunately, neither the *rate* of recruitment of weavers over the expansion years 1780-1820, nor the absolute *total* at the height of the trade, can be calculated with any accuracy; for by the time the weavers' problems had become a matter of urgent enquiry their numbers were already in decline, and their occupation had virtually vanished from some of the places where it had lately and briefly flourished.

If recruitment was spectacular, it is apparent from the trade figures that it must have been far from even and regular, for recurrent commercial crises before, after, and especially during the Revolutionary and Napoleonic wars meant that the cotton industry's growth came in a succession of sharp bursts, which were punctuated by periods of depression. In theory, the industry's output statistics ought to be of some help in making more precise calculations. However, neither the import figures for raw cotton nor the export figures for cloth will allow us to go very far in measuring the rise of the handloom labour force: for in the first place, not all the raw cotton which the industry consumed was actually woven in England – an increasing proportion of it being exported in the semi-manufactured state as yarn up to the 1830s; and in the second, the export figures can give us no indication of the extent to which the cloth woven in England was destined for the home market.

In estimating the weavers' total numbers, therefore, we have only the guesses which were bandied about at the time of the government enquiries in the early 1830s; for by the time the census returns give us a reasonably accurate occupational breakdown, cotton handloom weavers have pretty well vanished. These estimates suggest something of the order of a quarter of a million cotton weavers in England and Scotland; and if we judge by the fragmentary information as to the numbers in a few particular localities, this is probably not an overestimate of the situation when the trade was at its height, especially when we realize what a large proportion of the domestic weavers were women and children. We do know that handloom weavers came to dominate the occupational pattern very dramatically in some places: in the smaller villages of north-east Lancashire, where plain calico was extensively woven and where the weavers held out longest in large numbers, the number of looms amounted to between 40% and 50% of the total number of inhabitants, and the average household ran between two and three looms.

As to the distribution of cotton handloom weavers over the face of the country, it had already been suggested that the cotton industry in its early days expanded spatially over much of northern England, as well as having substantial centres in lowland Scotland and northern Ireland. Within England, Lancashire south of the Ribble together with some adjoining areas of Cheshire, Derbyshire, and the West Riding of Yorkshire was the chief producing region; but there was also a detached area in north Cumberland from Whitehaven to Carlisle. Individual places within these districts produced their own specialities – Bolton being famous for fine muslins, Carlisle for checks and ginghams, and so on; generally speaking, the finer and fancier goods were town-made, and the weavers in the villages and hamlets of the countryside stuck to the plainer and more common lines.

The division of the industry between town and country was one of its chief features. Within such growing towns as Bolton, Blackburn, Preston, and even Manchester in the early days, whole areas were occupied by weavers with their loomshops in cellars and garrets; and there can be no doubt that in these places handloom weavers contributed along with factory workers and the vast numbers employed in building, trade, and transport to the new way of life of the mushrooming cotton towns. But the remarkable thing about cotton handloom weaving was that, like older forms of textile outwork, it took its firmest roots in the surrounding countryside, and continued to be integrated there with farming, smallholding, and seasonal harvest work: it was in the upland villages of north and east Lancashire, around Pendle hill and in the forests of Rossendale and Bowland, that handloom weavers were most numerous in proportion to the total population, and their trade survived longest.

Naturally, there was a wide disparity of experience, environment, and life-style between town and country workers. In general terms, the pros and cons of urban living in the early nineteenth century form a subject still hotly debated, but if we consider the position of the town weaver simply in terms of his occupational advantages over his country cousin, it is clear that he got a better deal: his supply of work was probably more regular; he had a greater variety of potential employers to choose from, and a wider range of more skilled and better paid work to become adept at; and he and his fellows had better opportunities for collective action to maintain wages. The country weaver may well have had the benefit of a generally healthier environment, and a freer, more leisured life with an older local culture based on chapel and alehouse. In economic terms, however, he paid for these dearly in an irregular supply of work, which tended in any case to be of a less skilled and worse paid variety; in a greater degree of dependence on a single local employer or his agent; in an almost total inability to act collectively to defend his interests against employers; and, perhaps most serious of all, in a lack of alternative local employment, which kept the country weaver imprisoned in his trade and obliged him to accept· the pitiful rates of wages which prevailed in the last terrible years of the industry, during the second quarter of the nineteenth century.

Although the division between town and country in cotton weaving does not seem to have led to the manifestations of mutual distrust and even hostility between the two groups of workers which sometimes appeared elsewhere - as at Norwich and Coventry, for example - the differences in environment did lead to differences in values and responses in what might at first sight appear to be common predicaments for cotton handloom weavers. Whereas the town weaver might attempt through a trade combination to keep up an agreed list of piece-rates, and might reasonably hope within the urban context to be able to coerce undercutting masters and blackleg colleagues, the countryman was more of an individualist, whose surreptitious willingness to take work at low prices could not easily be exposed. Thus although the rural weaver might well be strongly conscious of belonging to the wider, total community of his village, his urban counterpart was liable to be more aware of the need for a narrower solidarity within his own economic or occupational group.

Apart from this basic disparity of experience and values, the cotton handloom weavers were a heterogeneous body in other important respects. Given that the numbers in the trade multiplied so rapidly in so short a time, it is clear that, at least in the plain branches, the work was not hard to learn. The simple techniques were widely imparted in workhouses and prisons throughout the cotton area, and although a certain dexterity was needed, there was a good deal about the job which was simply monotonous and repetitive. Apart from requiring little skill, most branches of the plain work called for little strength, and so could be followed by women and children as well as by adult men. Entry into the trade seems to have been largely unrestricted by formal apprenticeship requirements, and it is likely that most weavers learned the trade as children by seeing their fathers or mothers at work and by gradually joining in alongside them. This ease of entry meant, especially in the towns, a considerable turnover of workers, partly through the steady influx of existing weavers' children (many of whom might move out again to follow other trades as they got older), partly because new arrivals in these boom towns would find weaving an attractive proposition, even if only a temporary one, and partly because, once learned, the trade could be a useful prop to fall back on to anyone down on his luck. The attractiveness to immigrants helps to explain the predominance of the Irish among urban hand-loom weavers, especially in Manchester itself, and particularly in the last evil days of the trade, when most English urban workers were only too ready to give it a wide berth.

But in addition to a 'shifting' and fluctuating element, the labour force had a more stable core of permanent adherents. In the towns, this was probably supplied by the skilled and fancy weavers, such as the bedquilt and counterpane weavers of Bolton; these specialized branches took longer to learn, were male-dominated, and tended to have trade unions which could more effectively maintain entry restrictions and wage lists. In the country, too, the personnel was likely to be much more stable; for there, immigrants, whether from Ireland or elsewhere, were never numerous, and the limited range of job opportunities obliged the natives to think of weaving as a permanent part of their way of life. Through the co-existence of a volatile and a stable element, a further line of division appeared within the labour force: those with a deeper sense of involvement in their industry and of long-term commitment to it were far more likely to be actively concerned about its decline than would the shifting, shiftless pool of immigrants, idlers, and unfortunates who were forever drifting in and dropping out, and whose only response to the problems of their trade was a listless apathy.

One further element of disunity deserves attention when discussing the make-up of the handloom weaving labour force. A body of workers in which, in some areas, women and children probably formed the majority naturally contained a large element which was employed in only a part-time and casual capacity. Household duties, outside diversions, and the natural limits of strength and concentration all meant that many weavers simply did not follow their work full-time: their output, and consequently their earnings, were always low, and they saw their function as essentially one of supplementing the income brought into the family by the chief breadwinner, who might not even be a weaver himself. In the countryside, a part-time element appeared even among many of the adult men, for they frequently were involved to some degree in agricultural work, if only at harvest time; and sometimes in the towns, too, the followers of such seasonal trades as building might take to the loom in slack times. In some respects, this casual element, especially the women and children, divided the labour force – in terms of a sense of involvement in the problems of the trade – in a similar way to the split between the 'shifting' and the 'stable' components. But the two divisions do not coincide exactly: for an agricultural worker weaving part-time could still feel himself a 'permanent' weaver, who expected to find his livelihood at the loom at certain seasons, and to whom the loss of this regular by-trade would be serious; and conversely, a town weaver who wove full-time and had no other source of income might yet belong only to the 'volatile' element, in that he did not treat weaving as anything more than a temporary expedient which he would desert for something better if and when the opportunity arose.

This lack of homogeneity among the cotton handloom weavers was to crop up again and again among other groups of outworkers, and was to have many important consequences, not the least of which is the impossibility of making generalizations about large groups which had such diverse experiences and values. Diversity was particularly apparent in individual earnings – a circumstance which makes any definitive calculation of changes in the weavers' standard of living impossible. Like all outworkers, the cotton weavers were paid on a piece-rate basis, with each of the many varieties of cloth having its own special rate; what they earned was strictly proportional to the quality and quantity of the work they turned out. But the range of outputs which different weavers could attain was enormous, and the earnings of essentially part-time women and children, for example, were bound to be much lower than those of full-time adult men. Thus even if we could discover what the piece-rate was for a particular class of goods – and this itself is not too easy, because there were considerable local variations even for the same types of cloth – it would be difficult to establish a realistic multiplier by which to calculate how much work the average weaver would do in a week and how much he would earn. Moreover there is always the possibility that this multiplier would not be constant over time, since weavers might well try to increase their weekly output to keep up their total money earnings if the rate they were paid per piece declined. The periodic incidence of involuntary unemployment in slumps would add a further complication here, too.

If these difficulties could be overcome, the fact that certain incalculable deductions would have to be made from gross earnings for expenses connected with the workshop – maintenance and repair of the loom, flour for dressing and stiffening the warp threads before weaving, heat and light for the workplace, and possibly cash payments for ancillary workers who wound the weft threads onto bobbins – would still make the net figure very approximate. And, of course, any discussion of the changing standard of living would be meaningless if it failed to deal with the total income of a family in which there were several wage-earners, not all of whom were necessarily weavers.

Nevertheless, the sharp movements of those piece-rates for which a long-term series can be established do indicate the highly precarious position in which the cotton weavers found themselves. Not only was there a long-term downward trend in piece-rates from the late 1790s, so that, for example, the rate for plain calico in the late 1830s was less than a third of what it had been in 1815: but there were also savage short-term fluctuations, as piece-rates rose and fell when markets boomed and slumped. This short-term pattern was, indeed, well established long before the powerloom came into effective operation. For the market for textiles is notoriously susceptible to very short cyclical fluctuations, and the disruptive effects of the long war and its aftermath on the ordinary patterns of commerce intensified this natural instability between 1790 and 1820. Essentially the supply of labour in the industry could not hope to adjust smoothly to such bewildering changes in the state of the market: a chronic shortage of labour could give way within a year to a chronic over-supply. When demand failed and markets were glutted, manufacturers resorted to price-cutting competition, and reduced their costs by paying the weavers less; when demand revived, they had to raise piece-rates to attract a sufficient quantity of labour to enable them to seize the opportunities offered by the rising market. Insofar as the labour force did respond to changes in demand, it seems to have done so in a way which made the situation even worse: during depressions, the weavers seem to have tried as far as possible to keep up their incomes by increasing their output to compensate for the falling piece-rate, and so added to the over-stocking of the market until a period of virtually total un-employment followed; when an upward movement began again and the boom approached, however, it seems likely that individual output began to fall again, thus obliging the employers to put up their rates still further to attract additional workers into the trade. In each succeeding boom of the war years, more newcomers took to the loom; but in each ensuing depression they found great difficulty in getting out of the trade, and merely added to the increased competition for the dwindling quantity of work.

The last time that this situation worked to the cotton handloom weavers' advantage came in the early 1820s, when the long-delayed recovery from the post-war depression finally began. Low food prices at home stimulated the home-market, whilst the opening up of the South American republics offered a vast new export outlet for cottons. Weavers were again in short supply: their piece-rates rose, and they enjoyed in 1821 and 1822 an Indian summer of prosperity. But the favourable state of the market was such that some em-ployers were not going to be satisfied simply to try to take on more of the increasingly costly hand-labourers; instead they turned their attention to the complete mechanization of the weaving process on factory lines, which, they hoped, would greatly cheapen and speed up the production of cloth. The first heavy investment in power-looms was a key feature of the great trade cycle upswing which reached its peak in 1825; and the chief initiators of it were the big manufacturers in the immediate vicinity of Manchester, who al-ready owned spinning mills, and who thus had the necessary managerial and technical experience as well as the ability to furnish the required fixed capital. The process came to a sharp halt in the depression of 1826 - a date which marked the real turning point in the story of the cotton weavers. Thereafter the two rival systems co-existed, with the new gaining ground on the old; and although they did not necessarily compete directly in producing identical types of goods, the price of cottons in general came increasingly to be determined by the costs of producing them by power. Thus the generally downward trend in piece-rates continued even more sharply than before until the cotton handloom weavers virtually disappeared in the early 1850s. Even in this final desperate phase the process was not inexorable, for whenever in boom years such as

1834–5 factory production alone failed to keep pace with the increased demand, the remaining handloom weavers again found their services were solicited, and for a time enjoyed higher piece-rates. But such respites were temporary: and when, for example, Richard Muggeridge visited the village of Haggate, near Burnley, in 1838 on behalf of the Royal Commission on the handloom weavers, he found the gross weekly earnings of 171 families, numbering 968 people, and running 606 looms, all at work, averaged only 10s 0¼d per family.[21]

Why had manufacturers not considered the possibilities of the powerloom earlier? After all, there had been tremendous bursts of growth in the markets for cotton cloth at irregular intervals since the 1770s, and the Rev Edmund Cartwright, an academic dilettante from Cambridge, had foreseen the need for a weaving equivalent of Arkwright's water-frame as early as the mid-1780s. How are we to explain the fact that the first half-century of the modern cotton industry's history witnessed no development on the weaving side comparable to the spinning inventions of the 1760s and 1770s?

The obvious answer is that circumstances made it possible for the industry, in spite of its great overall expansion, to build up the necessary weaving capacity to meet the desired levels of output simply by the wholesale extension of the existing form of outwork organization. Until the early 1820s, entrepreneurs on the weaving side were never so constrained by the high cost and low productivity of outwork labour as the spinners had been in the mid-eighteenth century, and were never under overwhelming pressure to revolutionize the techniques or organization of their industry. Three factors were responsible for this state of affairs. In the first place, the efficiency of the handloom itself could be improved: Kay's flying shuttle and cotton came simultaneously to some of the old textile areas in the 1790s, and in later years improved forms of handloom, such as the iron-framed 'dandyloom' invented by William Radcliffe of Stockport, were used in some places, often in large workshops which had all the attributes of factories except for steam-power. Secondly, an abundance of suitable labour – including initially many who had previously been outworkers in the spinning branch – was available during the years of exceptionally rapid population growth which began about 1780. The inter-relationship of the expansion of outwork industries and the growth of population is a complex one, and will need to be discussed later; but it is clear that outwork as a form of capitalist organization is unlikely to spread rapidly unless accompanied by a sustained and substantial increase in numbers, and it may well be that the two processes are mutually reinforcing. Thirdly, although the output of the cotton industry rose substantially from 1790 to 1815, the irregular and uneven pace of its growth was hardly likely to be conducive to the confident investment of large sums of fixed capital by manufacturers: and it was probably the general long-term uncertainty of economic prospects which the protracted war engendered, rather than any actual shortage of investment funds which it might have caused, which was of importance here.

This reluctance to invest in change at a time when it was still possible to expand the outwork system without undue strain was powerfully reinforced by two other considerations. The first was the sheer practical difficulty of making a reliable and efficient powerloom, given the primitive state of the machine-making industry before men like Sharp and Roberts set up their Manchester works; and even after they had patented their improved powerloom in 1822, it took another two decades of piecemeal modification, during which the first machines quickly became obsolescent while the newer models became altogether cheaper to produce, before the various technical problems had been satisfactorily solved. It is not surprising, therefore, to find old and cautious entrepreneurs such as Samuel Greg of Styal who continued for many years to be sceptical of the real advantages of the still unreliable machine.

A second, though certainly less important, consideration was the hostility which the mere mention of powerlooms was likely to provoke among the handworkers. The first powerloom shed in Manchester, opened by Messrs Grimshaw in 1790 and using Cartwright's patent looms, was burnt down by an angry mob within two years; and when Cartwright successfully claimed compensation for his invention from the government in 1808, his supporters blamed this event for the lack of interest which manufacturers had subsequently taken in his machine. But timidity of this kind was not sufficient to deter entrepreneurs from looking hopefully to the powerloom in the early 1820s. For by then many of the technical difficulties had been overcome; glorious new markets were presenting themselves in Canning's brave New World; and the price of hand-loom labour was starting to rise again. Only the subsequent recurrent downswings of the trade cycle in 1826, 1829, 1837, and 1841 delayed the total replacement of handlooms by powerlooms in the cotton industry thereafter: and in spite of these delays the process was accomplished remarkably quickly, in comparison both with the slower progress of the powerloom in other branches of the English textile industry and with the much longer survival of cotton handlooms in Germany and France. For by 1850, the quarter of a million or so handlooms of thirty years before had been superseded by a quarter of a million powerlooms, each producing perhaps five or six times as much cloth per week as the old machines had done. According to the census of 1851, cotton handloom weavers were to be found at this date only in small numbers here and there: in the towns, little groups of survivors carried on in the fancy lines, such as the counterpane weavers of Bolton; and in the countryside, odd family groups were still treadling away in the more isolated farm-houses and hamlets. By the time of the cotton famine of the early 1860s, the old trade was to all intents and purposes extinct.

But what exactly do we mean when we talk of the 'extinction' of cotton handloom weaving? What really happened to the tens of thousands of people who followed this occupation when it was transformed in this way? The process of displacement may have been relatively swift, but did that make it any the less painful? Here again, the contrast between town and country is striking. Urban weavers were well placed to abandon their increasingly unrewarding jobs with relative ease: town life offered a wide range of occupational openings for men, women, and children, and the most appropriate of these openings were in the weaving sheds themselves. Handloom weavers have often been accused of having an insuperable repugnance to the regimentation of factory life, which was so obviously the antithesis of the freedom with which they could organize their domestic routines as outworkers: but the 'shock' of the new working conditions can hardly have been traumatic for town weavers (and even less so for their children), since at least they had lived cheek-by-jowl with mill folk and would have some appreciation that factory life had its compensations as well as its disadvantages. But it was not only that town weavers were better attuned to taking up mill-work; they also had abundant opportunities to do so in the booms of 1823-5 and 1834-6. These opportunities presented themselves first in Manchester and such neighbouring towns as Stockport, Hyde, and Stalybridge; but in the mid-1830s, the burst of new mill building gave similar openings in the larger of the more distant towns, such as Bolton, Blackburn, and Preston. By 1840, indeed, the number of handloom weavers had dwindled to only a few hundreds in most of these towns: other than Irish immigrants, hardly any newcomers can have taken up the loom seriously since 1826; most people already in the trade had managed to get out, either into factory work or in some cases into weaving other textiles on which the powerloom had not yet encroached; and the remnant probably consisted of two groups – the proud and elderly who stuck stubbornly to the more specialized types of work if they could, and the 'soft core' of ne'er-do-wells and social casualties who, as ever, drifted in and out of the low-class work and competed with Irish immigrants in the murky depths at the bottom of the pool of urban labour.

Things were very different in the villages of the countryside twenty to thirty miles north of Manchester. The local employers there were rarely men of such substance as the master spinners of the south Lancashire towns: most were small operators with no more fixed capital than their taking-in warehouse, and some were little better than commission agents for the big urban manufacturers and merchants; few could easily and quickly furnish the capital or summon up the credit with which to open a weaving shed. Many country weavers thus found no widening range of alternative and suitable work opening locally for them. If they wanted different jobs they had to move out and look for them – and many did just that, as the census figures for the upland townships of north-east Lancashire from 1821 testify. If they stayed at home, they and their wives and children were doomed to low wages and irregular employment, and there was little prospect of any permanent improvement for two decades after 1826. In these circumstances, it is small wonder that the remaining country weavers were so strongly attracted to the radical political doctrines of Chartism in the 1830s and 1840s.

In an extreme form, the story of the cotton handloom weavers – the first, the biggest, and possibly the most tragic group of outworkers to disappear – emphasizes what were to become recurrent themes in the history of the place of outwork in English industry in the nineteenth century. It shows that outwork was a form of capitalist organization eminently capable of rapid expansion, given an abundance of cheap labour; it shows that industrial production could still be widely dispersed and its roots firmly embedded in rural life; it reveals the vulnerable economic position in which

outworkers often found themselves even when their role was *not*
being undermined by new machines and alternative forms of organization: and it demonstrates that, even when some entrepreneurs
had found such novel alternatives to be more satisfactory, the older
system might still – for easily explicable reasons – take a very long
time dying in places. But most of all, it illustrates the extreme
diversity – in experience, environment, and outlook – of the great
army of individuals who, in different places at different times, found
themselves caught up in outwork; anyone who fails to appreciate
this heterogeneity, and who prefers instead to make facile generalizations, cannot hope to understand the nature and significance of
the 'outwork system'.

Outwork in the Woollen and Worsted Industries

So far as cotton textiles are concerned, a study of industrial outwork
in nineteenth-century England can confine itself almost entirely to
the weaving branch of the industry. But when we come to older-
established branches of the textile industry, and particularly to the
traditionally important wool-using section, we find a more complicated situation. Perhaps the root of this complexity lies in the
distinction which must constantly be drawn between the woollen
(or 'cloth') trade, which used wool of short staple, and the worsted
(or 'stuff') industry, where raw wool of longer staple was employed: for these different materials produced fabrics of quite
different appearance and texture, woollen cloth being rough and
matted, where worsted was smooth with a clearly distinguishable
warp and weft pattern.[22] In order to produce these two basic types,
not only did different kinds of wool have to be used, but processes
of manufacture had to be employed which were peculiar to one
branch or the other. Spinning and weaving were common to both,
but when the raw material was being prepared for spinning in the
initial stages, the wool intended for cloth had to be *carded*, whereas
that for worsted had to be *combed*. Similar differences were to be
found in the finishing stages, where there was a whole range of
processes unique to the cloth industry: to secure the felted or matted
effect, a piece of cloth had to be shrunk or fulled by being soaked in
a suitable liquid and pounded by heavy hammers; and after that,
the fine loose ends of fibre which stuck up from the rough surface
had to be sheared or cropped; neither of these stages was necessary to

the making of worsted. In addition to the basic division of the industry into these two branches, both woollens and worsteds came in many varieties and qualities, with the former ranging from superfine broadcloths for coatings down to coarse blankets: and in both branches, 'fancy' or mixed cloths, where a woollen or worsted weft was crossed with a cotton or silk warp, could be – and in the course of the nineteenth century increasingly were – manufactured.

In the late eighteenth century, the older woollen industry proper clearly illustrated – as did cotton – that outwork and factory forms of organization could co-exist in the succeeding stages of a great manufacture. Indeed, the fulling of cloth in water-powered mills might legitimately be called the first factory process in the textile industry, since it had been carried on on this basis since at least the thirteenth century. Other finishing processes such as cropping and dyeing, which were increasingly in the province of the merchant rather than in that of the manufacturing clothier, were also by this time being carried on chiefly in large workshops in such urban marketing centres as Leeds and Huddersfield. But until the great inventions which promoted the rapid expansion of the cotton industry after 1770, the preparation of the raw wool, the spinning of the yarn, and the weaving of the fabric seem to have largely conformed to the classic outwork pattern in both wool and worsted. Thereafter, however, the development of the two branches moved along different lines, both as regards the actual *dating* of the decline of outwork in each major process and as regards the order in which the various stages passed into the factory. Generally speaking, outwork survived longer in woollens than in worsteds, with one important exception: the carding of the raw material for the cloth industry was the *first* of the processes to enter the factory, whereas the comparable combing of the raw material for the worsted trade was the *last* stage to do so in that branch. The following is a rough indicator of the comparative decline of outwork in the two parts of the industry in the century after 1770, and provides a bare framework for the discussion which follows:

Development of factory production in the woollen and worsted industries

	Carding and Scribbling	post 1790
Woollen	Mule-spinning	post 1830
	Powerloom weaving	post 1850

	Waterframe spinning	1790-1820
Worsted	Powerloom weaving	1835-1850
	Combing	1845-1855

Not only did outwork persist at different stages and for different
lengths of time in the two principal branches of the wool-using
industry. For each division of the industry continued to be carried
on in several different parts of the country, and as a result of this
spatial dispersal the pace of industrial change also varied from area
to area. In the course of the eighteenth century, the relative importance of Yorkshire in both parts of the industry had increased:
the latest historian of the cloth trade, for example, has estimated
that Yorkshire produced 'nearly three times as much' as the West of
England by 1790.[23] But it was in worsted that the most spectacular
progress seems to have been made in the north; in the upper valleys
of the Aire and Calder, north and west of Bradford and Halifax,
the newer industry had mushroomed since the late seventeenth
century, and Professor Sigsworth claims that 'by 1770, the production of worsted in the West Riding was equal in quantity if not in
quality to the output of Norwich'.[24] Nevertheless, the persistence
of the industry in other centres in the early nineteenth century
must not be neglected: neither in the West Country broadcloth
industry, nor in Norwich worsteds, nor even in the more primitive
mid-Wales flannel trade was there sudden collapse or a failure to
absorb the new techniques and forms of organization which Yorkshire largely pioneered. The pace of change certainly differed –
particularly in mid-Wales, where jennies and even handwheels
survived in spinning until the end of the nineteenth century.[25] But
Miss Mann has shown that the West Country clothiers responded
vigorously to new opportunities in the 1790s,[26] and Dr Edwards
has warned us against following Sir John Clapham in pre-dating
the final 'transference of the worsted industry' from Norwich to
the West Riding.[27] Each area continued to have its own specialities
and its own markets, and entrepreneurs in each responded to their
particular situation in the ways they judged most appropriate. Thus
we should not be surprised to find that regional variations in the
persistence of outwork are more noticeable in wool textiles than in
the more compact cotton industry.

A final distinction which must be drawn between developments
in woollens and worsteds stems from the not inconsiderable differ-

ences in organization which had emerged by the eighteenth century, and which were especially marked in Yorkshire. The prevalence of small-scale master clothiers in the older woollen industry of the Leeds district is well known, and was immortalized in the report of the Parliamentary Select Committee which inquired into the state of the manufacture in 1806. Witnesses there spoke of the average small master in such a village as Pudsey employing only ten or a dozen workers at carding, spinning, and weaving; some would be members of the master's own family and household, but others might be outsiders working in their own homes.[28] It is clear, however, that this form of 'outwork in miniature' was peculiar to the woollen branch of the industry in the West Riding, and not universal even there, as the rise of big employers such as Benjamin Gott demonstrates. In the Yorkshire worsted industry, as in the woollen trade elsewhere, the entrepreneurs operated on a larger scale. They were organizers and co-ordinators, not practical workmen, and their employees in the various processes could run into many hundreds: John Foster, founder of the Black Dyke mills at Queensbury, who in his early days merely bought yarn which he put out to local worsted weavers, was said to provide work for 700 handlooms by the time he began his famous mill in 1835.[29] Moreover, by the end of the eighteenth century the relatively small number of worsted manufacturers had organized statutory regional committees to enforce the mercantilist legislation which fostered their trade and to protect themselves against troublesome or dishonest workers.[30] This difference in entrepreneurial scale and cohesion is obviously relevant to understanding both the differences in *timing* of the disappearance of outwork from the woollen and worsted manufactures, and also, to a lesser extent, the different patterns of labour relations in the two branches of the Yorkshire industry, for the small masters of the older trade were *less* likely to have the means or the inclination to change the basic pattern of organization, and *more* likely to enjoy a personalized relationship with their little band of workers.

Nonetheless, both in Yorkshire and elsewhere, the woollen industry was not slow in adopting those techniques which could easily be incorporated in the pattern of outwork and accommodated in an essentially domestic environment. Under favourable market conditions from about 1790, when government contracts for blankets and uniforms flowed in and when prosperous farmers turned themselves out in the best broadcloth, both the spinning jenny and the flying shuttle came into general use, essentially as devices which could enable the spinning and weaving sectors to meet the new demand without changing their organizational patterns.[31] By the time of the 1802 Select Committee on the industry, it was said that nine-tenths of the Yorkshire weavers were using the flying shuttle,[32] and it seems to have come into general use in the Witney blanket manufacture in the first decade of the nineteenth century.[33] Its adoption was slower, however, in the south-west, and especially in Wiltshire, where the weavers were still rioting against its introduction as late as 1822.[34]

The absorption of these new techniques into the outwork system at the end of the eighteenth century – thereby giving it a further lease of useful life – was accompanied, and indeed facilitated, by the simultaneous disappearance of the preparatory processes into the factory. As with the older fulling mills, to which they were often attached, the small and initially water-powered establishments in which scribbling mills, carding engines, and slubbing billies were set up at this time were, at any rate in Yorkshire, 'public' mills: that is to say, they served the needs of all the smaller manufacturers in a particular area, who took their materials to be prepared or finished there. Such mills were common in Yorkshire by 1800:[35] they began to come in in the south-west after 1790;[36] and, having been introduced in mid-Wales in 1789, they were 'despite local opposition . . . well-known throughout the region by 1820'.[37]

The co-existence of outwork sectors in spinning and weaving, taking full advantage of the jenny and the flying shuttle, with the newly factory-based preparatory processes appears to have lasted until at least the 1830s in the woollen industry. As with cotton after the great spinning inventions, we see again how industrial expansion in the early stages of the so-called 'industrial revolution' could be achieved by the simultaneous and complementary developments of both outwork and factory work. Whether this co-existence was entirely harmonious is unclear, for we know little about the effects of the re-organization of carding or the introduction of the new 'domestic' machines on the family economies of the workers in the woollen industry. A Wiltshire clothier complained in 1806 that the scribbling and carding mills had taken away much children's employment, though he qualified this with the admission that there was now more employment for women than twenty years before – presumably in jenny spinning, and possibly in handloom weaving, too.[38] It should be remembered, however, that, in compensation for any possible loss of children's earnings, the weavers in the family were likely to be bringing in considerably more as a result of both the higher quality of the yarn now available to them and the use of the flying shuttle. Overall it seems safe to conclude that the woollen industry still essentially rested on a viable outwork basis at the end of the Napoleonic wars. Where individual large 'factories' incorporating spinning and weaving, such as Benjamin Gott's in Leeds, had grown up – and the implications of their appearance were much discussed by the 1806 Select Committee – it must be remembered that they used the same machines and techniques as did the smaller domestic workshops. Thus the Committee was probably right to infer, from the evidence it heard, 'that the apprehensions entertained of [the domestic system's] being rooted out by the factory system are, at present at least, wholly without foundation'.[39]

From about 1830 this state of balance began to be disturbed, and the outwork basis of spinning and weaving in woollens began to crumble, though only slowly. The factory-based spinning-mule seems to have appeared in Yorkshire after it was made self-acting in the 1820s,[40] although it did not come to be used in Wales until the 1860s.[41] As with cotton, it was in handloom weaving that outwork survived longest in the woollen industry. Powerlooms seem to have been virtually non-existent in the 1830s, at a time when the Royal Commission on the handloom weavers produced the following figures for the different centres:

Leeds and surrounding villages	10,029 handlooms
Gloucestershire	1,303
Newtown (Wales)	688[42]

It is not certain when the absolute decline in the number of handlooms began, although in view of the particularly acute depression which struck the West Country industry after 1826 it seems likely that the number in that area had already begun to fall by 1840. Thus, when we read in the Royal Commission's report of the sharp drop in woollen weavers' wages since 1815, it is obvious that, as with the cotton weavers before 1820, we are dealing with a situation where the competition of hand and power does not arise: the explanation lies rather in the industry having a larger productive capacity than the slow-growing markets for a relatively unvaried and expensive product required. For two decades after 1826, the sluggishness of international trade and the competition which woollen cloth encountered from cheaper and more versatile fabrics created a bleak outlook. Given a labour force which was largely dispersed in the smaller villages and upland hamlets and which consisted predominantly of full-time and permanent male workers (for woollen weaving was in every way more demanding than cotton), it is not surprising that the supply of labour remained relatively fixed whilst the demand for its services fell in the repeated trade recessions of the 1820s, 1830s and 1840s. Far from looking to the powerloom in this situation, the small entrepreneur, who in any case may have lacked the necessary capital and who was obliged to keep the goodwill of the employees in whose close company he lived and worked, was much more likely to aggravate the difficulties by resorting to work-sharing and producing ahead of demand.

It was in the two decades after 1850 that the powerloom triumphed in the woollen industry, as the following figures show:

	England and Wales	Yorkshire only
1850	9,170 powerlooms	3,849
1870	37,356	24,033[43]

Free trade and rising real incomes helped to improve the industry's prospects and encourage innovation in weaving. Yet the last of the old woollen weavers were slow to disappear. In the early 1890s, an assistant commissioner visiting mid-Wales on behalf of the Royal Commission on labour reported 'one room in which old men and old women over 75 years of age are making all kinds of flannel with handlooms'.[44] Joseph Rhodes of Saddleworth, reputedly the last woollen handloom weaver in Yorkshire, retired only in 1905;[45] and the occasional use of the handloom in the Witney blanket industry seems to have persisted even after the First World War.[46] The survival of the handloom in the tweed industry of the Scottish highlands and islands right up to the present time is, of course, well known; but this is a rather special case of a small-scale industry establishing and maintaining itself under aristocratic patronage and with some degree of government encouragement.[47]

In worsteds, industrial changes came in a different sequence and on a different time-scale. The greater similarity of processes and products to the neighbouring Lancashire cotton industry was one reason why – in contrast with wool – the Yorkshire branch of the worsted industry tended to adopt the new spinning and weaving techniques from across the Pennines at an early date and in a relatively short period: but there is a good deal more to the story than that. Compared with its sister industry, Yorkshire worsted had experienced vigorous expansion throughout the eighteenth century, and exports were particularly buoyant in the decade of peace after American independence. Moreover, the capitalists who controlled its fortunes were men of substance. It is not surprising, therefore, to find water-powered mills which used an adaptation of Arkwright's frame taking over in spinning from about 1790. The process seems to have been gradual, because for some years the hand-spun thread continued to be of higher quality. But Professor Sigsworth concludes that 'in the West Riding, the hand spinning of worsted yarn was virtually extinct by 1820'.[48] As in cotton, the weaving branch of the Yorkshire industry expanded and survived on an outwork basis for a good deal longer – its adaptation to the increased output of the spinning side being again facilitated by the simultaneous adoption of the flying shuttle. The Norfolk trade, on the other hand, – increasingly concentrating on the highest quality goods and on fancy mixtures of worsted with cotton and silk – made much slower progress in both the mechanization of spinning and the adoption of the flying shuttle.[49]

The disappearance of handloom weaving from the worsted industry began at a point in time roughly mid-way between the corresponding developments in the cotton and the woollen industries. There were fewer than 3,000 worsted powerlooms in the West Riding in 1836, and when the Royal Commission reported at the end of that decade there were still nearly 14,000 worsted handlooms in the Bradford district and just over 5,000 on all kinds of fabrics in Norwich.[50] The big change-over came in the 1840s and – although some firms employed hand and powerlooms side by side for a time – it seems to have been accomplished remarkably quickly. By 1850 the number of worsted powerlooms had increased more than ten-fold in the West Riding since 1836, and by the late 1850s very few handlooms remained. To take one specific example, the number of handloom weavers in the village of Oxenhope, which adjoins the Rev Patrick Brontë's parish of Howarth, fell by 45% between the censuses of 1841 and 1851.[51] Again we must ask, why the intial delay in the mechanization, and why the final rush? The answer seems once more to be comparable to that already given for the cotton industry: for the handloom weavers' earnings seem to have slumped heavily during the course of the 1830s, in other words *before* the powerloom had come into widespread use;[52] and once again the very cheapness of hand labour during this decade might for a time have deterred entrepreneurs from mechanizing their weaving departments.[53] An over-large and relatively immobile labour force coincided with uncertain market prospects for fifteen years after the great slump of 1826, and the report of the Royal Commission of the late 1830s suggests a state of affairs very similar to that which afflicted the cotton weavers during and just after the war years. The worsted weavers included a higher proportion of women and children than their counterparts in wool, though they were not perhaps so numerous as in cotton; and in Yorkshire they were thickest on the ground in the country districts where alternative employment was not so readily available.[54] Only about 15 per cent of the worsted handloom weavers in the Bradford district lived in Bradford itself; and in proportion to the total population there they amounted to very little in contrast with the position in such out-townships as Denholm, Thornton, Keighley, Bingley, and Howarth.[55] In East Anglia oversupply of labour was obviously at the root of low wages, and the urban weavers of Norwich in the 1830s were particularly concerned to restrict the numbers in their trade by limiting the work taken out into the surrounding villages, where distressed agricultural labourers and their families showed no qualms about undercutting the wage rates which the Norwich weavers' union was striving to maintain.[56] Only when, from the mid-1840s, market prospects brightened, did the worsted manufacturers as a whole feel it worthwhile to abandon the rather questionable benefits of cheap hand labour for the more tangible advantages of factory weaving.

The worsted industry in the late 1840s had one residual category of outwork peculiar to itself in handcombing; but this rapidly disappeared in the following decade. Handcombing was not entirely an outwork process, for some spinning factories had combing shops attached to them; but the combers seem generally to have lived in the outdistricts and worked in their own homes or in small workshops. The work itself – drawing the locks of wool through the teeth of two heated handcombs – was both arduous and unhealthy, and was largely done by men. The threat of mechanization had indeed hung over the combers for at least two decades, and was the occasion of a major strike in 1825; but Professor Sigsworth maintains that combing machines were still 'rather legendary beasts of uncertain performance' until Samuel Cunliffe Lister successfully developed and patented one in 1845. Thereafter the combers' decline was dramatic: said to number 10,000 in Bradford and district in 1845, they had dwindled to 5,600 by 1851, and were 'almost extinct' six years later.[57] At first sight, theirs is a classic case of technological unemployment: yet even the combers, like the handloom weavers in cotton and worsted, experienced distress and falling wages *before* machine competition was effective. Once again, the explanation seems to lie in an over-large labour force – swollen in the later years by displaced country weavers[58] – which, under the repeated threat of mechanization and with its spirit broken by the failure of the 1825 strike, simply could not or would not defend its position by industrial action. And as before, the very cheapness of such labour may have discouraged the search for a mechanical alternative until the boom conditions of the mid-1840s led to a revived interest. In this respect as in others, the history of the coming of the factory in the worsted industry provides a salutary reminder of the dangers for the worker implicit in industrial outwork even when he was *not* actually being made redundant by new machines and new methods.

Outwork in Textiles: Linen and Silk

The lesser branches of the textile industry, linen and silk, showed several common features in their pattern of development in the nineteenth century. Most notably, their rate of expansion was low, compared both with their own performance under considerable government encouragement during the eighteenth century and with the contemporary progress of cotton and wool. Thus their relative importance within textiles declined, and they were under less pressure to change their techniques and forms of organization, with the result that handloom technology and an outwork basis survived in places until the end of the century. Moreover, because of their diminishing importance and slow mechanization, their history has attracted less attention both from contemporaries and later historians, and there is less information and statistical data about them.

In the case of linen, slow growth and ultimate contraction were clearly related to the tendency for this fabric to be replaced in many spheres by cotton from the 1780s onwards. In the last years of the

eighteenth century, the manufacture of the newer textile actually
replaced that of linen in such areas as south Lancashire and the
western lowlands of Scotland; and again in the later nineteenth
century, the only dramatic increase in output – in itself very
short-lived – came during the cotton famine of the early 1860s,
when the rival goods were in short supply.[59] In addition, there was
a long-term tendency over the course of the nineteenth century for
the industry to become concentrated in Ireland and, in the case of
jute, in Scotland; the English section was in absolute decline from at
least the middle of the century, and the numbers employed here fell
from over 27,000 to under 5,000 between 1851 and 1901. Nevertheless, even the English linen industry had had a period of vigorous
recovery in the early 1800s, following the successful mechanization
of flax spinning by the Marshalls of Leeds and others. Linen weaving on an outwork basis remained firmly entrenched in three towns
in northern England – Darlington, Knaresborough, and Barnsley –
until decline resumed in the late 1820s. As one weaver put it in
1839, describing the difficulties which began then, 'the powerlooms
throw many men out of employ in the cotton trade, and bring
them to the linen . . . and they have done the linen weavers much
injury. The powerlooms have also brought cotton into such general
wear by the cheapness of the price that there is less demand for linen
for general purposes'.[60] According to the Commission's report, the
handloom weavers at Barnsley survived best under these adverse
conditions: like their counterparts among the worsted weavers at
Norwich and the silk weavers at Coventry, the Barnsley men kept
up an effective trade union which attempted, by strikes in 1823 and
1829, to maintain agreed lists of piece-rates. But the Knaresborough
weavers were certainly in a sorry state by the late 1830s, with a
large-scale exodus to Barnsley and 130 cottages allegedly standing
empty; and the situation at Darlington seems to have been almost as
bad.[61] Thus it is not surprising to find less than 4,000 linen powerlooms in the whole of the United Kingdom in 1850, and to learn
that, even after the stimulating impact of the cotton famine, the
great bulk of the 31,000 powerlooms in 1868 were in Ireland and
Scotland.[62] The Royal Commission on children's employment of
the early 1860s reported that 1,000 weavers still found 'intermittent
employment' on 'coarse kinds of linen goods' in and around
Barnsley, but described the trade as being in 'a moribund state.'[63]

Unlike linen, silk was almost entirely an English industry, albeit a widely dispersed one; in 1851, as Clapham noted, 'in nearly every place where there was any textile manufacturing some silk was worked, and the industry persisted in a few places where there was no other.'[64] In addition to areas which specialized in the production of all-silk fabrics of different kinds, silk was used in 'mixtures' with cotton and worsted, for example, at Norwich and in the West Riding. More than any other branch of textiles, silk was vulnerable to the vagaries of female fashion; and in addition, it was the sector hardest hit by the adoption of free trade policies by Britain in the course of the nineteenth century, since its growth in the century before 1820 had been largely facilitated by the high tariff protection it enjoyed from French competition. The liberalization of the tariff by Huskisson in the mid-1820s had certainly caused much apprehension among silk producers, but English technical superiority in applying steam power to throwing and, in some areas, even to weaving enabled the industry to go on expanding until the total loss of protection after the Cobden treaty with France in 1860 revealed its real vulnerability. Thereafter the silk industry's decline was dramatic, in spite of the development of such new branches of the industry as those using silk waste and artificial silk. At its peak in about 1860, the industry employed around 150,000 people, possibly two-thirds of whom were still outside the modern 'factory' sector; by 1907, the numbers were down to 40,000.[65]

Until the collapse of the early 1860s, the various branches of the silk industry offer interesting examples of the shifting balance between outwork and factory organization during the classic 'industrial revolution'. The English silk industry received its first great stimulus from the Huguenot immigration of the late seventeenth century, which produced the remarkable community of weavers at Spitalfields in London, and in the eighteenth century this highly protected industry was further encouraged by the removal of the throwing sector – the equivalent of spinning in the other textile industries – to factories. After the Lombes set up their celebrated water-powered mill at Derby around 1720, throwing mills were gradually established elsewhere in the north – for example by Charles Roe at Macclesfield in 1743. Many of these provincial centres largely confined themselves to the provision of spun silk for use by the London weavers until the total absence of French competition nor uarter of a century after 1790 provided the whole industry with a further opportunity for expansion. Macclesfield itself only began

weaving silk 'about 1790', yet by 1817 the town had 12 manufacturers of woven silk and 28 throwsters, some of whom now used
steam power;[66] similarly, the last years of the war came to be known
in Coventry as 'the big purl time' when, according to the Royal
Commission on the handloom weavers, 'the demand for ribbons
with large purl edges was so great that . . . a great influx of hands
from other occupations ensued'.[67] However, one of the most remarkable areas of expansion in the first two decades of the nineteenth century was East Anglia. London manufacturers, anxious to
escape the high labour costs imposed on them by the Spitalfields Act,
began to establish throwing mills and put out silk weaving on the
Essex-Suffolk borders, attracted by 'an abundant supply of young
women and children, unemployed handloom weavers from the
woollen and worsted industries, some water power, a long textile
tradition, [and] proximity to London'.[68] There was, of course, a
serious recession in the industry during the immediate post-war
years, but in general growth began again in the early 1820s and was
sustained until the slump of 1826. Between then and the debacle of
1860, however, the picture becomes more confused, and the pace of
change and growth varies widely between the different areas in
which the industry was carried on.

In examining the survival of outwork in silk weaving after 1820,
it is necessary to remember that the industry had two main
branches: the making of ribbons, which was mainly carried on in
Coventry, Derby, Leek and Congleton; and the weaving of lengths
of broad silk, which was the traditional preserve of Spitalfields
and had more recently been developed at Macclesfield, in south
Lancashire, and in Essex. In the latter branch, the declining fortunes
of the old London industry were constantly contrasted with the
intermittently expansive experiences of the other areas after 1825: in
1856, it was said that there were only 7 or 8,000 workers left in the
Spitalfields industry out of the 25,000 in 1824 – these figures
apparently referring to ancillaries as well as to actual weavers.[69] The
Royal Commission of the late 1830s found about 10,000 looms in
Spitalfields, half of them worked by adult men, and there was an
average of two looms in each family engaged in the industry; but
the vast majority of the looms were engaged on velvets or plain
work, and only about five per cent were Jacquard looms, capable of
producing patterned goods.[70] A permanent oversupply of labour in
what appears to have been a dwindling, but still remarkably closed,

cultural community kept wages wretchedly low and militated against any attempt to mechanize the weaving process. Thus from the 1830s, the diminishing band of London silk weavers became notorious for both their poverty and their political apathy;[71] and the Select Committee on homework was still able to find sad specimens of this depressed class as late as 1907.[72]

In spite of several protracted periods of depression after 1826, things were different in the broad silk weaving districts outside London. The newly established East Anglian industry probably fared worst, for extreme poverty was reported there by the Royal Commission on the handloom weavers in the late 1830s: but even here, an enterprising firm like Courtaulds was able to remain in business by concentrating on specialized fabrics such as crape and by investing heavily in powerlooms (as early as 1838 they employed 178, compared with 441 handlooms).[73] Further north, Macclesfield did badly in the late 1820s and early 1830s, but enjoyed a further period of recovery in the 1840s. The handloom remained important in the industry there until the end of the century, and when, in Clapham's words, 'the leading firm in Macclesfield first got the order for silk handkerchiefs for the navy, in 1883, it made them all on handlooms'.[74] But it is said that, as early as about 1825, half of these handlooms were operated 'indoors' in the workshops and factories of the manufacturers, so that the claims of this industry to be regarded as a true outwork industry in the late nineteenth century are perhaps difficult to sustain.[75]

More progressive still was south Lancashire, for one of the main features of the silk industry's development in the first half of the nineteenth century was its expansion in and around Manchester. Clapham, discussing the occupational distribution revealed by the 1851 census, noted that 'there were more silk workers in . . . Lancashire than in any other county, whereas Lancashire had hardly been reckoned a silk county at all thirty years earlier'.[76] The second half of this statement is something of an exaggeration, for Wadsworth and Mann have chronicled the history of combinations among Manchester silk weavers in the 1750s and 1760s, and their analysis of trade directories for the town in 1773 and 1781 shows the existence of 5 and 7 'silk manufacturers' (as well as others with interests in mixed fabrics) in these respective years.[77] Similarly it is clear from the writings of Samuel Bamford, the radical leader of the Middleton weavers at the time of Peterloo, that broad silk weaving

was established in that area before 1820. Nevertheless, substantial
expansion certainly took place in the 1820s and early 1830s: in
Manchester, these years saw the building of about a dozen large
steam-powered throwing mills; and during the same period, many
former handloom weavers of cotton switched to silk, not only in
Manchester itself, but also in the area around Bolton and Leigh, as
their former trade became increasingly precarious.[78]

Turning to the ribbon branch of the industry, we find a development in Coventry before the collapse of 1860 which in many
respects marks the most interesting single episode in the history of
outwork in the nineteenth century: it has the advantage of being
particularly well documented, for it produced in the work of Joseph
Fletcher much the best report in the series published at the end of
the 1830s by the Royal Commission on the handloom weavers, and
in the life of Joseph Gutteridge, a silk weaver, one of the most
fascinating of working-class autobiographies. Until very late in the
eighteenth century, the Coventry ribbon manufacture seems to have
been organized by a few resident merchants, who gave out the
thrown silk to master-weavers or 'undertakers' in the town and its
neighbourhood who in turn employed journeymen and apprentices.
Originally, both plain and fancy ribbons were made on the traditional 'single' loom, which produced one ribbon at a time; but from
about 1770 the 'engine loom', capable of weaving several breadths of
plain ribbon at once, came into increasing use;[79] and according to
Joseph Gutteridge, the addition of the Jacquard device to this
'engine loom' in '1820 or 1821' made possible the multiple weaving
of all but the highest quality of figured and fancy ribbons, too.[80]
Neither of these new machines – though expensive to acquire – was
incompatible with the continued organization of the industry on an
outwork basis, but the use of both came to be mainly confined to
the male weavers of the city; the old 'single' loom persisted in the
1830s only in the surrounding villages, where it provided a meagre
supplementary income for the wives and children of the agricultural
labourers and others. According to an enumeration in 1818, three-
quarters of the 3,000 'engine' looms were in Coventry itself, as
against only a thousand of the 5,483 'single' looms; altogether, the
industry employed 13,346 people, nearly four thousand of them in
warping and winding, and among the actual weavers the men were
in a small majority.[81] Twenty years later, Fletcher found that
virtually all the 3,500 plain 'engine' looms were within the city, but

hardly any of the 7,500 'single' looms; the new Jacquard 'engine' looms, totalling 2,228, were divided between the two, with rather more than half in Coventry.[82]

The expansion of the industry in the later years of the war and in the early 1820s altered its organization as well as its techniques: an increasing number of the former small 'undertakers' began to take work direct from the great warehouses of London and Manchester rather than from the resident merchants, so that whereas Joseph Fletcher noted a dozen manufacturers in the late 1830s who each employed over a hundred looms he also found seventy who employed fewer than ten.[83] However, steam power was hardly employed at all as yet, thanks to the riot which ensued in 1831 when a manufacturer named Beck tried to introduce it.[84] Fletcher believed that the orginal 'undertaking' system only survived now in the 'single' loom work in the country: here, the master-weaver employing seven or eight looms was still responsible for fetching and carrying, warping and winding, and kept one-third of the price he got from the manufacturer as his share of the proceeds.[85] Within the city, however, the 'engine' trade was now dominated by the 'first-hand journeymen', operating on a smaller scale than the rural undertakers, but still employing their families on their own looms in their own houses, and working direct for manufacturers without the intervention of a middleman. Of 1,759 'loomowners' enumerated by Fletcher, 664 had only one loom each, and a further 452 had only two.[86] These independent 'first-hand journeymen' – often freemen of the city – were powerfully organized for industrial bargaining and, with the backing of local 'public opinion', were still able to force their employers to agree to price-lists for 'outdoor' piece-work at the time of Fletcher's report.[87]

But this dominance was already being undermined in the late 1830s by the appearance of 27 'factories' (not necessarily steam-powered) in the city, the owners of which not only employed the 600 or so looms which these factories contained, but also provided work for about three times as many 'journeymen's looms' outside.[88] As Gutteridge frequently makes clear, the factories were recognized as a threat by the independent outdoor workers, for greater mechanical refinements and further divisions of labour were possible in them, and weekly wages could replace piece-rates as the method of payment. Thus in the twenty years after Fletcher's report, the factory gained ground at the expense of the 'outdoor' first-hand journeymen, and the price-lists for piece-rates became increasingly difficult to maintain. In the 1850s the factories added the use of steam power to their organizational advantages;[89] and by 1859, the factory inspectors' reports spoke of 15 factories in Coventry with 1,250 powerlooms between them. But they also spoke of another development, which represents perhaps the most ambitious attempt to keep outwork alive in the whole of the nineteenth century. This was the appearance of the 'cottage factory', in which the families of outdoor weavers retained their 'freedom' by harnessing steam power to their own home-based looms. Steam engines were set up to provide power by a system of shafts and belts to the upper rooms of a whole row or group of houses, and families could thus, by paying rent for power, continue to compete with the factories whilst still working in their own attics.[90] In addition, the outdoor weavers succeeded, after a strike in September 1858, in obliging their employers to pay both their factory and their outside weavers on an agreed piece-rate basis.[91] This victory was short-lived, however: the ending of protection with the Cobden treaty in 1860 and the loss of American markets after the Morrell tariff revealed the high costs and uncompetitive nature of the English silk industry, and was quickly followed by heavy unemployment and by the repudiation of the 1858 price-list by the manufacturers. Although the weavers struck for eight weeks, they had no hope of success, and indeed only made things worse: depression deepened and a spate of bankruptcies followed, so that in 1866 the Royal Commission on the employment of children reported that 'during the last ten years the number of manufacturers in Coventry has been reduced from 80 to 26, and about 1,000 weavers have left the town';[92] Joseph Gutteridge himself was out of work for more than a year.[93] Although the 'cottage' factory did not disappear from Coventry, the industry as a whole never recovered its former level, and was of diminishing importance to the city's economy in the late nineteenth century. Thus, even when outwork in the silk industry tried ambitiously to harness the tools and techniques of the rival factory system, it was unable to prosper under the sudden onslaught of fierce competition and the dramatic loss of markets. Nevertheless, no other strong group of outworkers ever made such a vigorous defence of their way of life, or were prepared to go to such lengths to preserve the essentials of their traditional form of organization.

— 2 —
Outwork in Clothing

The Clothing Trades

Of all the manufactures encompassed in this study, none showed a greater variety of forms of organization or supplied a wider range of products to such a diversity of markets than the industries which produced items of clothing from the different textiles. Of course, even at the end of the nineteenth century, not everyone in Britain obtained all, or even the bulk of his clothing 'in the market': in country places especially, many of the poorer women made their own and their children's clothes at home – their efforts in some cases being supplemented by the charitable exertions of the better-off ladies in the village; and in addition to clothes run-up at home, there were the cast-offs, hand-me-downs, and other adapted second-hand garments which furnished a large part of the wardrobes of the poorest classes.[1] Even today, and at various levels in the social system, there remains a 'household' or 'subsistence' sector in the supply of clothing, which a highly organized, mass-produced, factory-based clothing industry has not wholly displaced.

At the other end of the social ladder, the majority of the better-off groups in society, both men and women, had their own clothes made to individual order by essentially local producers. The 'bespoke' tailor in the clothing trade proper (which supplied the requirements of adult men), or the high-class milliner and dress maker who catered for the ladies might, in a small country town, be simply a self-employed man or woman working in his own home-workshop; but many bespoke establishments were far larger than this, and in the major towns where there was a big fashionable clientele, the workroom behind the retail shop could house dozens of workmen or women, some of whom would be qualified crafts-men whilst others would be learners and apprentices. The workers in these sections of the clothing trades, although experiencing a great variety of conditions of work and of rewards, tended in the main to enjoy, by the standards of some other groups of workers in the nineteenth century, a reasonably high and comfortable status: it was the journeymen tailors of this stratum who formed the backbone of the Amalgamated Society of tailors throughout the century, who insisted on a proper apprenticeship and on the training of a journey-man to make a complete garment 'right through', who vigorously opposed the putting-out of bespoke work to those who did not come inside the master tailor's shop to work, and who tried to maintain agreed 'logs' of rates of payment in all the 'recognized' high-class houses in a particular town or city. There was no equivalent organization among their female counterparts, however, and girls remained more open to exploitation in the form of irregular hours and low pay. Nevertheless, high-class dress-making as an employment continued to be looked on with favour by those 'respectable' parents whose circumstances demanded that their daughters earned their own keep, in spite of the fact that the consciences of the rich were periodically stung by revelations of scandals: the amount of overtime worked by girls in the superior London shops at times of national mourning or immediately prior to some great social function, for example, was a recurrent theme in mid-nineteenth-century social criticism.

The essential concern of this study, however, is with that part of the clothing trades - especially the *men's* clothing trade - which fell between the home-made and the individually bespoke: for it was in the wholesale mass-production of cheap ready-made clothing, under an increasingly complex subdivision of labour in the different stages of manufacture, that the outwork system showed remarkable powers of survival throughout the nineteenth century. As the urban wage-earners became a more numerous element in the total popu-lation - both relatively and absolutely - and as their real incomes on average clearly rose during the second half of the nineteenth century, the potential mass market for inexpensive clothing in-creased enormously: for the urban worker was less inclined or less able to have his clothes made at home, and was unlikely to be content with someone else's cast-offs if he could possibly afford to buy new. On the other hand, especially when it came to men's coats, jackets, and trousers, this group of consumers could not run to the high prices of individual tailoring. With the subsistence sector of the clothing industries diminishing, but with bespoke work beyond the means of working-class customers, the way was open for a vast, and in some senses new, sector of these industries to expand in the course of the nineteenth century.

For many years, this sector was able to expand by practising an increasingly minute subdivision of the various processes which went into the making of an individual garment, and by repeating long runs of stock sizes and patterns. The individual worker thus carried out a simple repetitive task at just one stage of the long process of making up a garment. According to Lewis Lyons, a London tailor's machinist and part-time journalist in 1888:

> It is a remarkable thing how these people are unacquainted with the whole of the trade; the person who presses off a pair of trousers could not press off a coat, the person who presses a coat could not press off a waistcoat, but the one who presses a waistcoat could not press off a coat. So the labour is so much subdivided that the worker in the coat trade does not know the actual price given for the whole garment . . .[2]

Under such a system, unskilled workers, who never learned how to make a garment 'right through', could quickly become proficient at their bit of the job; thus the usual pools of cheap labour in nineteenth-century urban society - immigrants, women, and young people - could be readily employed at low rates of pay in work of this sort.

Closely allied to the subdivision of processes was the continued reliance on outwork organization. In 1864, the Royal Commission on children's employment described the organization of Messrs Cook and Son, wholesale clothiers of St Paul's Churchyard, London, in the following terms:

> The greater portion of the work is given out. The material is cut out here [i.e. at the central warehouse] and made up into bundles; this the outworker takes away, and brings back completely sewn to have the buttons put on. Some of these outworkers employ only a few, perhaps only their own family; others take a large building in a suburb where rent is low, or a little further out on some line of railway, and have a hundred or more . . .[3]

Thus we see a large wholesale house putting out the different making-up processes to a multitude of small masters and subcontractors whose own scales of operation might vary considerably, who might in turn subcontract some of the work, and who in all probability relied on some mixture of workshop and 'outdoor' production to get their particular batch of work done.

Subdivision of processes, subcontracting, and much home-working were common throughout the men's tailoring trade, although different branches of that trade had their own peculiarities. According to John Burnett, who made the first serious investigation of the 'sweating' system in the tailoring trade on behalf of the Board of Trade in 1887, genuine outwork was most common in the making of men's trousers and waistcoats and of boys' clothes, whereas coats and jackets tended to be made up 'indoors' under the direct supervision of the small workshop master.[4] But taking the trade as a whole, specialization and subcontracting meant that powered factories, workshops, and genuine homework establishments could co-exist in it for decades. And as R. H. Tawney discovered at the beginning of the First World War, when he examined the effects of the recent minimum wage legislation on the industry, these three forms of production 'do not . . . correspond to differences in the quality of the goods produced. If much clothing of inferior quality is made in factories, so also, to an increasing degree, is much that is excellent . . . while of the homeworkers, some are finishing trousers for kaffirs, and others are making clothing for court receptions.'[5] Thus a wholesale firm in the second half of the nineteenth century, whether in London or in one of the major provincial cities with a large local market of working-class consumers, might in fact rely on a combination of 'indoor' work done on its own premises and 'outside' work subcontracted to workshops of varying size, the smallest of which would be the living rooms of the homeworkers themselves. Cutting-out and basic machining were the processes most commonly done centrally, while needle-work, pressing, and finishing were often put out; but the possible permutations and combinations at the different stages of production were almost endless.

The relative shares of factory, workshop, and homework in men's tailoring varied greatly over time and from place to place. From the 1870s, it might be guessed that the amount of real homework was in absolute decline: Barran's, one of the major wholesale clothiers in Leeds, had 50 'indoor' and between 200 and 300 'outside' workers in 1864, for example, but thirty years later they claimed that 'the bulk' of their work was now done inside.[6] Periodically, however, the impact of revised factory and workshop legislation might ensure a renewed, if temporary, lease of life for the small domestic workplace where regulations and restrictions did not apply, or were less easily enforced: the passing of the Workshop Act in the 1860s, for example, was said to have led to increased outworking in the tailoring trade of Ashton-under-Lyne in the 1870s.[7] (See also Chapter 5, p. 241.) Conversely, Tawney reported a decline in home-working after the minimum wage legislation of 1909, which required that the piece-rates of homeworkers should be such as to permit the average worker to earn $3\frac{1}{4}$d an hour.[8]

An important aspect of the growth of the wholesale clothing industry, of its intricate subdivision of processes, and of its complex mixture of 'indoor' and 'outdoor' organization in the second half of the nineteenth century, was the adoption of the industry's principal technical innovation, the sewing machine. The first mention of its use in tailoring at a Parliamentary enquiry seems to have been in 1856, when its success was still uncertain:[9] but the dramatic impact of the new machine on tailoring, shirt-making, ladies' outfitting, and to a lesser extent on shoe making and other leather-using trades was highlighted in the report of the Royal Commission on children's employment in the first half of the following decade.[10] In this report the use of the sewing machine was extolled because it tended to be adopted initially in larger and better regulated work-shops, and because it could not be operated by youngsters; and where it competed directly on processes hitherto done by hand, the worker's weekly reward was greatly increased by using the machine. But it was also pointed out that 'the economy of production effected by the machine . . . has also led to a great increase in the number of hands', many of whom were, of course, finishing by traditional hand processes the larger volume of half-completed work which the sewing machine could turn out.

The sewing machine thus tended to increase the sheer volume of handwork (and therefore, potentially, of outwork) in the ancillary processes of those industries to which it could be applied in the mid-nineteenth century, just as the spinning machines had done in their own sphere in the late eighteenth century. By performing certain basic stages in the process of manufacture on the new machines, more work of a traditional sort was created for a larger number of workers in the subsequent stages; and as with handloom weaving between 1770 and 1820, there was no need to look to great technical innovation to perform these later stages, provided sufficient cheap labour was available to do them in the traditional way. According to the Royal Commission mentioned above: 'Among stay-makers two or three women working by hand are wanted for each machinist . . . at the Army Clothing Depot it was after trial found that two handworkers to one machinist was the best proportion.'[11] The additional ancillary workers were not necessarily homeworkers, of course; the earliest sewing machines were said to have been introduced by manufacturers and subcontractors on their own premises, and it was often most satisfactory to have the handworkers on the spot, too; but even in 1864, it was obvious that much work, ready machined, was being given out for needlewomen to finish at home.[12] Within a very short time, too, sewing machines themselves were appearing in the houses of the homeworkers, as their price dropped and their purchase by instalments became possible: the better-off workers acquired their own machines, for which they then sought to obtain outwork, and often became small subcontractors themselves by undertaking machining for their less fortunate homeworking neighbours who could not afford to buy or hire a machine for themselves. A Miss Hagley, of Whitechapel, told the Royal Commission how the purchase of a sewing machine for £11 (not yet completely paid off) had affected her family's economy: with her sister, her mother, and a neighbour to do the finishing, she herself machined trousers; working a fourteen-hour day in a one-roomed tenement they made twelve pairs of trousers a day at 10d a pair. 'We could get work enough for twenty if we had room for them here', she said, but her mother was unwilling to take extra work which would have to be put out to neighbours, as they could not be sure that it would be done properly.[13]

How did the fortunes of the different centres where the expanding wholesale clothing industry was carried on in the nineteenth century vary, and for how long did outwork form a part of their organization? The enquiries into 'sweating' in this and similar industries at the end of the century tended to stress the importance of subcontract and homework in London, which not only had a large local working-class market, but which also produced extensively for the colonial trade. Thus A. J. Hollington, whose wholesale house in Aldgate produced clothes for export to the colonies, told the Lords' Select Committee of 1888 that his firm had

60 or 70 men on the premises who cut out garments by hand and machine, and that the making up was entirely done outside by contractors; 'I have not the slightest idea how many are employed', he confessed.[14] One-third of the work given out by Hollington's in fact went to garrison towns and agricultural districts in Hampshire, Essex and Suffolk, where the garments were made up by the wives and daughters of soldiers and farm labourers. 'We send them down by rail at night, the man would receive them in the morning, and he would in all probability do the machine work upon his own premises, and take them out in a van, and deliver two to this cottage, two to that cottage, and two to the next; and this man would drive twenty miles through country lanes and deliver them in all the agricultural districts.'[15] It is interesting to note that in this instance the railway facilitated rather than inhibited the organization of production on the outwork system.

Outside London, it seems likely that the growth of urban working-class markets for ready-made clothing encouraged the expansion of a clothing industry to meet local needs in the main conurbations in the mid-nineteenth century: in addition to Leeds, Manchester, Liverpool, Newcastle, Bristol, and the West Midlands all seem, from the evidence given to various Parliamentary enquiries towards the end of the century, to have had extensive clothing industries. At Bristol, from example, the six large clothing factories under government inspection in 1893 employed 769 'indoor' workers, and had 2,000 homeworkers on their registers – each name on the register probably representing two actual homeworkers. The largest firm of all had twelve times as many 'outdoor' as 'indoor' workers.[16] In the West Midlands, the Dudley firm of Grainger and Smith had, about the same date, 180 to 190 'indoor' workers and about 100 named homeworkers on their books – the latter being chiefly the wives and daughters of colliers and metal-workers.[17] The large-scale employment of women, often on an outwork basis, in the ready-made clothing industries in the provinces seems to have been most common in areas where labour in the staple industries was predominantly male and where little industrial employment was otherwise available to women.

By the last decades of the century, however, the wholesale manufacture of men's ready-made clothing 'on the spot' was declining in some of the provincial cities and, in the north at least, was becoming concentrated in Leeds. The Lords' enquiry into sweating in 1889 was told that at Edinburgh, Newcastle, and Sheffield much less ready-made clothing was being made than a few years before, and the migration of the industry to Leeds, where it was increasingly carried on with the aid of steam power in large factories, was specifically mentioned as being responsible for the decline in each case.[18] In spite of this trend in the big provincial cities, however, London remained the seat of a large clothing industry in which outwork and homework continued to be a significant element until after 1900, and in and around certain towns in the 'non-industrial' south of England – such as Colchester, Bristol, Plymouth, and other places in the south-west – many women continued to add to family incomes by taking stitching and sewing into their homes right up to the First World War.[19]

The same reliance on outwork is evident if we consider other items of clothing which came to be mass-produced during the nineteenth century. Shirt-making furnishes another good example: its expansion, too, involved a considerable subdivision of processes, some of which were carried out centrally whilst others were put out to homeworkers, and the sewing machine was again an important element in the story. Cutting out, and the basic machining of collars, cuffs and other parts could be done in a central factory, with or without the aid of steam power, whilst the making-up, button-holing, and button-sewing could be finished outside by hand. Like their fellows in tailoring, London wholesale houses in the shirt trade sent their work into the country as well as to the East End; in 1843, Messrs Silver and Co. were employing 3,000 homeworkers from their depots at Portsea and Landport, and claimed that there were 'six or seven establishments of a similar kind' at the former place, 'in the heart of low-priced shirt-making'.[20] Their manager explained that 'this business is a great service to poor families, especially when, as often happens, the husband is at sea': it was also evidently of great advantage to the manufacturers, who paid 10d per dozen for stitching striped cotton shirts, for which they would have paid 2s 0d in London.[21] Other dockyard and seaport towns and their surrounding districts, such as Devonport and Poole, were also leading centres for outdoor needlework in the mid-nineteenth century, and government clothing contractors were often the leading employers.[22]

In the second half of the nineteenth century, however, the north of Ireland emerged as the leading specialist area for shirt-making in the Kingdom. Here too, although the 'factories' of Londonderry did the machining and the collar-making, the making-up and stitching employed a much larger number of farmers' wives and daughters in the country for thirty or forty miles around the town. A deputation from the shirt-makers of Derry told the Commission on the Factory and Workshop Acts in the mid-1870s that their industry had been in existence for twenty-five years, and that in addition to between 4,000 and 5,000 in the town itself there was a 'rural and suburban' labour force of between 12,000 and 15,000.[23] Even in the 1860s, Tillie and Henderson, the largest firm in Londonderry, claimed that their 1,000 'factory' workers were supplemented by 9,000 out-workers.[24] Outwork persisted into the twentieth century: a representative of Welch, Margetson told the 1908 Committee on homework that the firm's homeworkers outnumbered their 1,000 factory hands by two to one, and regarded this as the norm for the trade.[25] The rates of pay in the trade may have been low, but in the early days one Derry manufacturer boasted of the beneficial effects of outwork on the rural population: 'Many who had no employment at all before [are] now making threepence or fourpence a day and being thus very comfortable. They are of a class . . . that spend all the money on the spot where they live, which is a benefit by circulating so much money. That their condition is much improved is evident by the improvement in their dress and manner.'[26] By Irish standards in the mid-nineteenth century, these meagre earnings may have been a boon to the rural poor: but there can be no doubt that it was the very cheapness of labour which led to the rapid expansion there of shirt-making on an outwork basis. As one manufacturer told the Royal Commission on children's employment in the 1860s: 'The increased application of steam power will depend altogether on the price and supply of outdoor labour . . . With the present price of labour, the application of the sewing machine cannot be profitably extended. Many kinds of hand labour are cheaper than the same work could be done by the sewing machine.'[27] There can be little doubt that this continued to be the explanation of the remarkable survival of outwork in this industry in the north of Ireland into the present century.

True outwork was not perhaps so widespread in women's clothing as in men's, for the element of individual order remained more important here, and small-scale establishments and self-employed workers continued to be common. In the more fashionable urban houses there was a natural reluctance to let work outside the shop, for fear that it might be spoilt. As one Leeds dressmaker put it in 1864: 'We could not trust the delicate textures we make up out of our own shops. The dresses might be soiled, and great care is required in getting up the goods.'[28] But in sudden rushes, when work had to be finished in a hurry, some of the 'inside' 'women might take their work home to finish it off at night; and at the height of the season, a big establishment might regularly give out jobs to trained and trusted journeywomen who found it more convenient to work at home, rather than have them done by 'learners' in the workroom behind the shop. The lower the social level of the clientele, the greater the likelihood of outwork being relied on, at least in part: the same Leeds dressmaker quoted above admitted that 'in the case of more ordinary and cheaper goods, they could be made out, and are made out for many establishments. Work can be got much more cheaply done in the workpeople's homes than in our shops.'[29]

Headgear as well as clothing continued to be produced by a mixture of indoor and outdoor work until well into the nineteenth century; here the mass-production of standard shapes and sizes had always been more important than individual order. The making of straw-hats is dealt with elsewhere, but the making of men's felt hats in the Stockport and Oldham district is worth a mention here. Christy's of Stockport, for example, who claimed to be the largest manufacturers of felt hats in the country, producing between 500 and 700 dozen a week, had 370 workers on their own premises and 'a large number' of homeworkers besides in the 1860s. By that date, an increasing number of processes were being carried on 'inside' and only 'planking' was being given out. Nevertheless, whole families could still be found working in hot steamy sheds adjoining their homes, and where four of five were employed in a family it was said that their total earnings could amount to £3 or £4 a week.[30] In London, too, at the same date, the mass-production of children's caps and women's bonnets (though not their hats) seems to have been largely carried on on a domestic outwork basis: a maker of children's caps said that it was 'not the rule' to have the work done on the premises: '. . . they are got up so cheaply that it does not pay to have room and gas wasted on them, to say nothing of the trouble of looking after them. Very young children of both sexes are employed at home to help, some as young as seven . . . Sometimes a

woman who takes out work and has no children of her own hires
one or two, paying them 1s or 1s 6d a week.'[31]

It is very difficult to calculate the numbers in so diverse an
industry where casual work was so common, and the task is not
made easier by the frequent reclassification of the various sub-groups
in the general census category, 'dress'. But if it is difficult to estimate
the total numbers employed in the various branches of the clothing
trades, it is even harder to discover what proportion were homeworkers or outworkers. In London alone in 1861, the various
clothing trades (excluding boots and shoes) employed 107,000
women and 30,000 men; the former represented over 9% of the total
female population aged over ten years, or nearly a quarter of the
occupied female population. Thirty years later, the number of
women was 130,000 (still almost 7.5% of the female population over
ten years old), and the number of men was 37,000.[32] The second
great Royal Commission on children's employment, quoting the
census of 1861, claimed that, in England and Wales as a whole,
there were 286,000 women and girls employed as milliners and
dressmakers: this was roughly ten times the number of female
tailors, and four times the number of 'shirt makers and seamstresses'.[33] Figures for the proportion of outworkers become a
little more precise by the end of the century: the Select Committee
on homework of 1907 was told that about one-third of the women
in the various clothing trades were returned in the 1901 census as
being 'homeworkers'. In Manchester, for example, a total of 470
employers still had 4,115 named homeworkers on their books, and
some of these probably acted as intermediaries for relatives and
neighbours.[35] By the time the trade boards had come into being just
before the First World War, the picture becomes clearer still: in the
country as a whole in 1910, the women homeworkers in the men's
tailoring trade were just over 10% of the total number of women
employed in the industry. In Leeds, where the provincial trade was
by now heavily concentrated and carried on on a factory basis, only
570 out of nearly 16,000 women were working 'outside' – a mere
3.5%; but in London, with 32,000 women tailors, 11.4% were
outworkers, and in the garrison towns of Plymouth and Colchester,
with 1,634 and 5,032 women tailors respectively, the proportions of
outworkers were 21% and 38%.[36]

Although total employment in the clothing trades was expanding
only slowly in the second half of the nineteenth century, an im-

portant shift was taking place in the composition of the labour force, especially in men's tailoring. Like other industries which continued to rely a good deal on outwork, an increasing proportion of women workers came to be employed. Women had, of course, traditionally been employed in making women's clothes and as general seamstresses and needleworkers; but the new wholesale men's trade, with its minute subdivision of processes and its use of the sewing machine, seems to have taken them on in increasing numbers. Whereas in the 1881 census there were in England and Wales two male tailors to every female (107,000 to 53,000), the women actually outnumbered the men thirty years later (127,000 to 122,000).[37] The enquiries into sweating towards the end of the nineteenth century asserted that this trend had been especially marked in London: indeed, female tailors exceeded male tailors in Stepney as early as 1851.[38] The Lords' Select Committee was told of 'a growing practice in the East End of London for wives to support their husbands' on account of the 'precarious and uncertain and nomadic form of labour' which the dock labourers of that district had to contend with.[39] According to a Congregational minister from Bethnal Green, women were 'constantly coming into the market according to the rise and fall of the trades or the occupations that their husbands follow. If the husband gets good work they drop out of the market; if the husband falls out of work or it is casual work, they come back into the market.'[40] When Tawney examined the effects of the minimum wage legislation at the beginning of the First World War, he paid particular attention to the economic circumstances and social position of the women outworkers in wholesale tailoring. From a sample of 800 drawn from London and Colchester, he found that the majority were elderly or middle-aged women, and that two-thirds of them were married; among the married women, only 82 were the 'chief breadwinners' of their families, whereas 150 did not 'need' their own earnings at all for family purposes, and presumably worked for 'pin money'. Significantly, this last group actually earned more on average than those to whom outwork was 'essential' – presumably because the latter had a larger number of family commitments to their children or their ailing husbands, and were unable for various reasons to work as long or as hard.[41]

The principal exception to the growing employment of women in the clothing trades (and especially in tailoring) in the late nineteenth century lies in the rapid influx of immigrants from Eastern Europe - chiefly Jews from Russia and Poland - into these trades in London and Leeds in the 1880s. The number of Jewish workshops in Leeds was said by the local factory inspector to have increased nearly tenfold in the five years before 1889.[42] In the working-class districts of both cities, latent antisemitism was quickly aroused, as the Lords' Committee on sweating discovered, by the ease with which the newcomers picked up the simple work routines of the sub-divided clothing trade, by their readiness to accept low wages and long hours, and by their willingness as subcontractors to organize and 'overwork' both co-religionists and gentiles in the clothing and shoemaking trades. In the 1880s and 1890s, it became all too easy to attribute all the evils inherent in any industry where outwork and subcontract - the principal features of sweating - were rife to the effects of unrestricted Jewish immigration on the lower levels of the urban labour market. Of course, many of the allegations of the effects of cheap Jewish labour on the wages and conditions of native-born workers were exaggerated, and their numbers and influence overstated: within London, they were heavily concentrated in only a few districts of the East End such as Shoreditch and Bethnal Green and, according to Beatrice Webb, although they tended to monopolize the coat and jacket section of the men's tailoring trade there, they were conspicuously absent from the trouser and vest divisions.[43] Elsewhere in London, and generally in the provincial centres with the exception of Leeds, Jewish immigrants, male or female, were not at all a significant element in the labour force of the clothing trades.

Finally, what can be said about the earnings of outworkers in the clothing trades? Given such a diversity of products, such a variety of piece-rates, and such different levels of ability and application among the workers, it is clear that generalizations are more than usually difficult. The situation is not improved by the fact that much of the information about the effects of sweating on wages, which was collected towards the end of the nineteenth century, is not really relevant, as a good deal of it relates, not to genuine homeworkers on piece-rates, but to the 'indoor' workers in the dens of the sweating subcontractors, who were sometimes in fact paid on time-rates.[44] However, some kinds of work, paid by the piece, were done by both 'home' and 'inside' workers, and not surprisingly the indoor workers' earnings were generally higher: Beatrice Webb maintained that, even in the lowest quality of trouser work, for example, indoor hands could make 1s 6d a day, whereas home-workers would make only 10d or 1s.[45]

The root of the problem of drawing any really meaningful conclusions from the large but fragmentary body of information on piece-rates and earnings lies partly in the sheer diversity of both the products and the labour force, but it arises even more from the variety of piece-rates offered for what appear to be basically similar kinds of work. As in other outwork industries, it was the prevalence of undercutting at different levels in this highly competitive industry which was chiefly responsible. In the first place, within the increasingly national market for mass-produced clothing, different districts (some more reliant on outwork than others) competed with each other, and in order to 'keep the trade' in a particular place manufacturers had to offer attractive prices to the merchants. Secondly, competition for orders between the different subcontractors who worked for a particular manufacturer or merchant meant that some would be ready to tender for batches of work more cheaply than the rest. Finally, the same sort of competition would be repeated among the outworkers themselves when they sought work from the agents and subcontractors.[46] All this served to keep piece-rates low, but not uniform. To give some indication of the kinds of rates paid in the lower levels of the men's tailoring trade, here are some figures given for the West Midlands to the Lords' Committee on sweating in 1889:

> . . . for the cheaper kinds of boys suits, 2s; the coat and vest, 1s 6d, and trousers, 6d; men's suits, 2s 9d; moleskin trousers, 6½d; men's cords, 6d; boys, 4½d; youths, 5d; knickers, 2s 6d per dozen.[47]

A further difficulty in comparing piece-rates arises because the amount of work a homeworker had to put into the materials she received from the warehouse might vary considerably from place to place even for basically similar garments. As the Committee on homework discovered in 1907, the actual processes involved in 'machining' or 'finishing' a garment were not uniform between one manufacturer and another: sometimes, for example, outworkers who 'finished' had to make button-holes and press their work, but in other cases these were done after the goods came back into the factory or warehouse.[48] Similarly, the amount of work involved in 'finishing' shirts of different qualities varied enormously: cheap coloured export shirts, without stiff fronts, collars, or cuffs, might be paid as little as 10d per dozen 'making throughout' in London, whereas an Irish homeworker, engaged in finishing high-class shirts whose stiff fronts and collars were factory-made, might get 1s 9d a dozen.[49]

There are also the problems arising from the differing speeds of working between different homeworkers on piece-rates, and from the extent of involuntary and seasonal unemployment; both add to the already formidable difficulties facing any would-be researcher into the earnings of clothing workers. We must, of course, recognize that many homeworkers would never attain their theoretical maximum output, because many worked only casually, intermittently, or part-time; their needs and circumstances might not oblige or permit them to devote very much time to their work. The weekly earnings of outworkers employed by the Army Clothing Factory at Pimlico in the 1880s showed that 'permanent' workers averaged between 13s and 15s, where 'sick' (i.e. temporary or part-time) workers averaged only 8s or 9s.[50] But what of the homeworker who tried to earn as much as she possibly could by using her needle or sewing machine to the physical limit? Since the clothing trades were to some degree seasonal (even though mass-production of standard ready-made clothes to stock was fairly safe), and since the homeworker came at the end of a long chain of subcontract, it seems very likely that she could not be certain of a constant flow of work from week to week. Indoor hands in the sweatshops certainly complained bitterly to the Lords' Committee in the late 1880s of the irregular and short-time working which they were faced with for nine months of the year, whereas they were overworked at other times; this situation must have also affected homeworkers to some degree.

But the main and recurrent complaint of the needlewoman or tailoress in the 'slop' sections of the clothing industries was always of low piece-rates and insufficient earnings, rather than of the shortage and irregularity of work. And for the weakest groups of all – widows with dependent families and the like – net earnings could be so low as to require supplementation from the Poor Law; in the 1860s, for instance, it was reckoned that 'in the worst-paid branches of needlework . . . a woman of average ability and industry, working at home, earns from 2s 6d to 6s a week'.[51] At this level, there can have been few outworkers in greater distress. As Henry Mayhew said, in the introduction to his *Morning Chronicle* letters on the 'slopworkers and needlewomen' of London in November 1849: 'I had seen so much want since I began my investigation into the condition of the labouring poor in London that my feelings were almost blunted to sights of ordinary misery. Still, I was unprepared for the amount of misery that I have lately witnessed. I could not have believed that there were human beings toiling so long and gaining so little, and starving so silently and heroically, round about our very homes.'[52] Forty years later, the more thorough but prosaic investigations of Charles Booth and his associates showed that, essentially, Mayhew did not exaggerate.[53]

Framework Knitting

Among the industries which remained organized on an outwork basis until well into the second half of the nineteenth century, the production of knitwear is perhaps the one about which most is known. This fortunate circumstance is the result, firstly, of the wealth of material in the Parliamentary Papers of the middle years of the century, and especially in the massive report produced by commissioner Richard Muggeridge in 1845; but secondly, since the industry has come to be particularly associated with the counties of Leicestershire, Nottinghamshire, and Derbyshire, it has been excellently served by its regional historians from William Felkin in the 1860s down to F. A. Wells, J. D. Chambers, A. Temple Patterson, and their pupils in more recent years. If, therefore, the treatment of the industry which follows seems brief, it can be supplemented by further reference to the works of these authorities.

Although the industry is strongly associated with the East Midlands and with the widespread use there on an outwork basis of the complex knitting-frame which William Lee had invented in the late years of the sixteenth century, it should be remembered that the industry survived elsewhere on a much more primitive technological footing. Until very late in the nineteenth century, the hand-knitting of coarse socks and seamen's jerseys on needles remained an outwork industry employing the families of small farmers in the dales of the north Pennines around Hawes, Dent, and Kirkby Stephen;[54] and indeed, a similar industry has persisted in the Shetlands and the west of Ireland into the present century. Likewise, although it is common to talk of 'framework knitting' and 'hosiery' in the Midlands as if the terms were interchangeable, the knitwear industry in fact produced many different items of clothing, including drawers, shirts, and gloves, as well as stockings. Moreover, it was an industry which used a variety of fabrics and produced goods of many different styles to meet different demands: there was a tendency for the knitting of worsted to predominate around Leicester and of cotton around Nottingham, whilst the smaller centre of Derby was noted for its specialization in silk; but these divisions were not rigid. Thus it would be reasonable to expect some diversity in the development of so complex an industry, and some of the generalizations which follow ought, as a result, to be treated with caution.

The growth of framework knitting in the Midlands was a persistent process in the eighteenth century, and it has been admirably examined in the writings of J. D. Chambers.[55] The shift from London seems to have been motivated in part by a desire to avoid the regulations which the Framework Knitters' Company sought to impose there; but a more important influence was the search for cheap labour, which the small towns and villages of the Midlands could provide abundantly. According to Felkin, there were 2,500 of Lee's frames in London in 1727, and twice as many in the provinces: by 1812 there were 29,000 in the whole kingdom, and 25,000 of them were in the three Midland counties.[56] Associated with this long-term growth was the development of new styles of knitted fabrics through the improvement and refinement of the frame, especially after the introduction of ribbed fabrics by Jedediah Strutt in the late 1750s: new 'fancy' branches of the industry were thus constantly appearing, and demanding additional workers. According to Temple Patterson, this effect was very marked around Leicester from the late 1780s to the end of the Napoleonic wars and, as in the contemporary expansion of cotton handloom weaving elsewhere, it was accompanied by a phase of initially high wages and by the large-scale recruitment of new workers (including women) from outside the industry.[57]

Even at this time, and especially in its hosiery branch, the knitwear industry was vulnerable to sharp changes in fashion and levels of demand; but it is in the period from 1815 to the 1850s that adverse market conditions are usually thought to have inhibited rapid expansion or fundamental changes in technique and organization. Nevertheless, it seems that the workforce continued to grow during these years, if the apparently thorough censuses conducted by Felkin and Muggeridge in the mid-1840s are to be relied on. Their figures show some 20,000 knitting frames in Leicestershire (4,000 of them in Leicester itself); 16,000 in Nottinghamshire (3,500 of them in Nottingham); and over 6,000 in Derbyshire. In Leicestershire the principal centres (apart from the county town) were (in order of the number of frames) Hinckley, Shepshed, and Loughborough; in Nottinghamshire they were Sutton-in-Ashfield, Arnold, Hucknall, and Mansfield; in Derbyshire they were Heanor, Derby, Ilkeston, Alfreton, and Belper.[58] Taking Nottinghamshire as an example, we find that the 16,000 frames were dispersed among 4,600 workshops; the overall average of three or four frames per shop rather masks the fact that a typical shop in Nottingham itself would be about twice as big as one in the surrounding villages.[59] Even in the early 1860s, contemporaries still spoke of there being 40,000 hand-frames of different kinds in the three counties;[60] and only in the last third of the nineteenth century did the Midlands knitwear industry adopt steam power and a predominantly factory system.

It was not merely the direct working of the 40,000 hand-frames which provided outwork in this industry in the mid-nineteenth century: many ancillary processes provided additional employment in home-workshops, especially for women and children. As in the basic textile trades, there was the preparatory winding of the yarn onto bobbins before knitting in the frame could begin; but at a later stage there was a good deal of needlework to be done, in the form of mending, stitching, seaming, and 'making-up' of the knitting from the frame into appropriate articles. As early as 1819, it was claimed that a woman or a child was needed to do the seaming work for two or three stocking-knitters, and Felkin's later estimates seem to suggest that, as the actual knitting came increasingly to be carried on on 'wide' frames, and, later on, in factories with the aid of steam power, the number (and indeed the proportion) of 'outside' seamers and finishers went on increasing; for 1866, when the 'entire English hosiery trade' employed 50,000 frames of various sorts, he estimated that the ancillary workers would amount to twice this number.[61] The rates of pay were low, and long hours brought meagre rewards, but outwork at this stage of the knitting industry seems to have persisted on a large scale, especially in the country, until the end of the century; its survival again demonstrates that the gradual mechanization of one crucial stage in the process of manufacture could lead to an increase in the amount of outwork available in later and subordinate stages.

Until the coming of compulsory schooling in the 1870s, children were undoubtedly the greatest sufferers from the persistence of outwork in the final processes of the knitting industry. In the smaller villages, 'seaming schools' existed, similar to the straw and lace schools of the South Midlands, and Muggeridge was told by one clergyman in 1845 that the parents in his village refused to keep their daughters at the local National school because they were not allowed to take their seaming with them.[62] The testimony of William Hadden, aged seven, of Hinckley, to the Royal Commission on children's employment in the early 1860s is an appalling reflection of what this kind of outwork meant for the very young; William was not constantly at work, and could occasionally have a half-day at school, but essentially he had to wind for the three frames in the house, and was rarely in bed before 11 pm:

> Edwin [his brother, aged four] has only begun winding this week, and winds for two hours in the morning . . . and does the six bobbins which father sets him. Next week he will wind after dinner and leave off when it gets dark (it is December). I shall seam till candlelight, when Edwin gives over. Edwin will not wind by candlelight till he is almost as big as I am now. Little Emily [his sister] is going on five . . . She seams my father's legs from breakfast till tea at 5. She has begun for four weeks, and does ten legs in a day. (Seaming a dozen legs is less than twopence here, I am told.) Walter [another brother] is going on four; he has not begun any work.[63]

As well as this ancillary work, the frame itself provided employment for women and young people, and, as in cotton handloom weaving, adult men were apparently in a minority in the labour force in many places. According to Benjamin Elliott, who acted as middleman at Heanor for Morleys in 1854, 'My fine class goods are worked by able-bodied men, and the coarse work is done by women and children to fill up their time and assist their families. If I let a fine frame to a man, he applies for a coarse cotton frame for his family to work at . . . and they will assist in doing the winding and seaming, which helps to make the family comfortable.'[64] In the same year, the Sharnford (Hinckley) agent of Thomas Corah, one

of Leicester's biggest hosiers, managed 100 frames: as he put it in a
letter to his employer, 'These hands are as follows: 32 men hands, 22
stocking-makers' children, 30 agricultural labourers' children, 16
agricultural labourers' wives'; whilst another agent of the same
manufacturer employing a similar number of frames at Stoke
Golding (also near Hinckley) had 40 men, 26 women, and 30
children working for him.[65] Certainly in the country, outwork in
knitting was thus kept alive, as it was in so many other industries
until the last quarter of the nineteenth century, by the availability
of abundant cheap labour, willing to work casually and intermittently for very low earnings which were no more than a
supplement to total family income.

One feature unique of framework knitting among the outwork
industries was that the vast majority of the homeworkers rented
rather than owned the complex machines they operated; and one
complication arising from this was that the man who supplied them
with work was not necessarily the man from whom they rented
their frame. In the organizational structure of this industry, therefore, a distinction has to be made between the merchant entrepreneurs who provided the materials to be worked up by the
knitters and the 'capitalists' who furnished the tools on which the
work was done. Some individuals, of course, fulfilled both functions,
but it seems that many merchants provided work to more knitters
than they supplied with frames, and that conversely there was a
class of frame-owners who earned rent from frames but made no
attempt to provide work for them. Even the largest manufacturers
employed more frames than they owned: in 1854 Morleys of
Nottingham had 1,700 of their own frames and employed a further
1,000 'independent' ones; whilst Wards of Belper (whose labour
force included also 2,000 seamers, 800 winders, and 700 other
ancillaries) provided work in the three counties for 4,000 frames – a
quarter of them being owned by Wards, another quarter being
rented by them, and the remainder being 'independent'.[66] The
independent frame-owners were a numerous and diverse body: in
some instances they included the workers themselves, as in the case
of the knitters employed at Wingfield (north Derbyshire) by
Wards,[67] but many were obviously owned by the middlemen and
agents who were the key figures in the distribution of work from
merchant to knitter. Thus, George Loveday, of Wigston, near
Leicester, took work from at least three different manufacturers and

supplied it to fifty frames, half of which were his own, and two-thirds of which he kept in his own shop.[68] Frame-smiths such as Daniel Sansom of Leicester were another group who made money by renting out frames as well as by building and repairing them;[69] but there must have been many more private individuals, often otherwise unconnected with the trade, who put their savings into frames to provide a steady and easy source of income.

Although, as has been suggested, an average frame-shop in Nottinghamshire contained three or four frames and would thus provide work mainly for the family of whose home it formed a part, larger shops of 15 to 50 frames, belonging to both manufacturers and middlemen, were not uncommon, particularly in the larger towns and in the new 'cut-up' branch, which used wide frames. In several important respects the position of workers in these shops differed from that of genuine outworkers: they were liable to heavier charges on their wages for 'loom-standing', 'coal and candles' and so on; but they were also likely to work more regular hours and, in Muggeridge's opinion, to have net earnings of 2s 6d a week more than comparable 'outdoor' workers.[70]

Given the bewildering complexity of this system of organization, with its multiplicity of frame-owners, its large merchant entrepreneurs, and its different-sized shops, it is not difficult to see how the key figures in its smooth functioning were the hordes of middlemen or 'bagmen', who in themselves could vary greatly in the scale of their operations. Muggeridge reckoned that half of the fully-fashioned (narrow-frame) work and three-quarters of the 'cut-up' (wide-frame) work passed through middlemen; and certainly, in the mid-1850s three-quarters of the 2,700 frames employed by the Morleys were worked through bagmen.[71] A detailed example of the intricacy of the industry's organization can be found at Heanor in 1844: of the 647 frames in the parish (of which only 55 were 'independent') slightly more than half were worked to bagmen, and slightly less than half direct to the warehouses. Eight different employers provided work for these frames, the principal ones being Wards of Belper, Brettles of Belper, and Morleys of Nottingham. Of Ward's 258 frames, 56 worked direct to the warehouse, 142 were under one bagman and 60 under another; Brettle's 154 frames worked predominantly to the warehouse, but 35 were under a bagman; and Morley's 101 frames were fairly evenly divided, roughly half being split between two bagmen and the rest dealing direct with the warehouse.[72]

What was the role of the middleman, and how did he make his living? Apart from any income he might derive directly or indirectly as the receiver or collector of frame-rents, a middleman would make a straight deduction from the knitter's earnings for his trouble in taking in and delivering the work, and he might in addition conceal from the knitter what the true piece-rate for his work was, and pay him less than the warehouse price anyway; if he arranged for the seaming and mending for his knitters, he would make a deduction for this which he might not necessarily pass on in full to the women who did the work; if he ran a loom-shop, he would make charges for loom-standing and other purposes; and over and above all these, he might also keep a truck shop which his knitters would be expected to patronize.[73] With so many opportunities for penny-pinching and profit-taking, it is not surprising that bagmen were widely disliked. But nor is it surprising that the summit of many a knitter's ambition was to become a bagman himself. The importance and value of middlemen was, of course, repeatedly stressed by employers: the country workers benefited because of the saving of time in going to and from the warehouse, whilst the manufacturers were spared the trouble of dealing direct with many small employees and got the services of men who were in effect managers and foremen at no expense to themselves. The workers, however, were more aware of the middlemen's indulgence in dishonesty and fraud, and of the various deductions he contrived to make. It is impossible to say just how large these deductions – whether admitted or concealed – were, because many of these charges were far from standardized; but Muggeridge maintained that 'the hands complain that they have to work, on an average, two full days [a week] for the charges before they begin to earn one penny for themselves or the support of their families'.[74]

However, the framework knitters' biggest single grievance arising out of this system of organization concerned frame-rent. Both the value of knitting-frames, and the rent charged weekly for their use, varied in part according to their age, size, and condition; yet the relationship between value and rent seems to have been based on no fixed principle or scale. A brand new frame was said to cost of the order of £15 in the early nineteenth century:[75] but frames had a very long life provided they were used carefully and were repaired or 'recruited' every three or four years; and although few new narrow frames were being made by mid-century, a serviceable second-hand one could be had for £5 or less.[76] The normal rent for such a frame was about a shilling a week, and it was said to be possible in some of the poorer villages for a man to pay more in frame-rent than in house rent.[77] It is difficult to say how profitable frame-renting really was as a source of income both to hosiery manufacturers and to the small savers who put their money into 'independent' frames: the beneficiaries were often truculent or reticent when tackled about it in Parliamentary enquiries, and tried to understate the true sum. Their estimates ranged from 5 to 10 per cent 'clear profit on the capital invested' – presumably over and above the basic 5 per cent interest which they would expect – but this should be treated as a minimum figure, and it should be remembered that it was a very steady long-term return which carried little risk.[78]

The knitters complained not only of the high level of rents compared with the low value of frames, but also of their arbitrary nature and of the fact that rent was generally charged automatically, regardless of the skill of the worker, the amount and quality of the work done, or of the earnings made in any particular week. One Nottingham knitter told Muggeridge that the introduction of income tax in 1842 had led the employers to increase frame-rents by 3d a week;[79] and although in some places it was the custom to make reduced charges at holiday times such as Christmas and Easter or, by individual arrangement, during illness, these concessions were by no means general. But the real grievance went far beyond this, in two important respects. In the first place, as early as 1812 the practice of renting out frames was said 'to have been the means of introducing a number of frames in the trade belonging to persons not connected with the trade', and to have brought as a result 'many more hands in the trade ... than are necessary';[80] with income from frames an important element in the profits of both manufacturers and middlemen, it was in their interests to spread the available work around as many frames as possible – which was particularly disastrous for the knitters in any period of bad trade. Secondly, as the piece-rates for knitting generally fell in the long term because of the sluggish market and the oversupply of cheap labour, without there being any compensating reduction in the level of rents, the deduction for frame-rent (together with the other customary deductions associated with the bagman system) made proportionally heavier inroads on a knitter's gross earnings. The experience of William Felkin's grandfather, from whom the historian himself learned to knit, and who died in 1838 at the age of over ninety, indicates what this all meant in terms of a declining standard of living:

> When he began life, the usual hours of labour were ten, five days a week, and one Saturday was allowed for taking in work and marketing, the alternate one for gardening and domestic matters. In middle life, twelve hours' work was necessary. At its close, fourteen to sixteen hours a day scarcely sufficed for obtaining a bare maintenance by those who depended on this kind of labour.[81]

Under these circumstances, it is not surprising that the knitters constantly sought the regulation or abolition of frame-rents until the 1870s. Nor was there any economic reason why this could not be done by manufacturers of their own volition – the Biggs family of Leicester had abandoned rents on their own frames by the time of the 1854 inquiry, and had compensated by lowering their piece-rates *pari passu*.[82] In the end, frame-rents remained sanctioned for so long out of deference to private property and to the right of the individual to make as much profit out of his capital as the market would allow.

Although, as has been suggested already, the basic techniques of framework knitting did not shift decisively in the direction of steam power on a factory basis until the 1860s and after, there was nonetheless an important development, of which the knitters had become well aware by the end of the Napoleonic war, in the growing use of 'wide' (but still hand-powered) frames, usually housed in larger workshops and concentrated in the bigger towns. The old knitters complained, not merely that these new frames were capable of a much higher output, but rather that they made a low-quality product which was not fully-fashioned and shaped, as were the stockings produced on narrow frames. These 'spurious articles' were alleged to be a fraud on the customer and a threat to the reputation of British knitwear both at home and abroad, and in the second decade of the nineteenth century the knitters tried by fair means and foul to have the wide frames discarded and their inferior products banned. In 1845, a Leicester knitter described the development of this new 'cut-up' or 'straight-down' branch of the industry as follows:

The first of those spurious articles were produced about 1810 ...
At that time they used to take the scissors and cut a piece out
from the calf of the leg down to the ankle so as to form the
narrow and the same by the heels and the same with the foot,
and the parts cut out were entire waste. In consequence of the
worsted getting dearer, they could not afford to cut away that
part; they then introduced the leg-board now used, which is a
piece of wood shaped in the form of a leg. Then having made the
stocking straight all the way down and wetted it, they force the
board into the stocking, wet as it is, then they put it into the
stove and dry it, and then the leg-board is drawn out and the
stocking is left in the proper shape. As soon, however, as the
stocking is put into the water to be washed, the shape leaves it,
and that shape is not to be recovered unless it goes through the
same processes.[83]

By the 1840s, according to William Biggs, a leading Leicester hosier,
there was a clear distinction between the large towns, where most of
the work was of the 'cut-up' or 'straight-down' variety done on
wide frames and where the workers were better paid, and the
surrounding countryside where the old narrow frames, much
worked by women and children, produced 'wrought' or fully-
fashioned goods at very low piece-rates.[84] This distinction exactly
parallels the contemporary division in the Coventry ribbon trade,
where the newer 'engine' or 'jacquard' looms were concentrated in
the city, and the old 'single' looms persisted in the villages outside.
(See Chapter 1, p. 62.)

The parallel can be pursued even further, for when in the 1850s
and 1860s the great manufacturers of Nottingham such as A. J.
Mundella and Samuel Morley began to apply steam power on the
so-called 'circular' frames, it was the wide frames which the new
machines superseded, producing low-quality goods.[85] As one witness
told the Royal Commission on children's employment: '... the best
goods, the wrought, are still made on hand frames, owing to the
difficulty of forming the shape by steam power ... in the best class of
goods, in which the fashioning requires frequent stoppages, there is
no great advantage in the use of steam power.'[86] Thus there
remained a place for the hand-knitter even in the late nineteenth
century, just as the finishing stages of the manufacture continued to
supply a great deal of homework for women and children; and it is

not surprising to find outwork still visibly entrenched in the hosiery industry of the East Midlands at the beginning of the present century.

Why did steam power come so slowly and so late? Muggeridge was inclined to put much of the blame on the existing system of rents which seemed inseparable from hand frames: the manufacturer, he argued, 'is enabled to exact weekly from his workmen, in the shape of frame-rent and charge, an amount which may very possibly be considered more profitable to him than the probable advantage he would derive from the substitution of steam for manual power'.[87] His opinion was shared to some extent by a Nottingham manufacturer who claimed in 1863 that there were two reasons for the survival of hand frames: 'One ... the difficulty of doing certain things by machinery, or doing them equally well; the other, the great cost of factory frames ... coupled with the fact that the manufacturers, having property in the existing hand frames, do not like to throw them aside as useless ... But [he added] as the old hand frames wear out they are never replaced ...'[88] The complacent attitude of the manufacturers just before mid-century was perhaps best summed up by William Biggs' comment: 'We grow up to the trade as we find it, without seeing sufficient reasons for altering it ... We have no objection to the factory system, but on the other hand we have no sufficient reasons for adopting it ... The fair inference is, as a *prima facie* case, that the way in which a business settles ... and has been carried on in any locality for fifty years or more is, under all circumstances, the best way.'[89] S. D. Chapman was certainly right when he stated that 'the history of the English hosiery industry is a salutary reminder that the Industrial Revolution period was not uniformly one of impressive business leadership'![90]

Such remarkable evidence of undynamic entrepreneurship in this area of early Victorian industry is partly to be explained by the unpromising nature of the market for knitwear at this time. During the expansive days of the industry at the end of the eighteenth century, when long fancy hose were in vogue, being worn for instance with knee-breeches by men, the fickle dictates of 'fashion' had led to frequent changes in demand for different kinds of hosiery; thus the piece-rates paid for knitting a particular kind of stocking could rise and fall dramatically as demand changed, and in this sense there were always some branches of the industry which were in decline even before 1815.[91] But it was the change associated with the making of 'cut-ups' on wide frames from the second decade of the century onwards which had the most profound effects on the traditional marketing pattern of the industry. 'Cut-up' stockings may have been shoddy, shapeless, and short-lived, but they were very much cheaper to the consumer and they also brought a better weekly wage to the knitter: it was alleged in 1819 that one-fifth of the frames in Leicestershire were making 'cut-ups', that the price was rather less than half that of 'wrought' stockings, and that a knitter could produce more than twice as many pairs on a wide frame as on a narrow one.[92]

The rising market for 'cut-ups' was in part a reflection of changes in both male and female fashions in the first half of the nineteenth century. When men wore knee-breeches they also had to wear smart, well-made, and properly shaped long hose, but, as a manufacturer put it in 1854, 'now that trousers are worn, you cannot tell whether it is a straight-down stocking or a fashioned stocking that a man has on; it is not an article of dress that is seen, so that a person is not anxious to have an article that will make a show or appearance.'[93] The new preference among ladies of fashion in the early years of Victoria's reign for wearing long dresses and long boots out of doors was likewise said to have reduced the demand for high-quality women's stockings.[94] But it is perhaps more important to note that the availablity of much cheaper manufactured stockings in the market probably induced some working-class consumers, especially in the towns, to buy in the shops instead of knitting at home; as William Biggs told Muggeridge in 1845: 'The tendency of cheap stockings is to lead to an increased demand for them, and consequently to an increased employment for all those engaged in making them.'[95] In so far as the hosiery industry faced a rising market in the nineteenth century and had to adapt its techniques and structure to meet the new demand, therefore, it was clearly in this latter direction that growth occurred. But the process was a long and slow one: on the one hand working-class real incomes did not begin to increase noticeably on average until after 1850, and on the other the habit of home-knitting died hard, especially in the north of England and in the countries of the 'Celtic fringe' – indeed, it was sometimes alleged that the low quality of the early 'cut-ups' actually gave it a new lease of life.[96] It is not surprising, therefore, that Muggeridge commented in 1845, recalling Felkin's evidence, that 'upon the highest estimate ... the total produce of the whole number of frames employed in the United Kingdom in a year would be inadequate to furnish every one of the British population with more than a single pair of stockings and gloves'.[97] Under these circumstances, the apparently stagnant nature of the knitting industry until after 1850 was a reflection of the fact that it was gradually losing the 'quality' market as stockings became 'under' rather than 'outer' wear, but was only slowly making inroads into the potential 'mass' market.

The falling piece-rates, dwindling incomes, and general degradation of the knitters – especially those in the country – can be easily explained in this situation: the market for 'wrought' hosiery was declining, whereas the productive capacity of the industry was not, partly because of the immobility of the rural population, and partly because of the large number of workable frames which the owners still wished to keep in use. Muggeridge's report contains a good deal of information about the changes in piece-rates since the end of the Napoleonic war; and although there were naturally differences in the rate of change for different styles of goods, and although fluctuations were neither so volatile in the short run nor their decline so dramatic in the long run, as was the case in cotton handloom weaving, it was still true that the price paid for making a dozen pairs of most sorts of stockings in 1842 was not much more than half that paid in 1814.[98] Urban knitters were obviously less affected by this decline in piece-rates: in the first place they had greater opportunities for working on the wide frames in the expanding 'cut-up' branch of the industry, and secondly they were better able to act collectively to try to secure the acceptance of agreed 'statements' or 'lists of prices' by their employers. Country knitters may well have paid less in house rent and had the benefit of allotments and cottage gardens in some cases, as William Biggs argued;[99] but they were also more liable to be tempted into taking work below the 'list' price. This process was graphically described by William Appleton, a knitter from Belgrave in Leicestershire:

At bad times the men are in such a poor state they do not know what to do ... They stand at the ends of the streets; and some will go and beg for weeks rather than go and take the work at a reduced price ...; others will take to poaching ...; other men, who have been determined not to endure the suffering, have gone in a sneakish manner across the fields to Leicester with a bag over their shoulder to fetch out a bit of work, and do it at an under price, without saying anything about it, and kept it a profound secret.[100]

The disparity of supply and demand had a further effect on piece-rates in the long run, because as rates fell many knitters tried to work harder in order to earn more, and so intensified the overproduction. As early as 1819, it was said that 'where a man formerly made a dozen and a half or two dozen pairs of stockings he now makes, by extra exertion, three dozen at least'.[101] But this solution was self-defeating, and by the 1840s many knitters were clearly caught up in a vicious circle of low wages, insufficient diet, and consequently low productivity even when they tried to put in long hours. One Nottingham knitter, who managed six dozen pairs a week on a very wide frame by working from 6 am to 10 pm confessed that 'unless I lived well, I should not be able to work it. I am forced to have a good deal of beef' – a solution which few of the badly-paid country workers could have afforded;[102] and similarly when Muggeridge asked the physician of Leicester infirmary to account for the low physical condition of the average framework knitter, he was told that it arose mainly 'from the deprivation of the necessaries of life'.[103]

As a result of all these factors, average weekly earnings in the mid-nineteenth century were terribly low. There was, of course, a significant range of variation around the average: some classes of work were better paid than others, and some knitters were able to work harder and longer; there is also a special problem with this industry in knowing exactly how large the various deductions for frame-rent and other expenses were, when we seek to arrive at a figure for net or 'clear' earnings. But when all these allowances and qualifications are made, the evidence in Muggeridge's report suggests that the net income of most country knitters on narrow frames ranged between 4s and 6s a week, with the lower figure representing the norm for women and the higher figure that for men.[104] For 'indoor' knitters in large workshops and on the wider frames in towns, earnings of rather more than 10s seem to have been usual. Similarly, the highest classes of skilled 'wrought' work, where the hand-frame persisted after 1870, were better paid than the lower qualities worked by women and children: statistics collected by

Giffen in the late 1880s suggest that adult men in these branches could make 18s a week and upwards.[105]

The level of real earnings was affected by two other factors: the irregularity of employment, and the persistence of payment in truck. Like most outworkers in the countryside, framework knitters were inclined to celebrate 'St Monday', to take holidays at the time of the local wakes and fairs, and to turn out in the fields for a few weeks at harvest time.[106] But they were also liable to seasonal unemployment because peak demand for knitted goods, as for most kinds of clothing, tended to come at particular times of the year, so that in the slack season there might be very little work available in certain lines for weeks on end. However, knitwear was a multi-product industry, and different items did not necessarily have the same seasons: for example, the wrought cotton hose trade of Hinckley was said to be at its briskest between November and May, whereas the glove trade was active between January and April and again from August to November.[107] For town workers, who had a range of potential employers, middlemen, and fabrics to choose from, a certain amount of seasonal chopping and changing might thus be possible; but opportunities for this were likely to be much fewer in the country, where the knitters were a real 'reserve army' of labour, unless the men were willing to go away from home in search of work, as some evidently did.[108] The only compensation for this state of affairs lay, paradoxically, in the frame-renting system, which encouraged manufacturers and middlemen to spread the limited work available over as many frames as possible; but the result could hardly be called beneficial, for it tended, in Muggeridge's words, to keep the knitter 'on the borders of starvation, with just enough of work to prevent him seeking a more extended field of occupation, and too little to maintain either himself or his family in any state of approachinghqtohpomyolt5Ig2j109 Thirty years later, thanks to the abolition of frame-rents, the elimination of children from the labour force by compulsory schooling, easier migration, more alternative employment, and more stable markets, the situation of the remaining hand-knitters seems to have improved so far as regularity of work is concerned.[110]

In Muggeridge's day, the survival of truck payments was another feature tending to lower the real earnings of country knitters, for many middlemen continued to double as shopkeepers and truck-masters in spite of the legislation against trucking. One reason for this survival was that the wives and families of the knitters were actually in favour of the system of payment in kind, for, said Muggeridge, 'it effectually keeps the workman from the public house or beershop, because he is without money and therefore without welcome there; and it ensures that his earnings are expended at home, on articles almost exclusively consumed by his wife and children'; as witness to the deep-rootedness of the system he cited an instance at Oadby, where a knitter who had 'informed' on a local truck-master was burnt in effigy in the streets by his fellow workmen, who were apparently afraid that the middlemen would show their displeasure by ceasing to bring work into the village.[111]

The demoralizing effects of low earnings – even when one considers the total earnings of a family which ran two or three frames – can easily be imagined, and the accounts which individuals gave Muggeridge of their family economies make gloomy reading. Thomas Brown of Leicester, for example, told him that his Sunday dinner consisted of 'two pennyworth of meat and a pennyworth of potatoes', and went on to say: 'I have never tasted cheese, butter, or sugar the last twelve months. I have nothing for breakfast but what is called chickory ... that is a degree worse than coffee, and I drink that night and morning without a bit of cheese or butter or anything but dry bread ... Our earnings are so small that if we were to make broth it would be nothing. We are obliged to fry what we get in a pan and give the children two or three potatoes with the fat, and a bit of bread if we can afford it ... That is the chief of our living.'[112] But the general demoralization in this hopeless situation was perhaps even more depressing than the material poverty: it was alleged in the 1840s that the majority of framework knitters had lost interest and pride in their work;[113] that they were apathetic about the possibilities of improving their condition by any form of collective action;[114] and that they were unable to educate their children, attend church, or enlarge their minds, so that, in the words of one knitter, 'a man ... becomes more like an ass than a man from his excessive labour, and want of time to study and to learn, and to intermix with social society.'[115] But perhaps the most severe indictment of the stultifying effect a stagnant outwork system had on those enmeshed in it came from Richard Muggeridge ten years after the Royal Commission which he had conducted:

The advantage of putting out work ... has been dwelt upon a good deal, but it is to a certain extent an evil, for the workman never goes out of his own village, and is as ignorant as a carthorse of what is going on elsewhere ... He does not know when there is a demand (as there frequently is) for this or that class of labour ... he is working perhaps in Wigston or Knebworth ... where there are 400 or 500 operatives congregated together in squalid and miserable dwellings. The only man they look to see from week to week is one of these middlemen, who comes with his bag and brings an order to do something, and then there is a scramble among them for the work he brings ... and they would think that great hardship was done to them if a full week's work were to be given to one man while the man living next door to him got none. They would say 'Give us share and share alike, Master. Let us all have the same'.[116]

Admittedly, Muggeridge's words betray the impatience and in-comprehension of a middle-class political economist when faced with the apparent stupidity and the perverse values of the less-enlightened majority of the human race. But in highlighting the isolation, the apparent apathy, and at the same time the remarkable solidarity which prevailed in the poor knitting communities in the mid-nineteenth century, he had put his finger on one of the most powerful influences in the survival of outwork – an immobile and over-large labour force.

This was to disappear in the second half of the century. Muggeridge himself was aware in the 1840s that the town knitters avoided putting their children to the frame if they possibly could: at Derby he was told that the only apprentices taken on in recent years were the children of knitters from the country, and that in the town 'we are getting all old men nearly, now'.[117] It is clear, too, that migration out of the smaller towns and villages had already begun: the exodus from Hinckley, where trade had been particularly hard-hit in the early 1840s, was such that when the regular 'season' began again in November 1843 there was actually a shortage of knitters; [118] and from several villages there were reports of a decline in the number of frames in use, and of men moving away to take whatever jobs they could.[119] By the 1880s, even this had ceased to be necessary, for the power-driven hosiery factories, which had originally grown up in Leicester and Nottingham, now began to spread outwards to the smaller towns.[120] Diversification of employment in the big towns was also apparent by mid-century: in Nottingham there was the lace industry; in Leicester, the growing boot and shoe trade; in Derby, the railway and its engineering shops. All these provided new openings for the young, if not for the elderly. And for those whose circumstances made them prefer outwork, there was still seaming and mending in knitwear, and stitching and 'running' in lace – neither of which obliged their workers to bear the crippling expense of frame-rents – even when there was no remunerative work in knitting.[121] The problem of new employment was most acute for adult men in the villages, but some of their sons at least were able to find work in the collieries which were opening up in the north of Derbyshire and Nottinghamshire.[122]

Obviously, the process of displacement was not rapid enough for the material well-being of all the knitters, and the Select Committee on frame-rents in 1854 still found many of the problems which Muggeridge had described ten years before. But by the 1860s, where hand-frames persisted they tended increasingly *either* to be wide frames, as was said to be the case at Shepshed,[123] *or* to be employed in the finest quality of fashioned work. This remained the situation at the time of the Royal Commission on labour in the early 1890s, when the leaders of the hand-framework knitters – whom they estimated to number 5,000 in the three counties – still insisted that there was no comparison in quality between hand-made and steam-made stockings.[124] But the last remaining 'stronghold' of hand-knitting could hardly be described as high quality: with the inertia proverbially associated with administrators, the War Office at the beginning of the present century still insisted that the underpants supplied to the army be of a pattern which could only be hand-made; as a result, 1,000 old men were at work turning out long knitted pants to government specification as late as 1908.[125] Unwittingly, the State which had done so little in the mid-nineteenth century to alleviate the sufferings of the framework knitters was in the end providing an unintended form of 'outdoor relief' to the last survivors.

Lace-Making

The making of the various forms of figured and patterned lace,

chiefly for the decoration of women's dresses, cannot be precisely
categorized as either a 'textile' or a 'clothing' industry. But it is
convenient to tack it on to an account of knitwear, if only because
the two industries came to overlap geographically to a significant
degree in the early nineteenth century when the 'modern' sector of
lace-making established itself in Nottingham. Traditional lace-
making – where the thread was worked by hand around a number
of needles or 'points' which were fixed in a cushion or 'pillow' – had
flourished for several centuries in the South Midlands and in Devonshire; and, as we shall see, it was to survive there virtually un-
changed until very late in the nineteenth century. But the first
attempts to mechanize the manufacture came, in fact, in the hosiery
district of the East Midlands in the later eighteenth century for, as
Felkin put it, 'it was by various modifications of the stocking-frame
that lace was first made on machinery'.[126] From the 1760s, when
machine-makers in Nottingham were adapting the frame to the
knitting of ribbed fabrics, they were simultaneously trying to apply
it to the making of lace, and their efforts were successful in 1778,
when Thomas Taylor patented his 'point-net' machine.[127] There
followed nearly forty years of rapid expansion and development in
and around Nottingham, during which new outwork employment
was provided not only for those who worked the frames, but for an
even greater number who were engaged in various forms of needlework in finishing the 'nets' after they came off the frame. It was
alleged, however, that the quality of machine-made lace deteriorated in the course of the Napoleonic war as men tried to economize
on the amount of cotton thread used,[128] and cheap 'fraudulent
articles' were in danger of destroying the market – as in the 'cut-up'
branch of the hosiery manufacture. And certainly in 1815 the
making of point-net fell into a marked decline.

However, a speedy revival took place, and the fortunes of
machine-lace-making and the town of Nottingham continued to be
closely involved with one another. The key to this recovery was the
new 'bobbin-net' machine patented in 1808 by John Heathcoat. As
is well known, Heathcoat, disgruntled at the initial reception of his
machine in Nottingham, transferred his business to Tiverton, near
the traditional lace-making country of the south-west.[129] But in
the early 1820s there was an enormous boom in bobbin-net lace-
making in Nottingham, which Felkin described graphically: he
called the years 1823-5 'a time of unparalleled prosperity', when

'capital flowed into the business abundantly from bankers, lawyers, physicians, clergymen, landowners, farmers, and retail dealers in order to construct new lace machinery ... The inflation of the public mind was universal, and became a sort of local epidemic – a mania, acquiring in after-years the name of "the twist net fever."[130] These bobbin-net machines were not necessarily driven by water or steam power at first, but they were very expensive to acquire; thus although some were in the hands of small individual proprietors who housed them in their own domestic workshops, a good number were from the outset kept in large 'factories', where gradually, between the 1830s and the 1860s, steam-power came to be applied to them. Felkin told the Royal Commission on children's employment in the early 1860s that 'while in 1842 only one-third of the then existing machinery was worked by steam and two-thirds of these weighty machines were turned by hand, now, scarcely with an exception, all are turned by steam.'[131] The volatile nature of the market for lace, which suffered severe recessions in the late 1820s and again in the early 1840s, drove many of the small proprietors of the hand-operated machines out of business, so that by the 1860s the making of the actual lace nets was effectively a factory operation.[132]

However, the relatively early disappearance of the bobbin-net machine into the factory by no means saw the end of outwork in the Nottingham division of the lace industry. In the second half of the nineteenth century, the demand for inexpensive factory-made lace for both clothing and household purposes was buoyant; and a large export market was built up, too, which was taking about 70 per cent of the industry's output by 1900.[133] Although the making of the basic nets was done in factories, the various final processes of mending, 'running', 'scalloping' and embroidering the nets were unmechanized, and continued to involve much needlework by hand. Some of this work was done under supervision in large 'warehouses'; but much of it was done in private houses on an outwork basis. Once again, as in hosiery, we see how the mechanization of one crucial manufacturing process in the mid-nineteenth century led to an expansion rather than a decline of outwork in the succeeding stages of the same industry; the two types of organization continued to co-exist, and the growth of the new sector was, initially at least, accompanied by a further increase in the old.

The extent of outwork in lace-finishing in and around Notting-

ham, and the complexity of its organization, was first publicly
revealed in the report of the Royal Commission on children's
employment in the early 1840s. A Mrs Barber, who employed her
own family in seaming and 'running', said in evidence, for example,
that 'there are in Nottingham from 80 to 100 mistresses who take
lace to embroider; these mistresses employ young women at their
own houses, and on an average about five to ten each; they also
employ a number of women at Nottingham, Leicester, Derby,
Sutton, and the neighbouring villages; the women to whom the
work is thus given employ themselves, children and young persons,
and again deliver out a part of the lace to other parties, so that
sometimes the work goes through three and occasionally four
hands'; furthermore, she was of the opinion that 'each of the
first-hand mistresses to whom the lace is delivered from the warehouse employs either directly or indirectly 300 hands. Of the total
number of lace runners in this neighbourhood ... something less
than half are under 18 years of age.'[134]

It is impossible to estimate accurately how many people were
employed, full- or part-time, in this way. If Mrs Barber was right, it
would seem that the numbers were of the order of 24,000 to 30,000
but Felkin's estimates for 1865 were much higher: he reckoned that,
in addition to the 38,000 employed directly in the factories and
warehouses, there were 90,000 to 100,000 women and girls employed outside. According to his figures, there were 15,000 'brown
net menders', 'who usually receive nets from factories and free them
from foul, broken, or uneven threads', and who earned on average
5s a week; then there was an unspecified number employed in the
houses of 'mistresses' in the processes of drawing and 'scalloping';
and finally there were the 25,000 home embroiderers or 'runners' –
the survivors of a group which Felkin claimed once numbered
150,000.[135] Professor Church is inclined to regard some of these
figures as excessive;[136] clearly, with so complex an organization and
with so many casual workers, a precise count would be impossible,
but it is not unreasonable to assume that the 'outdoor' workers still
greatly outnumbered the 'indoor' in the 1860s. It is equally uncertain when this part of the labour force began to decline in
absolute numbers: work of this sort could be (and was, even in
mid-century) done in large warehouses, and it seems logical to
assume that the balance shifted increasingly in the direction of
'indoor' work from about 1870, when the younger children, on

whom the system relied so heavily, had to go to school. Nevertheless, 'outdoor' work seems to have remained perfectly viable at the end of the nineteenth century. The Royal Commission on labour in the early 1890s was actually told that 'a great quantity of work that was formerly done inside the factories [i.e. warehouses] ... is now given out at reduced prices', often bringing the workers as little as a halfpenny an hour in net earnings;[137] and the Committee on homework in 1907 heard that the industry in Nottingham still had 700 'contractors' (i.e. mistresses) and ten times as many outworkers.[138] Under these circumstances, given the low rates of pay and the opportunities for fraud by middlewomen, it is not surprising that lace-finishing came to be talked of as a sweated industry, or that it was one of the first trades to be given a wage-fixing board under the Liberal legislation of 1909.

In the middle decades of the nineteenth century, the fact that much of this work was done by young children caused particular concern. In 1843 it was alleged that they commonly began work at the age of six, and twenty years later one Nottingham middlewoman, who had also lived and worked in London and Manchester, expressed the opinion that 'there is no place where children work so hard for their parents and parents live so much on their children, doing little or nothing themselves, as here'.[139] The competition of child labour in reducing wages and depriving older women of work was, of course, eliminated with the coming of compulsory schooling; but the other evils inherent in the system persisted until the beginning of the present century. For one thing, the flow of work was highly irregular: fashions and styles in lace were constantly changing, so that in some years the form in vogue might require a great deal of needlework to be put into the 'net', whilst in others very little work of this sort would be needed;[140] furthermore, warehouses often supplied the mistresses with work at very short notice, and relied on an easily expansible pool of homeworkers to cope with rush orders.[141] Then again, after the consolidation of the Factory and Workshop legislation in the 1870s, conditions and hours in home-workshops were less regulated, and were generally admitted to be much inferior to those in genuine factories and large warehouses. Finally, the miserable earnings of a few shillings a week reflected the frauds and the undercutting of piece-rates that could all too easily be perpetrated on the vulnerable homeworker. From at least as early as 1841, the lace runners tried to get the manufacturers to agree to lists of piece-rates, to affix tickets stating the price to all their work, and to pay their agents a standard rate of commission for the work which passed through their hands.[142] The admitted need for a wage board in 1909 merely shows how unsuccessful all the previous efforts in this direction had been.

Outside Nottingham, the manufacture of the older form of 'pillow lace' persisted as an outwork industry until the second half of the nineteenth century. Like the hand-knitting of the Yorkshire dales, it provides a remarkable example of how a rural industry using very cheap casual female labour could survive for years in competition with an urban and factory industry which was technologically vastly superior. Traditional lace-making had two main centres: the South Midland counties of Buckinghamshire and Northamptonshire, with the adjoining areas of Oxfordshire and Bedfordshire; and the south-west of England, particularly the districts around Honiton and Colyton. In both places, it seems to have been established before the eighteenth century, and according to legend it grew up in the Midlands under the encouragement of Catherine of Aragon.[143] Eden found lace-making firmly entrenched there in the last years of the eighteenth century, and discovered that women and girls could earn an average of 8d a day.[144] These earnings were enough to make women unwilling to work in the fields, and were said to be a cause of annoyance to local farmers for this reason;[145] indeed, it was even claimed that, in the depressed 1830s, adult men found lace-making a more rewarding employment than farm-labouring.[146] In Devonshire, too, it was alleged that boys as well as girls made lace up to the age of about fifteen, and that sailors returned from sea would often take to the pillow again during their spells on land.[147]

Pillow lace-making, as it survived in the mid-nineteenth century, represented outwork in one of its most primitive forms. The industry in the Midlands was said to be chiefly in the hands of three or four large manufacturers, one of whom, Thomas Gilbert of High Wycombe, gave a full account of his business to the Royal Commission on children's employment in 1863:

> I employ about 3,000 persons. They are not absolutely engaged by me as workpeople, but I sell them the materials, i.e. patterns and silk or thread; and there is a mutual understanding, though

no legal obligation, that I should take all the lace for which I have sold the patterns, whether there be demand for it or not, and that the lace-makers should bring it to me and not to any other buyer . . . The value of the lace brought in by each lace-worker is entered in one column in a book in this way (*shows book*); in another column is the amount of fresh material and patterns taken out; in another, the amount as goods as grocery and drapery if the lace-maker likes to take any instead of money; and in another the balance paid in cash. From some I buy in their own villages, travelling round for the purpose . . . in some places I do not deal directly with the lace-makers themselves, but through the agency of small buyers, to whom I supply the materials and patterns, and who in turn deal with the lace-makers in the same way as myself . . .[148]

Gilbert confessed that, with the introduction of cheap machine-made lace, the older industry could only survive by 'constantly introducing new designs and kinds of lace as the old are made on the machine'.

The features of the industry as revealed in this account seem to have generally prevailed in Devonshire. There, too, the home-workers bought their materials and patterns at the manufacturer's or agent's price, often allegedly an exorbitant one; local middle-women were employed as agents by big manufacturers or merchants; and in the smaller villages, these agents were often small shopkeepers who paid in truck.[149] All things considered, it is hardly surprising that the clear earnings of these village lace-makers were minute: the 1843 Royal Commission on children's employment claimed that in the Midlands 'a young woman must work hard for fourteen or fifteen hours a day to earn 3s 6d a week;'[150] whilst its successor twenty years later found that children under ten would often be lucky if they made as much as a shilling a week net.[151] Apart from being poorly paid, the work was also bad for the eyesight, the workrooms in cottages were overcrowded and ill-ventilated, and the stooping posture adopted in sitting at a pillow was bad for the physique.

One feature of the industry common to both areas were the so-called 'lace-schools', where young children both learned the art and practised it under supervision. A payment of a few pence a week was made from gross earnings to the 'schoolmistress', who was often a middlewoman. Descriptions of these establishments, which rarely pretended to teach anything but lace-making, could sometimes wax lyrical, as in this example from south Devon in the 1870s:

> Here, hard by ruddy cliffs and a blue sea in a land of luxuriant foliage, and under a roof which, even if dilapidated, is probably picturesque, a party of little maids, demure and cleanly, employ their tiny fingers after a fashion which, however irksome in reality, looks more like pastime than serious work. The mistress sits among them, or goes and comes, rebuking sometimes with a look only, sometimes and no doubt sharply with her tongue; but ill-treatment there is none, while cleanliness is usual and order invariable.[152]

But against this are the facts that the workplaces were small and overcrowded; that children were sent to them as early as 6 or 7 years old; that the standard working day of ten hours for an older child could bring an income of no more than two shillings a week; that 'to escape the cane, they have to put in ten pins a minute, or 600 an hour'; and that the only relief from monotony came in the mindless chanting of doggerel verses.[153] Some children, of course, were taught and kept at home; but the advantages to a hard-pressed housewife in a small cottage, in being able to get some of the children out of her way and at the same time to be sure that they were out of mischief and earning their keep, meant that this travesty of education was all that many girls in the lace areas received until the 1870s.

As in the other types of outwork which relied on children, compulsory schooling finally killed the 'lace schools' and the industry which they had supplied with cheap labour. But it seems likely that the industry was in decline even earlier, about the middle of the century, for several witnesses at the Royal Commission on children's employment in the 1860s spoke of the dwindling number of lace schools and of the falling attendance at those which remained.[154] Similarly a Commission of 1888 which enquired into the decay of the Devonshire industry found a labour force which had greatly diminished and much aged in the preceding twenty years;[155] one mistress at Branscomb, who now employed half a dozen where she had once had between forty and fifty, complained bitterly of the effects of the Education Acts in depriving the industry of new recruits: 'I think', she said, 'our country will come to feel it some day, if they don't now, what with our children being put to so much schooling and not brought up as they used to be to a trade or occupation.'[156] Attempts were made to revive lace-making in the Midlands as a 'picturesque' and 'artistic' aspect of village life under wealthy patronage in the last decade of the nineteenth century. A group of 'Lace Associations' organized the production and marketing of high-class pillow lace, and by 1914, according to their recent historian, 'they had staved off the industry's elimination from the East Midlands'. The industry, however, was merely perpetuated, not revitalized; and the main 'achievement' of the Associations – a questionable one, at best – was to keep a few very old ladies in a much-boasted 'independence' outside the workhouse.[157] It was left to the First World War to administer the final *coup de grâce* to this ancient and long-declining industry.

— 3 —
Other Outwork Industries

Boots and Shoes

During the nineteenth century, the making of footwear for the mass market developed along lines very similar to those already observed in the clothing trades. As in men's tailoring, the range of products was wide and the markets diverse, and the organization of production to meet different types of demand had its own characteristics. At one extreme there remained a superior bespoke branch which supplied high-class shoes for well-to-do ladies and gentlemen to individual order: in workrooms behind display shops in the fashionable parts of town were groups of highly skilled craftsmen whose boast continued to be that their shoes were hand-made right through. At the other, especially in the smaller towns and villages in the earlier part of the century, the poorer classes wore rough, locally made footwear, including clogs and pattens as well as shoes, which were supplied and repaired by a host of self-employed cobblers: a genuinely 'home-made' subsistence sector was probably not so important here as it was in the case of women's and children's clothes, but a good deal of repair and maintenance was certainly done at home. However, as in the clothing trades, the significant development was the growth in the course of the century of an ever-widening market between these extremes for mass-produced, ready-made shoes. To meet this demand, a capitalist-controlled shoemaking industry expanded, localized in a few major manufacturing centres, which depended on the strict division of labour between the various processes, which utilized both skilled and unskilled workers, and which for long combined factory and outwork production in varying proportions in the successive stages. It is with this section of the boot and shoe industry that the present study is concerned.

Mass-production of boots and shoes for a more-than-local market was not, of course, new to the nineteenth century. Although there was a 'resident' boot and shoe industry in the capital, the large-scale needs of an urban community the size of London had long been met, at least in part, by wholesale production elsewhere, especially in and around Northampton. Furthermore, the regular requirement of the armed forces for large quantities of footwear provided another wholesale market, which again the Northampton makers were supplying from the time of Oliver Cromwell;[1] and army contracts were a continued stimulus to the industry in both old and new provincial centres throughout the eighteenth century. Military demand was especially important in the Revolutionary and Napoleonic Wars when it made the fortunes of established merchants such as William Hickson of London and Northampton,[2] and when it promoted the emergence of new contractors like Thomas Gotch of Kettering.[3] But the late eighteenth century equally witnessed a rising civilian demand, at home and in North America, which led to the growth of new wholesale shoemaking centres in other places: James Smith, the so-called 'founder' of the industry in Norwich, began producing ready-made shoes to stock sizes there in 1792, and William Horton, who opened the first boot and shoe 'factory' in Stafford in 1787, was said to be employing a thousand workers by 1806.[4] It was increasing civilian demand, too, at home and in the Empire, which brought the industry to yet more centres in the mid-nineteenth century: among the major towns where wholesale production now took root, Leicester was especially important; of negligible significance in 1830, it had more shoe-makers than Northampton by 1871.[5] Leeds, too, was a relative late comer. By mid-century, some of the provincial centres such as Kendal and Street were small and dominated by one producer, whereas others such as Leicester and Norwich had a large number of manufacturers. In many respects, of course, the various centres competed with one another for the growing mass-market, but each also had its specialisms – whereas Northampton continued to be chiefly noted for men's boots and shoes, Leicester and Norwich went in for the lighter shoes for women and children.[6]

It is interesting that the mass-production industry expanded in places where other outwork industries had formerly flourished, and indeed the rise of boots and shoes tended to coincide with the decline of older staple trades. This was true of Kettering as far back as the 1790s, when the woollen manufacture was in decay; it was equally the case from the 1830s at Leicester, Leeds, and Norwich.

Clearly, this was more than mere coincidence: given that the successful mass-production of shoes required a strict subdivision of processes, cheap labour, and a combination of centralized and out-work production, declining outwork centres were the ideal places in which to expand.[7] As the historian of the Norwich industry put it, with a touch of exaggeration inspired perhaps by civic pride: 'The decline in textile manufacture set free a supply of labour which, by virtue of skill transmitted by many generations of weavers, was endowed with just that lightness and dexterity of hand required for manufacturing the finer type of footwear for which Norwich is so justly famous.'[8]

What was this division between outwork and factory on which the industry based itself, and how did the balance between the two shift over time? To answer this question, it is necessary first to look briefly at the process of shoemaking. A shoe has two basic parts, an 'upper' of soft leather, and a 'bottom' or sole of rougher, harder material. Each part is made up of a number of pieces which have to be individually shaped and then fixed together. First of all, the pieces which make up the 'upper' and the 'bottom' have to be cut out and prepared from the appropriate qualities of leather – a skilled process which is known as 'clicking'; then the 'upper' is made, the process of stitching together the various pieces which compose it being known as 'closing'; this 'upper' is placed on a last and attached to the 'insole' by means of a welt, to which the sole and heel are then fixed before the last can be removed – this series of operations being called 'lasting' or 'making'; finally, there are a number of finishing stages. Given the sharp distinction between the various stages of manufacture, it is easy to see how mass-production based on cheap unskilled labour and the division of processes was especially suitable for the industry, and how, in particular, central-ized production in the skilled stages such as clicking could be combined with outwork in the closing and making stages. Further-more, the distinction of processes meant that the industry's com-plete mechanization would depend on a series of quite separate technical developments, since each process would need its own special machine: machines for stitching would be quite different from those used in cutting out, and the mechanization of so complex a process as lasting would be particularly difficult. Since such varied machines were unlikely to be perfected simultaneously, it is not surprising that some branches of the manufacture remained labour-intensive and well-suited to outwork organization, long after others had been mechanized and moved into the factory.

Until the middle decades of the nineteenth century, and especially in the older centres of the wholesale boot and shoe manufacture in London and Northampton, the outwork system seems to have flourished with little subdivision or specialization of processes. The materials for both uppers and bottoms were cut out in the warehouses and workshops of the manufacturers, and from there delivered to the outworkers, who brought them back in a virtually finished state after completing the various processes. Throughout the period when outwork was a feature of the foot-wear industry, it is important to remember that the outworkers supplied in this way could vary considerably in the scale of their operations. The 'single-hand' men were genuine piece-rate workers who sought work simply for themselves and their immediate families; but there were also bigger subcontractors, known in some towns as 'garret-masters', who acted as agents and middlemen controlling larger groups of workpeople, and who might also at times produce on their own account, ahead of demand, in order to keep their workshops in full operation. In London in the 1880s and 1890s, the subcontractors of this sort were alleged to be the per-petrators of the worst evils of 'sweating' in the boot and shoe trade. Whatever the scale of operations, however, each individual out-worker or contractor practised some division of labour which suited the size and composition of his own group of assistants. Within the purely household setting, for instance, children were extensively employed in the earlier part of the century in preparing wax and thread and in stabbing holes in leather with an awl, ready for stitching; the womenfolk, on the other hand, often did the closing of the uppers, whilst the men were responsible for lasting and finishing.[9]

The mechanization of shoemaking, which transformed it from a trade essentially characterized by a mass of hand-stitching, came in two distinct stages in the nineteenth century: the first, which made it partly mechanized but also left it on a predominantly outwork basis, came in the 1850s; the second, which transferred it almost totally to the factory, came at the very end of the 1890s. In the 1850s – under the pressure of a greatly increased export demand from Australia during the gold rush and from the army during the Crimean campaign[10] – the most important development was the adoption of the sewing machine in the stitching of uppers. But there were also innovations in the cheapest classes of footwear which, for example, dispensed altogether with sewing in the fixing of soles to uppers. In the late 1840s, 'pegged work' was introduced from America, whereby sole, insole, and upper were joined by small wooden pegs. A few years later Thomas Crick, 'founder' of the industry in Leicester, perfected a machine process for fastening soles to uppers with iron rivets. As with several other innovations in cutting out and stitching in which Crick was interested, the riveting machines were intended to be steam-driven and factory-housed. However, although Crick's own business expanded dramatically in the 1850s and 1860s – his annual turnover grew from £3,500 to £100,000 between 1853 and 1868 – he was almost alone as yet in using the steam-engine extensively. Even in 1871, when 145 shoe 'factories' claimed to use some steam power, a total of only 400 hp was in fact employed.[11]

Indeed, the sewing machine, increasingly used in all the centres of the industry in the 1850s, served rather to bolster up outwork than to undermine it – as was the case also in the clothing trades; for it was a tool which could be well accommodated in a domestic workplace. Evidence offered to the Royal Commission on children's employment in the early 1860s shows very clearly that some big manufacturers actively favoured the use of the sewing machine in the home, and that a number were actually reducing the amount of machine-work done on their own premises.[12] Typical among them was Mr Stanyon of Leicester, who reported that:

I have had as many as 120 machines on my own premises, but I now much prefer to give my work out, and have only about 20 females here for any special or sudden order. I let out my machines at a fixed rent of 1 shilling a week; some have two, and a few three of them. The cost of a machine is £11 or £12, and reckoning they get knocked to pieces in two or three years, still it answers my purpose. In some cases I have arranged to let them purchase the machine at the end of a year, allowing the rent they have paid. I would not go back to the old system, for I get by this means a better class of girls, whose parents would not like them to work in a factory.[13]

The marked unwillingness of the adult male shoemaker to work in factory conditions, which was expressed in a series of massive strikes in Northampton and Stafford in the late 1850s, was perhaps a principal reason why the manufacturers were prepared at this time to accept a compromise whereby the sewing machine came in fairly quickly, but by and large the factory did not.[14] From the early 1860s to the 1890s, indeed, as one witness said in 1864 to the children's employment Commission, 'everything [was] still transitional in the trade'.[15] The expansion of the riveting process, the development of more sophisticated cutting machines, and the application of the sewing machine to making as well as to closing following the introduction of the 'Mackay' or 'Blake' sole-sewing machine in the early 1860s, all encouraged a gradual, but not a dramatic, tilting of the balance between outwork and factory. But outwork still flourished in most centres around 1890, and, as elsewhere, it is possible that the laxer regulation of working conditions in domestic workplaces as opposed to factories and workshops helped to give it a further lease of life.[16] Certainly, the Lords' Committee on sweating in the late 1880s heard a lot about the evils of small-scale subcontracting at the cheaper end of the London boot and shoe trade, whilst the Royal Commission on labour a few years later was told that the Cooperative Shoe company at Kettering had about half its work done in the factory and about half at home, and that the industry at Kingswood, near Bristol, was still almost wholly 'domestic'.[17]

This compromise between outwork and factory, which meant that identical processes were often being carried out in employers' factories and in the workmen's shops, and that the industry in some centres was far more mechanized and production more centralized than in others, was, however, becoming an increasingly uneasy one in a world of more competitive national and international markets. It was unsatisfactory both for the workmen, who were anxious to defend their position and enjoy uniform conditions through national collective action, and for the employers, who faced stiffer competition at home and abroad from an American boot and shoe industry which was more highly mechanized.[18] By 1890, the men's unions, which had split in 1874 into two bodies representing respectively the older 'hand' and the newer 'machine' operatives, were finding the division between 'indoor' and 'outdoor' working an increasing source of weakness. Outworkers had traditionally enjoyed, and their successors wished to go on enjoying, payment by the piece, whereas in factories the employers were increasingly anxious to maximize the advantages of new machine-processes by paying time-rates; with more mechanization and subdivision of processes, an increasing amount of unskilled and 'boy' labour was taking over in areas formerly the preserve of adult men; and, to circumvent the urban unions' insistence on agreed lists of piece-rates for outwork, it was believed that some employers were sending more work out into the remote villages where the workers were unorganized and the agreed rates did not apply. The employers, for their part, felt that the men were being deliberately obstructive in their attitude to new machines, and were minimizing the potential gains to productivity.[19]

The crisis came to a head in the early 1890s. About 1890, the shoemakers' unions decided on a new national policy: in future there was to be no outdoor work at all, except possibly for women in closing. The employers must provide workshop space at no charge for *all* their men: in this way, the union could keep up wage rates by eliminating the 'independent' under-cutting outworker and subcontractor, and could also more effectively control the introduction of new machines. Although the employers were willing by this stage to go over as quickly as possible to a factory system, in order to speed the mechanization of such processes as clicking and lasting to which American machines had by now been applied, they had no intention of giving their workmen control over the pace and the consequences of mechanization. The result of this impasse was the major lock-out in the boot and shoe industry in 1895, which affected the centres where the union was strongest; the upshot was a severe defeat for the union, followed by the almost complete mechanization of the industry – chiefly using machines leased from the American-owned British United Shoe Machinery Company – on a factory basis by the outbreak of the First World War. Thus transformed, the industry became much more competitive, and enjoyed a substantial export boom.[20] Outwork did not wholly disappear, however: as a means of providing extra capacity at peak times it still had its uses for the big manufacturer; and it still allowed the ambitious small man to get a first foothold on the lower rungs of the entrepreneurial ladder. Thus there were 'at least forty of the old garret masters' active at Norwich in 1910, and it continued to be the boast at Northampton that 'one room and a five pound note were sufficient to start boot manufacturing'.[21]

Before the great changes of the 1890s, the balance between indoor and outdoor work varied from town to town. But the situation was especially complex in London, because of the co-existence there of a large high-class bespoke trade and a not inconsiderable cheap ready-made industry: and as in the capital's tailoring trade, the dividing line between the lower reaches of the former and the upper end of the latter could not be drawn with precision, because the different levels of quality in the market were not sharply differentiated. The highest-class trade continued to specialize in hand-sewn articles made in the 'first and second class houses' in the better part of town, where the workers, like their brethren among the amalgamated tailors, had long been unionized: as such, their traditional object was to ensure that the shops which they designated 'first and second class' paid agreed list prices for specified types of shoes, and did not resort to outwork. But between this aristocracy of the trade and the unskilled and unorganized victims of 'sweating' in the wholesale trade of the East End there was, as the Lords' Select Committee discovered in the late 1880s, an enormous gulf. In the mass-production trade, where subdivision of processes, some mechaniz-ation, and much subcontracting were the rule, it was far more difficult to get agreed lists of piece-rates, and less easy to persuade the big employers to abandon subcontract and set up their own factories.[22] For each 'sweater' or subcontractor, sometimes relying heavily on unskilled Jewish immigrant labour, had his own sub-division of work processes and his own system of piece- and time-rates for those whom he employed as 'specialists' in the various stages in his little workshop. So long as outwork and partial mechanization were the general characteristics of the ready-made trade, as they were from mid-century until the 1890s, the boot and shoe industry remained a significant feature of the economy of parts of London's East End.[23] But with the accelerated mechanization and the transfer to the factory in the chief provincial centres in the twenty years before the First Word War, the London wholesale trade declined in importance: by 1911, East London had 8,699 male and 3,567 female shoemakers, whereas the town of Leicester alone had 15,715 and 7,780.[24]

Estimating the number of outworkers is certainly no easier for the nineteenth-centry boot and shoe industry than for any other. Occupational data supplied by successive censuses from the middle of the century suggest that the absolute number of shoemakers of all kinds remained fairly stable until the early twentieth century, which is to say that their relative importance declined considerably – an unsurprising development, given the rise of heavy industry and services (as opposed to basic consumer goods industries) during the period. In 1851, they appear to have been about as numerous as coalminers, whereas by 1911 the latter outnumbered them by four to one. However, because of changes in census classification, even these totals are not strictly comparable from one census to the next: sometimes the figures include 'dealers' in, and 'menders' of, boots and shoes as well as 'makers'; and sometimes they include the workers in other branches of footwear such as clogs and slippers. But if it is difficult to be sure of exact totals, it is impossible to discover what proportion were outworkers, as opposed to 'indoor' bespoke and 'factory' workers on the one hand, or the still important self-employed village and back-street cobblers on the other. Nor is it clear how fully the totals reflect the often casual and part-time assistance given in a domestic workplace by the outworker's wife and family. All these reservations must be borne in mind in the discussion which follows.

The total number of shoemakers in England and Wales appears to have been the same in 1911 as in 1851 – about a quarter of a million. But whereas in the earlier year only 6% of master shoe-makers employed more than ten men each (as one might expect in a situation where the self-employed man, the outworker, and the subcontractor predominated), by the latter one has, at least in the mass-production trade, a factory labour force.[25] And if the distribu-tion of workers as between different types of work units changed, so too did their location around the country following the rise of the wholesale production centres. The numbers in the country as a whole grew by 11% between 1881 and 1891, but in Northampton, Leicester, Leeds, and Norwich they increased by 55%; and in the following decade, when the national increase was under 1%, it was 14.5% in these towns.[26] Indeed, the 1880s seem to have witnessed the only significant overall increase in the numbers in the industry; for there had been some decline between 1861 and 1881, and there was virtual stagnation again from 1891 to 1911.

In most of the expanding provincial centres of the ready-made industry, such as Norwich, Leeds, and Kendal, the mixture of outwork and factory production which persisted until the 1890s seems to have been a largely urban phenomenon. But in the Midland centres of Leicester and especially Northampton, the industry maintained a vigorous existence in the satellite towns and villages of the surrounding area: one recent historian has gone so far as to claim that 'the villages of Northants and Leicestershire became even more caught up in outwork for the riveted and machine-sewn trade than they had been in the hand-sewn trade'.[27] In 1911 in Leicestershire, about a third of the 33,000 workers in the industry were still outside the county town; and only about two-fifths of Northamptonshire's 42,000 boot and shoe makers were in the borough of Northampton.[28] This is not to maintain that by this date the factory was dominant in the big towns and outwork persisted in the country, for there were also factories in the smaller Northamptonshire towns such as Kettering. But in the earlier days, when factory and outwork production co-existed in both town and country, the same kinds of hostility and suspicion which we have noticed between townsmen and their country cousins in some of the textile and clothing centres were sometimes voiced in these East Midland centres of the boot and shoe trade. As elsewhere, the unorganized country workers were said to be guilty of accepting work at lower rates than the 'lists' which the town unions were trying to maintain.[29]

When the organization and location of the industry gradually changed in the second half of the nineteenth century, so did the make-up of the labour force. The old hand-sewn trade had rested on the assumption that the cordwainer or cobbler, however rough and ready, was a versatile handicraftsman who needed to be properly taught his business, preferably by serving some form of apprenticeship. With the introduction of machinery some attempt was still made to have young machinists apprenticed after the 1850s, but the system became increasingly informal and irrelevant.[30] The more the work could be reduced to a sequence of simple repetitive processes and the more the workers operated as a team rather than as individuals, the greater was the scope for employing unskilled workers who required only a short period of minimal training: Samuel Wildman, a refugee from Hungary, told the Lords' Committee on sweating in the late 1880s that he was promised on his arrival in London that he would be able to learn boot and shoe finishing in four weeks.[31] Furthermore, although opinions might vary as to whether the typical ready-made shoe of the period was particularly serviceable, few would have commended it for its elegance. As Dr Head has said: 'Nineteenth century footwear ...

was often badly made, and rarely distinguished between left and right; the range of fittings was limited, and in the absence of accepted standards each manufacturer had his own sizes.'[32] To produce such articles, no great artistry or long training was called for. The wholesale trade could use a good deal of unskilled labour, therefore, and it seems to have obtained it from four principal sources. In the first place, although the coming of compulsory education deprived the 'singlehand' outworking shoemaker of the services of his young children for ancillary purposes, employers found great scope in their own workshops for employing boys fresh from school at low wages in some of the new subdivided processes. Secondly, especially in London, the trade had its obvious attractions for foreign immigrants, which resulted in an influx of Jewish workers in the 1880s, as in the tailoring trades, and provoked anti-semitic feeling among some trade union leaders which was out of all proportion to the numbers involved, estimates of which varied between 2,000 and 4,000:[33] Charles Freak, president of the National Union of Boot and Shoe Operatives, for example, told the Royal Commission on labour that 'these Polish and Russian Jews that come over seem to me in respect of their conduct to be to England quite as undesirable as the Chinamen in respect to California, and I believe they will gradually undermine our trade unless something is done'.[34] Thirdly, there seems to have been an increase in the proportion of women workers in the labour force, expecially as machinists in closing – a process which continued as the industry moved into the factory at the end of the century.[35] Finally, the list of provincial towns which became centres of the ready-made trade indicates clearly that workers accustomed to outwork in other industries moved readily into outwork in boots and shoes: when framework knitting declined in and around Leicester, or weaving in Norwich, Leeds, and Kendal, shoemaking seems to have provided many with an acceptable alternative.

Because wholesale boot and shoe making exhibited a remarkable mixture of indoor and outdoor working, because the subdivision of its processes became so complex, because subcontracting as well as 'singlehand' outwork was widespread, and because the industry was carried on in a number of independent centres, generalizations about the level of earnings are particularly difficult to make; and indeed there is not at present much information on this subject. Whereas the outworker in the hand-sewn trade in the first half of the

century was a piece worker, many of the employees in subcontractors' shops in the days of the sewing machine were on time-
rather than piece-rates: for example, Mrs Porter, a subcontrator of
Hicksons' in the 1860s, had a shop off the City Road in London
which she regarded as 'a fair average specimen'; in a room ten feet
by twelve she had five sewing machines and also employed 7 or 8
tackers. 'The machinists were paid 12 shillings a week, that being by
the day. The handworkers, tackers and basters, were paid by the
piece, they earned in a week nearly as much as the machinists but
had to work two or three hours more than they to do so.'[36] A
quarter of a century later in London, Samuel Wildman, previously
mentioned, maintained that 'taking it all through the year if a man
is a very quick workman he can make his wages 15 shillings a
week', but this average was based on the assumption that he would
make double this amount for a few weeks during the 'busy time'.[37]
Irregularity of work and earnings were features of outwork in this
industry as in others, although sharp seasonal fluctuations may
gradually have diminished outside London as big manufacturers
could afford to make a few standardized types to stock throughout ·
the year once total normal demand had become fairly predictable.[38]
The mechanization of the industry undoubtedly contributed to the
process, but those workers who remained outside the factory continued to be particularly vulnerable: there were apparently still 'over
a thousand' outworkers in Norwich in the early years of the present
century, and the women among them were said 'not to earn more
than 3 shillings a week on an average through the year, though
when busy they can earn from 9 to 10 shillings a week, and in
exceptional cases as much as 15 shillings. Men taking the year
through cannot average more than 12 shillings weekly.'[39] By this
stage, of course, the outworkers in the ready-made trade in the
provinces had become a reserve army, liable to be fully employed
only when the factories were overflowing with orders.

Before leaving the boot and shoe industry, we should look briefly
at another leather-using industry which also survived on an outwork basis, glove-making. It should be remembered, of course, that
gloves were also knitted and made from woven fabrics such as silk.
The mass-production of gloves was particularly associated with the
wives of agricultural workers around Worcester and in the south-
western counties, especially around Yeovil, and the organization of
the industry was described very fully to the Royal Commission on

children's employment in the 1860s by the manager of Morleys, one of the large London houses in the trade:

> The material is sent in the piece from London to the agent in some central place in Somersetshire, Devonshire, Worcestershire, as the case may be. On his premises a few men are employed to cut out, and then the various parts of the glove are given out to be sewn together. The people who do that are wives and daughters of agricultural labourers scattered throughout the neighbouring country. It is purely domestic work; there is no such thing known as a woman getting ten or a dozen people to do the work which she has received from the agent there. If they live near they bring in their work as it is finished; if far off, probably someone goes round once a fortnight and collects all that is ready, bringing it in for a small percentage. The girls are taught by their mothers; a girl of 14 becomes very useful, at 16 she will often earn as much as her mother, or even more, because she will not be occupied with household matters so much. There are whole villages of born glove makers; it is quite a hereditary talent, and families generation after generation are celebrated for their peculiar skill. We have had as many as 6000 names on our books of persons employed in this manufacture by us in one year. About 70,000 dozen [pairs] a year are cut for us.[40]

Although, as implied in this account, the occupation was part-time and casual for many, there do appear to have been 'glove schools' in some places – comparable to the establishments also encountered in lace and straw; and the curate of Evesham complained bitterly to the same Royal Commission of the evil 'moral' effects which work in these 'gossip shops' had on the female population, who became 'either too proud or too lazy to follow more arduous employments', among which he numbered domestic service.[41] With so casual an industry, estimates of numbers and earnings are particularly vague: there were said to be 'at least' five or six thousand in the immediate neighbourhood of Yeovil in the early 1840s, and 'at least' three or four thousand in the Worcester area thirty years later; and the Select Committee on homework as late as 1907 claimed that, because of the need to supplement low agricultural earnings, 'every house was gloving' in the Yeovil area.[42] With 8,000 women and 3,000 men recorded as glove-makers in the 1911 census, this was obviously not a large industry;[43] but the survival of outwork in its most characteristic forms throughout the nineteenth century is a vivid reminder of the amazing persistence of this type of industrial organization.

Straw

The straw-using industry of Bedfordshire, Hertfordshire, and Buckinghamshire had two distinct branches in the nineteenth century: first, there was the making of lengths of plait from the splints of straw, which was carried on in many of the villages of these counties; and second there was production from straw-plait of various items of consumption – chiefly hats and bonnets – in and immediately around the towns of Luton and Dunstable. The origins of both parts of the industry are obscure; although it may have existed in this area before the eighteenth century, it seems that its rapid and large-scale expansion on an outwork basis came about in the last decades of that century, when it displaced spinning as the staple employment for women. Writing of Dunstable in 1797, Eden described straw-work as having 'given employment for the last twenty years to every woman who wished to work', and spoke of the earnings as being 'exceedingly great'.[44] Why it should have grown so much at that particular time and place is uncertain: the invention of a simple straw-splitting machine in about 1785 made possible the cheap and speedy production of splints of straw from which plait could be made, and its adoption in the South Midlands was 'largely due to the suitableness of the soil for the production of the quality of straw best adapted in colour and texture to the needs of the industry'.[45] But it is likely that other factors on the supply side, such as the availability of cheap unskilled labour, were important, in addition to the stimulus from demand during the French wars at the turn of the century – a result both of changes in fashion and of the lack of foreign (chiefly Italian) competition.

Plaiting straw was a simple repetitive activity, which called for nimble fingers, but required little strength or concentration. Like the knitters of the Yorkshire dales, the women straw-plaiters in Bedfordshire villages could be seen working as they gossiped at their doorways or walked along the street.[46] As with the lace-making industry of Buckinghamshire, with which it almost overlapped geographically, the organization of production of straw-plait was fairly primitive, and it is perhaps doubtful if it can be described as a true outwork industry. For the plaiters seem generally to have provided their own materials, buying sometimes from local farmers and sometimes from travelling merchants. They worked ahead of any known demand, and they often took their finished work in person to sell in the street markets held weekly in such towns as Hitchin and St Albans – although some also dealt direct with manufacturers and their agents who went round to the villages. In all cases they were paid so many pence per length of plait – the usual lengths being knowns as 'tens' (i.e. ten yards) or 'scores' (i.e. twenty yards). By the later nineteenth century the rates of pay were very low, and in any case it was said that 3½d out of every shilling went to buy the straw; under these circumstances, the hourly net earnings of a woman plaiter were unlikely to exceed a penny.[47]

As in the nearby lace industry, children as well as women supplemented family incomes by plaiting, and they were often both instructed and supervised in their labours at the so-called 'plait schools', which according to one estimate numbered 'not ... less than six hundred'.[48] Like the lace schools, these establishments made no pretence of providing general education: they existed to ensure that the children learned the art and were kept at their task until they had finished a daily stint fixed by their parents. The problems of overcrowding, cruelty, and mental stultification implicit in such a form of education should need little elaboration; but the testimony of Joseph Dorvell (aged twelve) to the 1843 Royal Commission on children's employment is worth quoting in full:

> Can read, can't write; go to Mr. Payne's Sunday School. Been working at the plait for two years and a half; I didn't begin so soon as most boys, because I went to a farm; sometimes attended plough, sometimes herded sheep; liked farming best, because you could lie down while your sheep and things was eating. Come to work pretty nigh always at nine in the morning, leave off at six in the evening if we've done our set, if we aren't we sit till we've done; my work is six tens a day (about 60 yards) of willow; earn about 1s 6d a week, from which I pay 3d schooling; Mrs. Demock teaches some on 'em to read, not me. Work is very easy; sitting so long makes my back ache; sometimes tired, not always; play is best. Father is out of work; mother works at the bonnet; one brother works at the willow here also; bread and butter for

breakfast, no milk; for dinner, sometimes get meat; mistress whacks with a stick when they sit idle; never whacks me. Holidays at Christmas, Easter, and Whitsuntide, and two days at fair time. Play at marbles after work; have an hour sometimes for dinner; go home to it.[49]

Once again, it was compulsory schooling in the 1870s, together with attempts to use the Workshop Acts to limit the number permitted in each workplace (which made many of the schools uneconomical to their mistresses) which killed this terrible adjunct to the organization of straw-plaiting; and even then, some schools continued to open in the evenings, and evasions of the law were connived at by parents.[50]

Given a labour force which contained many workers whose participation was casual and part-time and whose individual earnings could vary from a few pence to several shillings a week, it becomes impossible to calculate with any accuracy either the average income or the total numbers of the straw-plaiters in the nineteenth century. In 1861, according to the census figures, Bedfordshire contained over 21,000 workers in the two trades of plaiting and hatting – these presumably being the adult or 'full-time' element; there were about half as many in Hertfordshire, and a further 3,500 in Buckinghamshire. If, as was suggested in 1864, 'one sewer would sew up as much as four plaiters could make', then the Bedfordshire plaiters might have numbered about 16,000, as against 4,000 or so actually making hats and bonnets. But forty years later, the number of plaiters in the county was down to under a thousand, whereas the hat and bonnet makers exceeded 10,000.[51] The president of Luton Chamber of Commerce gave a three-fold explanation of this dramatic change and of the virtual extinction of straw-plaiting to the Royal Commission on labour in 1893: first, the old plait schools had been put out of business by the educational reforms of the 1870s, and child labour was no longer available; secondly, cheap plait from China was being imported from 1873 to provide the basic material for hat and bonnet making; and third, as he put it, 'sewing machines were introduced in 1874, and women could then earn more by machining imported plait than by plaiting'.[52]

The urban industry of making hats and bonnets grew considerably in the second and third quarters of the nineteenth century. In addition to being longer-lived than plaiting, it was also more highly

organized on a capitalist basis, and combined elements of outwork
and factory or large workshop organization even after the end of
the century. The trade at Luton and Dunstable contained a substantial number of small masters who both employed workers on
their own premises and gave out some work to others to perform at
home. W. Tapley of Luton, who gave evidence to the Royal
Commission on children's employment in the 1860s, regarded himself as typical of this class: he had a dozen women in his shop to sew
the plait and to do the lining and trimming, whilst he himself did
the 'blocking', i.e. the stiffening and pressing.[53] At the other
extreme, however, there were large London-based firms such as
Hunt and Brown, which employed 200 women and 15 men on
their own premises, where steam power was used for pressing, and
which also provided outwork for a further 300 to 500, as well as
buying goods from some of the small masters.[54] The position of the
small men was precarious, especially in the late years of the
century, when the plait they used had to be bought from merchant
importers in bulk: this meant that many little manufacturers were
in debt to the merchants, and also that they not infrequently had
stocks of plait on hand which exceeded the orders they had for
hats; as a result they were obliged to use up their surplus materials
in making goods on speculation, which they then had to sell off
quickly at low prices.[55]

If excessive competition among small masters and subcontractors
was one of the perennial features of outwork which cropped up
again in the straw-hat industry, the reliance on a predominantly
female labour force was another. In 1864, it was said that 'it may
be taken as a rule that 250 females [engaged in sewing the plait]
keep about 20 men employed in blocking, etc.', and that as the
industry expanded, sewing displaced plaiting in the villages nearest
to Luton and Dunstable, whilst plaiting receded into the more
remote districts.[56] But in addition to the sewers who remained at
home in the surrounding villages, it was said that 1,000 young
women migrated to the towns from the out-districts and lived in
lodgings or in the houses of their employers; their immigration,
which created a sharp disparity in the sex ratios in the age group 10
to 30 years in both Luton and Dunstable, was one of a seasonal
nature, because when the making of hats fell into its slack period in
the summer the girls were turned off, and usually went home for a
few weeks.[57] If we assume that the main motive behind this

curious migration was in fact to secure full-time work and higher earnings, it would follow that the supply of work to the country outworkers was highly irregular, and their incomes as a result were very uncertain. The industry's historian claims, in fact, that 'it is doubtful if there was another industry depending so much upon fashion and at the same time so seasonal'; and a factory inspector estimated, in 1912, that the average homeworker would have twenty weeks in the year with full work, twenty-two weeks with some work, and ten weeks with no work at all.[58] As in many other outwork industries, vigorous competition among a large number of small hard-pressed employers, coupled with a casually employed female labour force, meant that wages were vulnerable to frequent reductions, and that the workers had little chance to protect their position: an attempt to unionize them in the early 1890s was evidently a failure, for the organizer admitted to the Royal Commission on labour that he had been able to get only 72 members on his books.[59] Yet if earnings were low, living and working conditions were, as assistant commissioner Miss Collet discovered, much superior to those in the domestic industries of London: as she put it, 'to anyone accustomed to a district in which the majority of working class families are content [sic] to live in two rooms, the four- or five-roomed houses in Luton seem spacious, even though hats may be drying in front of the kitchen fire and lying about on the sitting room tables and chairs ...; nor ... did I see anything which for discomfort and unhealthiness could equal the conditions which obtain in every small house on washing days'.[60] Thus, if in the last years of the century the remaining outwork industries had degenerated into the terrible sweated trades, it would seem that some, in certain aspects at least, were less terrible than others.

Nail and Chain-Making

No industrial region in the nineteenth century presents greater problems of definition to the historian of outwork than the hardware district of the Midlands to the north and west of Birmingham. The area had long been the country's chief centre for the making of a vast range of small finished metal goods including weapons, locks, screws, nails and a host of others, and much of the production was characteristically carried on in small workshops and forges in conditions luridly described in Disraeli's novel *Sybil*. Subcontract and outwork were dominant features of many of the Black Country trades until the last quarter of the nineteenth century: but in many cases the subcontractor was a 'small master' with his own shop of employees sometimes producing on his own account, rather than the genuine 'single-handed' outworker carrying on his trade as a piece worker in essentially domestic surroundings, who forms the subject of this study. In at least two of the hardware trades, however, outwork remained well established in its basic form: at the beginning of the nineteenth century, nail-making was, in terms of the numbers employed, almost certainly the largest of these trades; and at the opening of the present century, the persistence of outwork in chain-making – a smaller and newer industry – created sufficiently serious problems to entitle this manufacture to one of the first batch of trade boards set up to regulate wages under the Liberal legislation of 1909. In order to complement the inevitable concentration of this study on the place of outwork in textile and clothing in the nineteenth century, a brief examination of nail- and chain-making will show how similar problems and conditions could arise in quite different industrial contexts.

The hand-made or 'wrought' nail trade was said, in a survey of the Midland industries published to mark the meeting of the British Association at Birmingham in 1865, to be 'one of the oldest trades in the Midland counties'.[61] It had considerably expanded on an outwork basis before and during the eighteenth century in the towns and villages of south Staffordshire and especially in Dudley, and it produced a wide range of products to meet the differing needs of housebuilders, shipwrights, shoemakers, blacksmiths and others, both at home and abroad. The great merchants in the business delivered out rods of the appropriate types of iron to the workers, who forged and hammered them into nails in their own domestic workshops, and who were paid according to the quality and quantity of the work done. As a wholly outwork industry, it probably reached its greatest extent about 1830, when it was generally said to have employed about 50,000 workers throughout the district.[62] But from then on, not only did it meet some competition from foreign-made wrought nails, but it also had to adjust to a situation where a growing number of different types of nails were being machine-made, initially in factories in Wolverhampton and Birmingham, but towards the end of the century in Warrington and Leeds. Thus the market for hand-made nails was steadily falling – except for brief spells of exceptional general prosperity as in 1870-75[63] – whereas the productive capacity of the industry did not contract so rapidly. In this situation, the old industry became debased as disagreeable new features emerged; and the remaining nail-makers, as repeated Parliamentary enquiries from 1842 made clear, became a Midland equivalent of the handloom weavers, and a by-word for poverty, depression, and exploitation. Essentially, three inter-related developments came to affect the trade adversely after 1830. In the first place, as the industry became more marginal, the large merchants and manufacturers tended to get out of it, and more control passed to a mass of middlemen, 'foggers' (i.e. factors), and truck-masters who engaged in cut-throat competition and were able to play upon the vulnerability of an over-large and disunited labour force.[64] Secondly, as the wrought nail trade became less secure and remunerative for men, it came to serve increasingly as a mere supplementary source of family incomes, and (except for specialized branches of the trade such as horse-nails, which were made in Dudley itself) to rely more and more on women workers. Thirdly, the location of remaining centres shifted somewhat from the Black Country proper north of Birmingham to the more remote and often semi-agricultural villages on the Worcestershire border around Bromsgrove.[65] By the time of the great Parliamentary enquiries of the second half of the nineteenth century, therefore, on which this account is largely based, the industry was dying: its lesser entrepreneurs were desperate and disreputable, and its workers disorganized and demoralized; geographically and economically, it existed nearer and nearer to the margin of a great industrial region. Yet it certainly took a long time to die. As late as 1876, a junior factory inspector estimated that there were 10,000 domestic workshops in the nail and chain trades combined, and that there was an average of between three and four workers in each: but this may be something of an exaggeration, in view of the fact that the 1871 census recorded a total of only 17,700 nailers (including those in factories) in the three counties of Staffordshire, Worcestershire, and Warwickshire.[66]

A comprehensive picture of the last years of nail-making can be pieced together from the evidence given to successive Parliamentary enquiries by George Green, a partner in the nail and chain firm of Eliza Tinsley and Co., one of the last remaining large enterprises: in 1876 they employed between 1,800 and 2,000 in the two industries,

made up of about 600 adult men, 400 women, and 800 young
people under 18; by the end of the 1880s, this number had fallen to
between 1,200 and 1,500, about half of whom worked exclusively
for the firm, whilst the rest presumably worked for other employers
as well.[67] In the former year, the business was 'entirely a workshop
trade', where the domestic nail and chain-makers were supplied
weekly with 60lb bundles of iron from half a dozen warehouses
strategically situated around the district; by the latter date, although
about 15% of their production came from their own large workshops, the rest was still being put out in the traditional way.[68]

George Green told the Lords' Committee on sweating that there
were 42 'large nail-makers' in the trade, but it is not clear exactly
what he regarded as 'large', or whether some or any of the ubiquitous middlemen or foggers who figured so much in the industry in
its decline were included: he did, however, provide a graphic
description of the fogger's place and function:

> Supposing these men who work in their own small shops are
> good workmen to start with, then the time does come when the
> [big] manufacturer cannot go on delivering iron to them because
> he has no orders and his stocks are as large as he cares for them to
> be; then these people will go on working in their own shop;
> although they have no iron from the manufacturer they have
> some in stock themselves or will manage to buy it or get it on
> credit; the product they will take to these large shopmen [i.e.
> foggers] and sell it to them at a less price than they would to the
> manufacturer.[69]

It is clear therefore that the nail-makers were to some extent
independent producers, not bound to one employer only, and were
prepared to produce ahead of demand; in a period of slack trade,
they would accept iron from anyone who would give them credit,
and would sell to anybody who would take finished work off their
hands. It was this situation which gave the fogger his opening, and
this which also accounts for the link frequently pointed out between
the fogger and the truck system, which was so firmly entrenched in
the nail and chain districts that a Parliamentary enquiry in 1871
reckoned that about two-thirds of the workers were paid wholly or
partly in kind. For the fogger was no mere middleman or putter-
out (although such men existed in the trade); he might be a small
shopkeeper, a publican, or any kind of local petty capitalist willing

to act as a small-scale dealer in iron and nails for the 'convenience' of his neighbours. Because of their periodic dependence on such men for materials and markets, the nail-makers had to accept the sharp practices to which the fogger resorted in order to boost his profit margins in a competitive situation: they bought their provisions at his shop; they paid his price for fuel, carriage, or tools; and they kept quiet about the faulty weigh-scales in his warehouse.[70]

The shops in which the nails were made were usually attached to, or behind, the nail-makers' dwellings; the best ones were purpose-built along with the houses, but sometimes people wishing to take up the trade built their own – the results being described by William Price, leader of the Halesowen Nail-makers' Association, as 'mere sheds – four posts, and they nail small boards onto them, something like you see an orange box'.[71] Within each shop was a central hearth in which the iron was heated, and separate benches or stalls for the workmen, each having an anvil, hammers, and other tools. To make a nail from a strip of iron, the red-hot end of the strip was first placed on the anvil and 'pointed' with a hammer; the sharpened end of the strip was then placed over a 'hardy' or fixed chisel on the bench, and, at a point appropriate to the required length of the nail, the tip was almost wholly severed from the rest of the rod; the point of the tip was then inserted in a 'bore' or vice in the bench and the rest of the rod of cold metal was twisted from it, leaving an end protruding from the bore; to complete the operation, this end was flattened to form the head of the nail by blows from a heavy hammer – whimsically named the 'oliver', after Cromwell – which was operated by a foot treadle.[72] Opinions differed as to the amount of physical effort needed to do the work (especially to operate the oliver), and as to its suitability for women. Unsubstantiated accusations were made by one clergyman to the Royal Commission on the Factory and Workshop Acts in 1876 about the prevalence of ruptures among women workers; but a number of the Commissioners visited some of the workshops for themselves, and found that the olivers were of varying sizes, none of which seemed to them 'very different from, or more distressing than, a sewing machine worked by the foot'.[73] Indeed, one gets the impression that the moral dangers which arose when men and women worked in these shops, rather than the physical risks, seemed the more reprehensible to well-to-do observers: situations in which people took their clothes off because of the heat, or where a boy and a girl operated a particularly heavy oliver by jumping on and off the treadle simultaneously, were clearly fraught with unpleasant possibilities! When taxed with the matter by the Lords' Committee on sweating, however, one nailer observed that 'as regards immorality, I do not hear much of that, but I expect there is some middling language used in the places'; and Mr Hoare, the Wolverhampton factory inspector, commented – although their lordships may not have appreciated the reminder – that 'you may certainly see far more indecency in the stalls of a London theatre than you see in a chain and nail shop, in the way of clothing'.[74]

The calculation of earnings in the hand-made nail trade presents all the usual difficulties; indeed, in a situation where fierce competition, under-cutting, and trucking were common, even the actual piece-rates are difficult to establish. But for these semi-independent outworkers, there are two particular problems: first, the number of hours habitually worked and the actual weekly output which was possible, and second, the level of expenses which had to be incurred in order to keep up a shop. On the first point, it was said that the nailers, as well as including many seasonal and part-time workers, normally worked irregularly, and kept up 'St Monday' – although in their defence it was maintained that they sometimes had no chance of starting on a Monday, either because the iron had not been ready for them at the warehouse on Saturday when they took in their last work, or because their tools had to be altered to make a different type of nail. It was also alleged that they were in the habit of taking a long break at midday in warm weather, so as to avoid the worst of the heat. Although the nailers themselves complained of the long hours they had to put in to make any sort of living, the Commission on the Factory and Workshop Acts in the mid-1870s did not believe that the average working week exceeded the legal maximum for those workers whom the law protected, which was 60 hours.[75] As regards necessary working expenses, the rent of a serviceable workshop would be an extra over and above the dwelling house, although some of this might be recouped by a householder who let empty stalls in his shop to workers from outside his family; then there was the cost of the coke fuel – known locally as 'breeze' or 'gleeds' – needed for the hearth, plus the cost of buying and repairing tools and any charges for the carriage of goods and materials; and there might have to be out-payments to assistants who worked the bellows for the hearth, if this was not done by the children of the family. Thus John Price, an elderly man who had been an active leader of the nailers in their trade disputes for over forty years, told the Lords' Committee on sweating that his necessary expenses came to 2 shillings a week, out of gross earnings for himself of 10s 6d and for his wife (a woman of 68) of 3 shillings.[76] Other evidence at the same enquiry suggested that women workers on common nails averaged between 4 and 6 shillings per week gross, whilst adult men on horse-nails averaged from 14 to 16 shillings.[77] Four years later, following a strike which was said to have raised piece-rates by 25%, George Green told the Royal Commission on labour that the *net* earnings of his adult male workers now averaged 18s 5d, of married women 9s 8d, of young unmarried women 10s 5d and of youths 11s 9d.[78]

In theory, the earnings of the nailers derived from the published lists of piece-rates for given quantities of nails of particular types which the principal manufacturers drew up from time to time; but in view of the general decline of the trade and the extent of under-cutting by foggers, these lists were often short-lived. Although there were many strikes against individual masters who habitually underpaid, and although some of the specialized workers such as the horse-nail makers of Dudley tried to keep up a permanent association to restrict numbers in their trade (and in particular to keep women out of it), formal machinery for collective bargaining seems not to have existed. As Joseph Rudge, a Halesowen nailer put it in 1876: 'I was never in a union; but we collected money and helped one another in different districts to support our own trade against the masters. That was when the masters used to beat us down, so that sometimes we used to have what we call partial strikes. We should collect money then, and we should be paying out of our small earnings a small portion to the men to keep them on strike, lest they should come under another reduction.'[79] Some major disputes did occur: the violence which attended the great strike in Dudley in 1842 is said to have discouraged the big manufacturers from attempting to maintain price lists, and, indeed, to have been the crucial factor in persuading some of them to give up the trade altogether.[80] The big disputes later in the century seem, like the 'partial strikes' described by Joseph Rudge, to have been conducted on an *ad hoc* basis, and to have relied on funds subscribed by sympathizers elsewhere: on two occasions – during the trade-cycle upswings of the early 1870s and the early

1890s – they seem to have enjoyed some success, albeit temporary, in raising piece-rates. In 1872, after a turn-out lasting just over three weeks, the workers' demand for a general increase of 20% was accepted at a meeting at the Dudley Arms Hotel where, as John Price the nailers' leader described it, 'the masters treated us with plenty to eat and plenty to drink, and very good feeling'.[81] But this Indian summer of affluence was brief: an unsuccessful twenty-week strike in the downturn of 1876 exhausted the funds and broke the union, and there seems to have been no other general turn-out until that in the winter of 1891-2, which resulted in the increase mentioned above.[82] By that time, the advantages which would arise from permanent conciliation machinery for the industry were generally acknowledged, and an old manufacturer like George Green was even prepared to recommend wage-fixing by some statutory body, such as the newly established county councils, as the only way of protecting the nailers from exploitation. [83] But it was another fifteen years before wages were fixed by law in the sweated trades, and by then it was too late, for nailing (although not chain-making) was virtually extinct.

The decline in the number of hand-nailers accelerated from the late 1870s: the census figures for the three counties of Staffordshire, Warwickshire, and Worcestershire, which included factory workers, showed them to number 17,700 in 1871; 7,900 in 1891; and 3,200 in 1911.[84] These totals may be an underestimate, in that some seasonal or casual workers, or some of the juvenile ancillaries, were omitted; but it is not possible to check the figures from any other source, because the manufacturers' wage books, for instance, might list only the heads of families, whilst at the same time many families would be on the books of more than one master.[85] By the time of the Lords' Committee on sweating and the Royal Commission on labour, witnesses were agreed about the general decline in numbers, and the local factory inspector told the former inquiry that there were now only 650 chain and 550 nail shops liable to inspection under some section or other of the Factory and Workshop Acts, together with a further 550 chain and 500 nail shops not liable to inspection, presumably because no person in the various 'protected' categories worked in them.[86]

As has been suggested earlier, the labour force came to include many part-time and seasonal workers as the trade declined and withdrew into the more remote districts. J. S. Parry, of Catshill,

Bromsgrove, told the Lords' Committee that 'fully one half of the men in our district are independent of the nail trade in the summer, and they will not make them at any price; they simply use it in the winter when they cannot get outdoor labour'; in summer the men had their own allotments or worked in the market gardens, and 'consequently we have no one left but the women and children'.[87] The growing tendency to employ women – initially on small and light varieties such as hob nails and tacks, but increasingly on the heavier spike nails – was noted by the Royal Commission on the Factory and Workshop Acts in the mid-1870s as a cause of the general depression of wages.[88] It is thus hardly surprising, given this over-large and unorganized labour force that the trade, apparently on the point of extinction for decades, was never quite defunct.

Nail and chain-making co-existed in the same area of the Black Country, and there were basic similarities between the ways the two industries were carried on and between the problems they created for their workers: home workshops were numerous, women were an increasing element in the labour force, and middlemen and foggers were active. But there were also a number of differences between the two: for example, chain-making was largely confined to a small area within two or three miles of Cradley;[89] also, because the work tended to be heavier, the domestic chain-maker had extra problems of transport and carriage for the greater quantity of iron he used.[90] More significantly, although the work was done in 'factories' as well as in domestic shops, there was not, as with 'wrought' [hand-made] and 'cut' [machine-made] nails, any difference between the techniques used in the two places: at the time of the Royal Commission on labour it was said that 'more than 45%' of the trade was carried on by 'home industry', but the chief difference was that the home-workers were mainly women, whereas the 'factory' workers were exclusively men.[91] This was confirmed by R. H. Tawney in his 1914 study of the effects of the trade board on the industry: out of the 3,000 to 3,500 who worked in the industry's nine hundred-odd domestic shops, 2,000 were women; whilst all the 1,500 factory employees were men.[92] This division between men-in-factories and women-at-home also reflected the distribution of different types of work between the two. Chains came in a great variety of sizes, ranging from ships' anchor cables to horses' harnesses: the bigger and heavier the chain, the more it called for a man's strength; further-more, because of the high cost of transporting heavy chains, the largest work had necessarily to be done in the manufacturers' own shops. Even on the outwork side, there was a distinction between men's and women's work: women by and large were confined to the lightest and smallest chains whose links could be formed by using hand-hammers; 'dollied' and 'tommied' chains, which required the use of heavier tools for striking the links, on the other hand, were the preserve of male outworkers. (The 'dolly' was a hand-operated tool; the 'tommy' a treadle-operated tool.)[93]

However, the principal difference between nail- and chain-making was that the former was an old-established industry in more or less continuous decline from about 1830, whilst the latter was only introduced 'about 1824'[94] and continued to expand – admittedly at an irregular pace – throughout the century right up to the First World War; indeed, Tawney said in 1914 that the trade 'had never been so prosperous as it has been during the last three years'.[95] The census figures bear out this pattern of growth: they show 2,896 chain-makers in Staffordshire and Warwickshire in 1861, and 6,550 in 1911.[96] Given the growing use of chains in agriculture, and more especially in shipping, during the second half of the nineteenth century, this expansion should cause no surprise; it is perhaps rather more surprising to discover that at least half of the industry's output was exported, and that Cradley appeared still to enjoy a virtual monopoly in most colonial, and some foreign, markets right down to the outbreak of war.[97] The industry's difficulties cannot therefore be explained in exactly the same terms as those of nail-making: nevertheless, if the market for chains was growing in the long run, it fluctuated widely in the short term, not least because shipbuilding, its biggest customer, was a particularly volatile industry.[98] A measure of outwork production obviously suited the entrepreneurs in such an unpredictable trade, but it inevitably created problems in slack periods for the workers whose small capital was embodied in their home-workshops and whose livelihood depended on their continued operation: in particular, it placed them at the mercy of middlemen and foggers. In short, the predicament of the 'outdoor' chain-makers closely paralleled that of the handloom weavers during the erratic expansion of the cotton industry in the period 1790 to 1820: unaffected by machine competition, they nonetheless formed an unorganized source of labour which could expand rapidly to meet a rising market, but could not contract or restrict its activities during a period of depression.

In terms of the actual work involved, chain-making was not unlike nailing. The outworker obtained bundles of iron bars between 3 and 8 feet long and of a thickness appropriate to the particular chain he was making. To make a link, the end of the bar was heated in the hearth and bent, cut away from the rest of the bar on the 'hardy', twisted round the last-made link in the growing chain, and finally closed and welded with blows of a hammer, 'dolly', or 'tommy' of appropriate size.[99] In order to make the thickest bars workable, very great heat was required; this in turn necessitated larger hearths, more fuel, and the services of a full-time assistant on the bellows to provide the blast. Measured by weight, the weekly output per worker varied, not only according to the time put in, but also to the thickness of the metal and the size of the links: thus a full-time woman on very small chain might make a hundredweight in a week, whereas an adult man on half-inch chain would make seven times this amount. Not unnaturally, the rates of pay per hundredweight varied inversely with the size of the links, so that fine chains might be paid at 10 shillings a hundredweight, and thick chains at 5 shillings.[100] One seventeen year old girl who made very small chain told the Lords' Committee on sweating that she could make one foot of chain, consisting of seventeen links, in about ten or fifteen minutes.[101]

As already indicated, chain-making was an expanding industry right up to the First World War: and although its markets contracted thereafter, both because of technical advances in welding and because of the loss of outlets at home and abroad, it was still possible for G. C. Allen, surveying the development of the Black Country in 1929, to report that 'much of the industry is still conducted by outworkers or shopowners'.[102] Although expanding, however, it suffered from periodic excess capacity and a glutted labour market; and changes in the composition of the labour force were partly responsible for this depressing state of affairs. As in nailing, the proportion of women steadily increased: the census showed 572 women to 2,324 men in 1861, but 2,102 women to 4,447 men in 1911.[103] Although they tended to be confined to particular sections of the outwork trade so as to reduce their competition with men, the union of Walsall chain-makers in the mid-1870s (who excluded women totally) was nevertheless alarmed at the growing employment of women in unorganized outdistricts such as Cradley.[104] It is clear that the women workers were not merely the wives and daughters of chain-makers, but often workers in their own right, who found the finer kinds of chain-making the only work conveniently open to them.[105] A further source of competition in the labour market, which resulted directly from the decline of the nail trade, came from ex-nailers who moved readily into chain-making as offering a better livelihood.[106] With so disorganized a labour force, even in an expanding industry, it is not surprising to find the workers highly vulnerable to wage-cutting, or to discover that they were among the first beneficiaries of the trade board system just before the First World War.

Just how badly off the chain-makers were in the late nineteenth century remains a little uncertain: some of the information published by the Lords' Committee on sweating in 1889, for example, was said at the time to represent 'the worst cases, the worst examples of the trade', and in a sense this was true.[107] George Green, in his evidence to that Committee, pointed out that the gross average weekly earnings of his own outwork employees were 8s 2d for married women, 9s 4d for young women, and 12s 7d for youths, from which one-eighth would have to be deducted for workshop expenses; on the other hand, the net earnings of the adult men inside his factory averaged 26s 11d.[108] This enormous contrast between the 'indoor' and the 'outdoor' workers was confirmed by Tawney when he surveyed the development of the industry over the twenty years between the Lords' Committee and the establishment of the trade board: during that period, 17 of the 25 rates offered for hand-hammered chains (on which women outworkers were employed) had been reduced, by amounts ranging from 21% to 32%; and 14 of the 17 rates for 'dollied' and 'tommied' chains (the preserve of male outworkers) had also fallen, by comparable proportions in the worst cases. But 'the earnings of the men working in factories rose in the same period considerably, owing, it is to be presumed, to organisation'.[109]

As to the effectiveness of their organization, there can be little doubt. As early as 1892, the secretary of the National Amalgamation of Chain-makers said that 'there is not a man in the cable chainmakers who is not a society man. The employers are not so well organised. I wish they were better organised, so that we could meet and discuss questions with them'.[110] Nothing could better demonstrate the contrast between the weakness of outworkers and the strength of factory workers, or between the rewards of female and male workers. It was the plight of the *former* which justified the establishment of a trade board for the industry; indeed, chain-making was not originally included among the four trades scheduled under the 1909 bill, and it was largely thanks to the lobbying of Mary MacArthur, secretary of the National Federation of Women Workers, that it was inserted during the debates in place of the ready-made blouse trade.[111]

It is perhaps fitting, in conclusion, to refer briefly to the effects of the trade board on chain-making, and in doing so to acknowledge the work done on this subject by that great economic historian R. H. Tawney in one of his earliest publications. Looking back over the first four years, Tawney concluded that, in general, the board 'had the effect of defining industrial relationships by substituting general rules which have been reached after discussion for usages dictated by the convenience or necessities of particular individuals', and that it had 'put all producers in respect of the price of labour upon an equal footing'.[112] Contrary to earlier fears, the setting up of the board had *not* led to a decline in outwork; its minimum rates had *not* become the maximum rates; and the customers were *not* apparently unwilling to have the higher cost of making chains passed on to them in the form of higher prices.[113] Nevertheless, the board was hardly extravagant in its definition of what the much-vaunted 'national minimum' should be, and Tawney declared that 'in practice the board's proceedings are characterised by a caution surpassing that of government departments'![114] In its first awards of 1910, which became obligatory the following year, it decreed that, for women in the 'hammered' chain trade, piece-rates should in future be sufficient to ensure that the 'average' worker made at least $2\frac{1}{2}$d an hour if she had workplace, tools and fuel supplied by an employer or middleman, or $3\frac{1}{8}$d if she worked in a domestic shop; for men on 'dollied' or 'tommied' chains, the rates were fixed so as to ensure hourly earnings of between 5d and 7d or $6\frac{2}{3}$d and $9\frac{3}{4}$d, respectively – the differences in these cases depending on the diameter of the iron being worked; for a full-time worker, all this should have meant a minimum net weekly income of 11s 3d for the average woman, and between 20s and 28s for the average man. In order to produce minimum earnings at this level, the actual median increase in piece-rates for 'dollied' and 'tommied' chains was 35%, and between 50% and 80% for some of the worst-paid hammered chains. Even with the minimum set at the ungenerous level of $2\frac{1}{2}$d an hour, and with the remarkably explicit assumption that a man should earn twice as much as a woman for an hour's work, the effects of this particular trade board, at least, could not be described as negligible.

Miscellaneous Outwork Industries

In addition to the major industries already examined, there were many others in which production was organized on an outwork basis in the nineteenth century. Often, of course, the place of outwork was genuinely marginal: that is, factory or workshop owners saw it as the most convenient way of coping with an overflow of work during 'the busy season' or of despatching a sudden 'rush' order. Even in so long centralized an industry as earthenware in the Stoke district, it was still the practice at the end of the century to have a limited amount of the decoration of china done 'outside' at busy times.[115] A similar situation arose in the London bookbinding industry, because the peak publishing season fell in the winter months. In these circumstances, outwork was often really a form of overtime and a means of evading the limits on working hours imposed in the Factory and Workshop Acts; for the outwork was often simply extra work taken home and done after hours by the indoor workpeople.[116]

This resort to outwork in busy seasons is hardly surprising in view of the obvious advantages this type of production offered for a sharp, short-lived, and inexpensive increase in capacity in trades where there was a good deal of light, unskilled, but labour-intensive work. Rather more surprising is the wide range of small and miscellaneous manufacturing industries, especially in London, of which outwork was a *permanent* feature. These trades rarely existed solely, or even largely, on an outwork basis, since most could equally be carried on, with or without the aid of some machines, in workshops of varying sizes: but genuine homeworkers were sufficiently common in them, even in the early years of the present century, to attract the notice of the 'anti-sweating' lobby and to be investigated by the Select Committee on homework in 1907. Some of the trades in question were really subordinate branches of the clothing industry: one good example was the making of coloured artificial flowers of silk or muslin for the decoration of dresses, which in the 1860s employed some 11,000 people (mainly young girls, and predominantly in London) and in which an experienced hand on piece-work could make 12 shillings a week during the three- or four-month season.[117] Others involved simple assembly work with the homeworker fitting together various small parts to make a completed object. Brush-drawing was typical of this group: according to Miss R. E. Squire, a factory inspector who gave evidence to the 1907 homework Committee, it comprised 'putting the tufts of bristle into the holes in the wooden back and drawing the tufts through with wire and fastening them at the back', a hard and dusty task calling for great dexterity but earning rates of pay which rarely exceeded a halfpenny a brush.[118] Even less wholesome were such occupations as fur-pulling (again, an adjunct of the clothing industry) which, according to Miss Squire, consisted in removing the unwanted long hairs from rabbit skins: the worker 'presses the skins between her knee and the table ... and pulls the long hairs from the skin. These hairs float everywhere and fill the room, everything is grey with the hair, ... everything becomes covered with it, and the smell of the skins is most nauseating'. For this task – 'dusty, dirty, unpleasant, and insanitary – wholly unfit for a dwelling' – the worker got between one and two shillings a 'turn', which consisted of sixty skins.[119] Many similar trades were exposed in the long campaign against homework in the first decade of the present century: most, predictably, were located in London and the other great cities, and catered for the miscellaneous wants of different segments of the vast urban population;[120] but some, like brush-drawing, provided basic household items in general use throughout the country, and were more widely dispersed – in Devonshire, for example, 'whole villages of women' were said to be employed in tooth-brush drawing.[121]

The demands for which this host of miscellaneous industries catered may – on a long view – have been small and relatively stable. But many of those trades were of quite recent origin and grew steadily in the late years of the nineteenth century in response to the gradually rising affluence and the changing tastes of various social strata in late Victorian Britain. Their entrepreneurs tended, however, to work from small beginnings and were unlikely to be faced with a sudden mushrooming of demand; thus it is not surprising that they played safe and stuck to handicraft and out-work methods of production, at any rate in part, for as long as possible. The mass-production of chairs in High Wycombe provides a good example of such an industry: although essentially carried on in workshops and small 'factories', certain processes – notably the making of chair bottoms from canes or rushes – were also done domestically by women and children, and continued to rely partly on homework right up to the First World War.[122]

Another area where the trend of rising affluence made itself particularly evident was in the packaging, presentation, and distribution of common household items and provisions. Professor Charles Wilson, in a famous recent article[123] has drawn attention to the remarkable rise in Britain of mass-production consumer goods industries in the last quarter of the nineteenth century and to the nationwide revolution in retailing and distribution which was associated with them: and the present study has indicated how part of this process involved the decline of outwork production in favour of the factory in such mass-production industries as ready-made footwear and clothing. But if outwork was disappearing from the manufacture of the items themselves, it still had a part to play in their distribution and display. Ready-made shoes and shirts which were nationally advertised and universally available needed to be securely wrapped and attractively packaged, just as machine-made buttons and other items aimed at the careful housewife needed to be sewed in dozens onto cards before they crossed the counters of corner shops in the great industrial towns and cities. Initially, industries like paper-bag and cardboard-box making met the new demands which this 'affluent' society put upon them by expanding labour-intensive processes which lent themselves easily to outwork production; as such, their history in the nineteenth century provides yet another example of the versatility and value of the 'outmoded domestic system' in *growing* areas of the industrial economy.

Box-making was perhaps the most interesting and important of these 'new' industries: it attracted the attention of the homework Committee in 1907-8, was one of the industries granted a trade board under the Liberal legislation of 1909, and came under the scrutiny of R. H. Tawney and his colleagues when they studied the workings of the first group of boards at the beginning of the First World War; thus there is a reasonable amount of fairly accessible information about it. One manufacturer, C. E. Watts, who was a witness before the homework Committee, provided some interesting infomation about the industry's origins and development: his own firm had been in business in London since 1842, and he knew only two others which went back beyond this; he believed there were now some 400 firms in the industry, as compared with a mere 70 two decades previously; his own establishment, which in the previous year had produced as many as 4,500 different kinds of boxes, still relied on a fluctuating band of between 300 and 400 homeworkers in addition to indoor hands, largely to cope with seasonal demand and to avoid having empty workrooms in slack seasons, 'which in a place like London is a costly thing'.[124] Further information about the industry is provided in M. E. Bulkley's study of the working of its trade board published in 1915: most of its employers operated on a very small scale – of 281 in London in 1913, 55 employed fewer than 10 workers each (including home-workers) and another 70 employed between 10 and 20. The census of 1911 showed that the total number of box-makers in England and Wales was now about 4,000 men and 26,000 women, with a further 1,000 and 8,000 respectively in the associated paper-bag industry; although the largest concentration was in London, the industry in fact existed in all the major provincial conurbations, because the firms in it tended to have grown up close to the factories where the goods to be 'boxed' were made.[125] By the early years of this century, genuine homework was fast disappearing except in London and Birmingham, as the scale of operations expanded and more and more of the simple repetitive processes became mechanized. Yet the old and the new still co-existed, and there was no clear distinction between the kinds of boxes made by machines in factories and those still made by hand or at home: fancy boxes, or 'novelties', such as those for quality chocolates, continued to be hand-made, yet even such basic items as match-boxes were still made at home as well as in factories.[126]

Clementina Black gave a graphic picture of the low-paid drudgery of the domestic match-box maker in her book *Sweated Industry*:

At first sight it is a pretty enough spectacle to see a match-box made; one motion of the hands bends into shape the notched frame of the case, another surrounds it with the ready-pasted strip of printed wrapper which, by long practice, is fitted instantly without a wrinkle, then the sandpaper or the phosphorus paper, pasted ready beforehand, is applied and pressed on so that it sticks fast .... The finished case is thrown upon the floor; the long narrow strip which is to form the frame of the drawer is laid upon the bright strip of ready-pasted paper, then bent together and joined by an overlapping bit of the paper; the edges of paper below are bent flat, the ready-cut bottom is dropped in and pressed down, and before the fingers are withdrawn they fold over the upper edges of the paper inside the top. Now the drawer, too, is cast on the floor to dry. All this, besides the preliminary pasting of wrapper, coloured paper, and sandpaper had to be done 144 times for 2¼d; and even this is not all, for every drawer and case have to be fitted together and the packets tied up with hemp. Nor is the work done then, for paste has to be made before it can be used, and boxes, when they are ready, have to be carried to the factory.[127]

It is not surprising to learn that the domestic match-box makers were the biggest beneficiaries from increased rates of pay under the new trade board.[128] Yet the board in its early days was hardly revolutionary: faced with the enormous range of different types of boxes produced, it simply confined itself initially to fixing a minimum time-rate of 3d an hour for women (and 6d an hour for adult men). Manufacturers were left to adjust their own piece-rates so that the 'average' worker could make this amount by an hour's work, and workers were expected to inform their employers (and ultimately the board) if they were unable to get through enough work to earn this sum at the prevailing piece-rates; however, it seems that many women were afraid to complain that the rates were still too low to enable them to make 3d an hour, lest they should be dismissed as inefficient.[129] Although the board's early years saw the continued decline in the number of outworkers in this rapidly changing industry, it is doubtful whether the creation of the board had much to do with it: Bulkley argued that the Lloyd George insurance schemes bore at least as much of the responsibility, since 'some firms seem to have deicded that their home-workers were not worth employing [and having contributions paid for them] unless they turned out a given amount of work a week'.[130] Summing up the board's effects in his introduction to the Bulkley report, R. H. Tawney wrote, rather sadly:

The truth is that the minimum wage, at any rate as applied hitherto, is a much less drastic measure than its critics - or even its advocates - sometimes seem to suppose .... The mere fact that it is a minimum means that it has but a slight effect on the better paid districts of the industry, and the real criticism to be brought against the proceedings of the Boxmakimg, as of the Tailoring, Board is not that it has fixed the minimum rates too high, but that it has fixed them considerably below what many employers were already paying without difficulty before the Trade Board was established.[131]

The carding of buttons, hooks-and-eyes, safety-pins, and hair-grips in the Birmingham district was another outwork industry stimulated by the selfsame mass-production and retailing 'revolution' in the late nineteenth century, although here again factory machines were fast taking over from the homeworkers by 1900. Birmingham's chief factory inspector told the homework Committee that '7 or 8' firms gave out buttons for carding to some 700 women, and that half-a-dozen hook-and-eye manufacturers did the same for a further 1,100, many of whom were small subcontractors who distributed the work among their neighbours 'in a perambulator or wheelbarrow, or anything they can get to carry it in'; because of the extensive subletting to casual workers in this way, the inspector reckoned that between 15 to 20,000 might be employed in this group of trades at one time or another.[132] Button-carding was said to be the most depressed of these trades, and the one in which factory machines had made the most progress: rates of pay were as low as half-a-crown to 3 shillings per *hundred gross* of buttons, and average net weekly earnings (when allowance had been made for needle and thread) were between 2 and 3 shillings;[133] hook-and-eye stitching, on the other hand, was still 90% unmechanized, and better paid. It seems that this kind of outwork was very much part-time and casual, being resorted to only when there was acute financial difficulty in the home; and in so far as outwork survives in manufacturing industry right up to the present time – in the painting of toy soldiers or the assembling of ball-point pens, for example – it often does so under essentially similar circumstances.

One final aspect of outwork deserves a brief mention. So far we have considered outwork as something associated with manufacturing industry, but it is worth remembering that it has had a place in the provision of many different services as well as in the making of a great variety of goods. Of course, many who have traditionally provided services in their own homes – like the self-employed craftsman in industry – are small independent entrepreneurs rather than wage-earners: groups as varied as prostitutes, washerwomen, landladies and music-teachers all come under this heading. Yet even they, at some levels, have been organized and controlled by agents and rings, so that it is not entirely fanciful to equate the pimp, the tout, and the proprietor of the bureau or agency with the putter-out, the fogger, and the bagman. At the present time, too, outwork still survives in the service sector as well as in manufacturing: typing agencies who distributed work to home-based secretaries are obvious examples. Even more, it is increasingly well established today in retailing and distribution: the young housewife on the new estate who holds a clothing party, sells make-up to her friends, or runs a mail-order club, is as much an outworker as her ancestor who spun at the wheel, sewed buttons, mended lace, or hammered nails; she is impelled to seek work by precisely the same forces, and her necessities offer precisely the same incentives to employers to take her on. These arguments also apply, it should be added, to her schoolmaster husband who devotes the first fortnight of his summer holidays to marking scripts for some examining board!

Thus outwork did not die with industrialization, it merely changed its forms: it disappeared in one area, only to crop up in another. Indeed it is probably indestructible, for the circumstances which have kept it going in the past show no signs of vanishing: so long as there are women who find it hard to make ends meet as they strive to run their homes, there exists a cheap and docile labour force for anyone who wishes to use it; the only requirement is that the work provided should be such as can conveniently be done in the home. Outworkers have long formed a distinct stratum among 'the poor' in our industrializing society: and like the poor in general, they seem fated to be always with us.

Conclusion to Part One

Before moving on to discuss some of the economic and political implications of outwork in nineteenth-century England, it would be appropriate to pause and sum up. Until the last quarter of the nineteenth century, the outwork system still had an important role in the mass-production of a wide range of producers' and, especially, consumers' goods. Although by then it had virtually disappeared from some sectors where it had traditionally been important, it had taken firmer root in others: and although no major industry now existed *exclusively* on a basis of outwork organization, many were carried on by some complicated combination of factory production and outwork, with the two effectively complementing each other. Technical progress did not immediately displace putting-out in the nineteenth century by any means: certain new machines which were themselves well suited to factory operation – such as the early spinning inventions, the mechanized knitting-frames, or the cutting machines for cloth and leather – actually increased their industry's reliance on decentralized production in the associated processes, at least for a time. Thus semi-manufactures and the basic stages of many finished products, which required simple, heavy, and repetitive work-routines, readily lent themselves to mechanization and factory methods and dispensed with outworkers at a relatively early date; but the more delicate and small-scale operations in the finishing stages – relying sometimes on the quick judgement of the experienced eye and always on the subtle and instinctive adaptability of nimble fingers – continued to employ them. By 1870, the home-based worker was no longer the characteristic industrial operative, as had been the case a century before. As a proportion of the industrially occupied population, such workers were in a minority compared with those who laboured in the more disciplined and mechanized environment of large workshops and factories; but they were still to be numbered in hundreds of thousands, if not in millions.

In the 1760s, outwork is generally associated with textiles: numerically, spinners headed the list of domestic workers, followed at a considerable distance by weavers. Because the industrial revolution eliminated the outworker from these two activities by about the middle of the nineteenth century, it is sometimes assumed that outwork had an ever-diminishing role in Britain's industrial structure from the time of the great spinning inventions of the 1760s and 1770s. But at the same time that outwork was disappearing from textiles, it was increasing its importance in the vast range of clothing trades - hosiery, men's clothes, lace, straw, footwear, and gloves. Thus if eighteenth-century outwork was epitomized in the distaff and wheel, mid-nineteenth-century outwork relied largely on the humble needle. Stitching and sewing became the characteristic activities of the homeworker, as spinning had formerly been, and the popularization of the sewing machine in the third quarter of the century did not immediately alter this position; for it was a device which did not need a power-source, and it could be accommodated within a home-workshop. Of course, the stitching trades were not the only outwork industries to survive: old-established occupations such as nail-making, which used quite different materials and techniques, remained well entrenched in their particular regions. But most of the traditional industries which continued to rely on outworkers, as well as some new ones which grew by using them, essentially consisted in the repetitive assembling and fixing of separate pieces of material - usually by means of needle and thread, but sometimes using glue - so as to form finished articles. Some of these materials were rough and heavy to work, as in the case of shoemaking, but the majority were textile fabrics or other light-weight items such as paper or card. Because of this essential 'lightness', most outwork industries could rely largely on women workers.

There was nothing new in this: if the needle-using domestic industries of the nineteenth century used women workers, so too had the textile industries of the eighteenth. Light work, such as women were well able to do, was the kind best suited to a putting-out system because of the transport problem associated with decentralized production: if the sheer mechanics of putting out and taking in became too costly in time and money - as would be the case if bulky items were involved - the system would cease to be viable. Homework *had* to be light work, because the homeworker had to be able – if only in an emergency – to carry the unassembled materials or the finished products between home and warehouse in a bag over the shoulder or a bundle under the arm. Moreover, homework meant work for the house-bound – for those, in other words, whom domestic responsibilities, age and ill-health, paternal discipline, or social convention kept confined to the domestic hearth. Of necessity, the *supply* of outworkers was bound to consist largely of women and children – of grandparents, wives, unmarried and widowed sisters and daughters, and young boys; and among these the female element predominated. As we have seen, those industries which continued to rely on outwork in the course of the nineteenth century, or which expanded for a time by using it, almost invariably increased their proportion of women workers. This was true in cotton handloom weaving at the beginning of our period, and of men's tailoring, shoemaking, and even nail- and chain-making later on. In the nineteenth century as in the past, outwork meant industrial employment for women. The sort of work likely to come into the home-workshop was in most cases very suitable for women to do; and the effort, time, and skill which the household could offer the entrepreneur was largely that of its women members. Not only were most outworkers women: until the last quarter of the nineteenth century, most of the women who worked in industry probably did so as outworkers.[1]

The link between outwork and women's work is emphasized by its geographical distribution in the second half of the nineteenth century; by the timing of its eventual elimination as a form of industrial production; and by the low earnings habitually associated with it. By the 1850s, in contrast with the position reported by Defoe and Eden in the previous century, the homeworker had virtually disappeared from the north of England. Industry there was increasingly concentrated on the coalfields, the population was highly urbanized, and large centralized units of production were the norm both in the textile districts and in the areas of heavy industry. Where outwork still survived in the industrial north by the third quarter of the nineteenth century, it did so chiefly in the mass-production clothing trades of the great provincial centres – Leeds, Manchester, Sheffield, and Newcastle.

Things were still very different in the Midlands, however. To the west, the old nail-making and the newer chain trade continued the outwork system on the fringe of the Birmingham area. But it was to the east (and especially the south-east) – from Nottingham through Leicester, Coventry, and Northampton down to Luton – that the principal provincial centre of homeworking was to be found in the 1850s and 1860s; for here, footwear, hosiery, silk, lace, and straw were variously located in and around the area's major towns. Smaller provincial concentrations of outworkers – in clothing, textiles, and footwear – were also still to be found in East Anglia and in parts of the south-west. In most of these places, it was a case of outwork surviving in some long-established industry – although we must remember that new and expanding trades such as footwear were perpetuating the outwork tradition in some cases. In many of these areas, too, outwork retained its largely rural setting in the smaller towns and villages, rather than the cities.

London housed the other major concentration of homeworkers in the second half of the nineteenth century. Most of the industries of the capital were workshop industries; and, as Gareth Stedman Jones has said: 'The effect of the Industrial Revolution on London was to accentuate its pre-industrial characteristics.'[2] Not all such industries were depressed, nor were their workers impoverished: in the words of E. H. Hunt, the metropolis 'contained some of the best – and the worst-paid labour in Britain'. Indeed, men's wages there were generally well above the national average: but in parts of the East End, the combination of casual dock labour for men and homework for women provided a notable exception.[3] Right to the end, London remained the largest single centre of outwork production: and although the number of homeworkers almost certainly declined over the long term in the forty years before the First World War, it is possible that the process may have been reversed for a time around the turn of the century.[4]

Clearly, the conditions which made for the survival of outwork in certain provincial areas in the second half of the nineteenth century would not necessarily be the same as those which operated in the capital, as we shall see. Unique factors were at work in the London labour market to perpetuate homeworking in some parts of the city. But most of the remaining outwork centres did have a number of features in common. They were remote from the areas of heavy industry, and were at best on the fringes of the major coalfields. In most of the provincial outwork districts, unskilled men's wages were below the national average, and in London, although men's wages were higher, so too was the cost of living, and especially the cost of housing. Factors such as these made women's (and children's) supplementary earnings especially desirable to the family.[5] But for a woman seeking work in these areas, the option of the factory remained much less common than in Lancashire and Yorkshire: domestic service or some form of paid work within the family home were still the principal alternatives. Compared with her sisters in the industrial north, the woman who needed or wanted work in much of the Midlands and London after mid-century would be more likely to have to think about taking such outwork as might be locally available, however poorly rewarded.

Yet if outwork was still a prominent feature of the economy of these places in the 1850s and 1860s, it was fast disappearing in the 1870s and 1880s, as straw-plait and pillow-lace were superseded, and hosiery, clothing, and footwear followed the basic textile industries into the factory. Official statistics of outwork collected at the beginning of the present century show just how unimportant the old 'domestic system' now was to the mature industrial economy. The 1901 Census tried to enumerate all those 'working at home'; but since this definition also includes both employers and the self-employed, the resulting figure is much greater than the number of genuine wage-earners. Even when inflated by these other categories of 'home-based' workers, the total was only 371,000 (278,000 of them women) for the whole of England and Wales; and 283,000 of these were employed in 'other wearing apparel', where the self-employed and the small employer were still important, as compared with a mere 54,000 in men's tailoring.[6]

More meaningful figures became available a few years later, when Local Authorities were obliged by the Factory Acts to collect lists of outworkers' names from employers. Clearly these were incomplete, and difficult to interpret, but for 1907 (when the Commons' Select Committee on homework was beginning its deliberations) they provide the 'approximate total' of 105,633 registered employees working at home in England and Wales. The 'making of wearing apparel' employed 86,000 (over 80%) of them. The next largest industry to employ homeworkers was lace, with 5,362, followed by paper bags and boxes, with 2,572; no other industry returned more than 2,000 employees. London contained exactly one-third of the national total, with the great bulk (30,000) in the clothing trades and in paper-bag making (2,236); whilst among provincial cities, Nottingham and Manchester headed the list, with between 4,000 and 5,000 registered homeworkers each.[7] Even multiplying these figures by a factor of 3 or 4 to make generous allowance for deficient returns cannot help us to escape the conclusion that homework, however monstrous the suffering it might still entail for individuals, was statistically insignificant in the first decade of the present century. And at the risk of being branded a heartless revisionist, one cannot avoid reiterating E. H. Hunt's judgement, after discussing the sweated women workers of London's East End, that the attention lavished on them, by contemporaries and by some later historians, has been 'highly disproportionate'.[8]

By the time Parliament was at last prepared to do something to help the low-paid workers in the sweated trades, therefore, outwork had ceased to be a major social and economic problem. The trade boards established in the first experiment of 1909 included the three most important of the limited number of industries in which the homeworker still played some part.* Three of these boards - lace, paper bags and boxes, and chains - covered industries of little national significance, which were concentrated in one particular locality (Nottingham, London, or the Black Country) and created special problems there. The fourth - men's tailoring - dealt with a larger and more dispersed trade, in which factory and workshop had by now reduced the homeworker to a very marginal role. Perhaps it was the very fact that the homeworker's lot, though 'intolerable', was also rather rare which made it possible for conservative Parliamentarians to accept the radical notion of the minimum wage.

Whether the establishment of the trade boards between 1910 and 1914 actually hastened the further decline of outwork is questionable; but it is clear that the process was accelerated by the First World War. Since the 1870s, it seems certain that compulsory education and the growth of the economy in consumer goods and service industries were combining to widen the range of women's employment in many parts of the country,[9] whilst it is probable that social attitudes were becoming less hostile to the notion of a woman working full-time outside the home. This process was speeded by the special circumstances of the Great War, which - if only temporarily - offered women of all social classes a variety of employments hitherto unknown. Homework never regained even its pre-war hold on women workers thereafter.[10] Only the house-*bound* would now resort to it; and the more unfortunate social

---

*For an account of the trade boards, see Chapter 5, pp. 242-7.

casualties who constitute a large element of this group - the elderly, the widowed, and the sick - have increasingly been released from the harsh economic necessity of taking low-paid work by the gradual extension of State welfare provision.

Low pay provides the final link in the chain connecting outwork and women's work. In nineteenth-century England, *all* women's work was poorly paid compared with men's: and a society which traditionally deemed it appropriate that a woman should receive only half a man's wages could see little intrinsically wrong when women who worked at home earned as little as two or three shillings a week. In fact, of course, all outworkers, male and female, were likely to be relatively badly paid, for a variety of reasons. In the first place, those who worked at home were as a rule unorganized and incapable of resisting wage reductions, with the result that the piece-rates for most types of outwork tended to move inexorably downward over the years, even in industries where the outworker was not facing competition from factory-based machines. Secondly, average earnings were bound to be low wherever the average reflected the presence of a mass of casual, part-time and seasonal workers (predominantly female) who outweighed and concealed the achievements of a minority of full-time regular hands. Because of these twin elements in the labour force of many of the industries covered by this study, it is likely that outwork earnings fell into two broad bands for much of the nineteenth century: the higher of these, averaging say 10 shillings or more a week, contained the full-timers; the lower, perhaps averaging only 3 or 4 shillings, represented the part-timers and casuals.

Compared with the earnings of most adult men, which ranged 'round about a pound a week' towards the end of the nineteenth century, these figures, whether for full- or part-timers, are certainly low. The very fact that a rate of 3d an hour was thought to be a suitable *minimum* by the trade boards established after 1909 indicates that some sweated homeworkers were earning even less than this. When we recall the various pressures which tended to push piece-rates down, it seems certain that most homeworkers would find their money earnings declining over time. In an age which, in retrospect, enjoyed remarkably stable prices, such a drop in money income meant a declining standard of living: and it was no consolation to discover that one might keep up one's income in real terms by working longer hours and with greater intensity. 'Sweating' became a social problem in the late nineteenth century precisely because it combined low pay and long hours in a world where average real incomes had risen and where the shorter working day of nine or ten hours had become almost universal.

The debate about 'the standard of living' in the nineteenth century has caused unending controversy among economic historians, and it is necessary, however tentatively, to conclude by fitting the outworker's experience into the general pattern.[11] It is probably unprofitable to try to devise a meaningful concept of a changing standard of living as applied to a part-time and casual homeworker, except to say that such a worker would probably have to put in longer hours and a greater effort by the last years of the nineteenth century if he or she wished to keep up the real value of his contribution to total family income (much of which would be derived from occupations where the conditions which affected outwork earnings did not apply). But it seems safe to conclude that the likely experience of the average *full*-timer solely dependent on homework would be of a standard of living which at best stood still, and at worst deteriorated sharply. By contrast, the long-term experience of most wage-earners, certainly from the early 1840s, was one of intermittent improvement in the real purchasing power of their pay. This means that the *relative* decline of the outworker's position was even more drastic than the absolute deterioration; and it was this widening gulf between the *general* lot of the Victorian wage-earner and the increasingly *exceptional* fate of the dwindling band of outworkers which finally caught the attention of social reformers towards the end of the century. This contrast between 'progress' for the majority and stagnation (or retrogression) for a few is well captured in Charles Masterman's vivid (if somewhat mixed) metaphor:

> Somewhere festering at the basis, round the foundations of the great mansion of England's economic supremacy, are to be discovered the workers of the 'sweated trades'. At intervals of ten, fifteen, or twenty years the dredger is let down to scrape up samples of the material of the ocean floor: in Royal Commissions, Committees of the House of Commons, or the House of Lords. It is always the same there, whatever tides and tempests trouble the surface far above: a settled mass of congested poverty shivering through life upon a margin below which life ceases to endure.[12]

In the end, when it became clear that the existing economic system could do nothing to improve the lot of the outworker, the State was obliged to interfere in areas hitherto regarded as sacrosanct. But it is an interesting commentary on the process of social reform that it did so only when outwork was almost defunct. In the middle of the nineteenth century, when outwork was still a regular feature ofeconomic organization and social life in several parts of the country, the problems associated with it were accepted in a matter-of-fact way as normal, inevitable, and unalterable. Not until this type of employment had become very rare and highly localized did it receive attention: low pay, long hours, and bad working conditions only became intolerable when they became abnormal. The final campaign against sweating and homework around 1900 illustrates clearly the truism that today's scandals were yesterday's common-places. An abuse was suddenly discovered and judged ripe for reform because it represented an ugly, moribund survivor in a world whose norms, values, and expectations had changed. We must now turn our attention to the economic circumstances which had enabled it to survive, and to the developments in political institutions and ideas which called, in the end, for its extinction.

Page 152 is a blank

Part Two
ANALYSIS

— 4 —

The Economics of Outwork

Having described the role of outwork in various branches of industry in nineteenth-century England, we must now turn to some more general analytical problems. From what has been said in the descriptive chapters so far, it should be clear that outwork had many serious drawbacks for both the capitalists and the workers who were involved in it. A manufacturer who relied on outwork, for example, often had only slight control over the quality of the work made for him; he was liable to incur extra costs because the workers might embezzle some of his materials; and he could never be sure of keeping up regular production schedules or of meeting delivery dates. The experience of Courtaulds, who put out silk-weaving in Essex to workers whom they also supplied with looms, during a trade revival in 1837, vividly illustrates some of these disadvantages:

> Mr Courtauld began soon to observe that the work came very slowly back, and in fact he was much annoyed at being unable to supply the goods which he found that he could sell. He was obliged to get bills printed and stuck up in his warehouse and distributed amongst the weavers, calling upon them to 'take notice' that every weaver who took out work must consider that there was an obligation to finish at least one piece a week; that whoever did not do so were [sic] liable to have the looms called back altogether, and at all events the names should be entered on a book and they should be the first to be discharged when trade became slack.[1]

If an employer who provided his workers with the actual tools of their trade experienced these difficulties on occasions, how much greater must the frustrations have been of manufacturers who lacked this additional hold over their labour force?

Similarly, we should not need to stress that outwork was rarely conducive to the overall long-term well-being of its workers: from the handloom weaver to the nail-maker, the depressing story of

hard work and low wages shows little variation. And, as Joseph
Fletcher, secretary to the Royal Commission on the handloom
weavers, noted, the deprivation suffered by rural outworkers in the
1830s and 1840s could be cultural as well as material. He wrote:

> Their sole connection with the great community around them is
> their weekly resort to the master's warehouse, which is assuredly
> no powerful means of civilisation; and beyond this they are
> almost alienated from all society. The influences which reach
> them are those only of a religious character; and the feebleness of
> these has already been shown [in an extended survey of the
> educational facilities available to the Coventry weavers, which
> was a major feature of Fletcher's report]. The great body of the
> weaving and framework knitting populations are similarly dis-
> persed and similarly depressed; and the *absenteeism* of so many of
> the employers, except agents who are not the real capitalists, will,
> I doubt not, be found everywhere to have a great, though not
> always an obvious, effect on the condition of the labouring
> people ... through the want of the moral bonds which should
> attach them to society at large.[2]

With the passage of time, outworkers became more of an urban and
less of a rural phenomenon: but similar problems of isolation and
social control merely reappeared in the new context. In addition to
being as vulnerable in material terms, the 'sweated' women workers
of London were as much hidden from the knowledge and concern
of polite society until the repeated exposure of their wretched
condition from the 1880s as the provincial knitters and weavers had
been half a century before.

Yet with all these imperfections for both sides, what has emerged
from this study so far has been the amazing persistence – even
vitality – of this antique 'system' in the nineteenth century. Over
the century, undoubtedly, the long-term history of outwork is one
of gradual retreat, so that by 1900 its role was extremely limited;
but the very gradualness of its decay, and its capacity to go on
cropping up again – sometimes in unexpected places – shows that it
had some inherent advantages, too. What then were the reasons for
outwork's continued viability and vitality? Why did manufacturers
in some industries go on sending work out into people's homes, and
why were workers willing to take it in? Obviously, the innate
conservatism of economic man – epitomized in the words of the

hosier William Biggs quoted earlier (see Chapter 2, p. 90) – and his willingness to make do with things as they are and as he has become accustomed to them, might go some way towards explaining this glaring example of the survival of the apparently unfit. But what was the final deciding factor in any given case? What was the critical point at which the balance of advantage and inconvenience shifted decisively against the old and in favour of the new, and led to the final extinction of the outwork system? Is it possible, out of the still confused mass of experiences in different industries, to suggest a general explanation of the economics of outwork and to indicate how long it might expect to survive and when and why it would finally die?

Most attempts to explain why outwork remained an integral and important part of industrial growth under private capitalism in the nineteenth century have seized on two main points: first, that outwork is above all a labour-intensive method of production, and therefore its essential prerequisite is abundant cheap labour; and second, that the industries in which it became most firmly rooted were highly competitive, and contained a multitude of debt-ridden small entrepreneurs struggling viciously to stay in business. The final report of the Royal Commission on labour in the 1890s put these points in reverse order when it explained the existence of 'sweating':

> The evils in question seem to be dependent upon two conditions, first, that in these occupations an excessive number of small masters are competing against each other to an extent which makes it necessary for each of them, in order to live himself, to reduce the cost of production to the utmost; and next, that an overcrowded and unorganised mass of workpeople ... are competing with one another for employment. The oversupply of labour renders it difficult to establish effective organisation among the workpeople ... and the absence of organisation in its turn deprives them of that protection which is possessed by workmen in trades requiring greater skill or energy. Thus a vicious circle of interacting causes is formed.[3]

But we need to go a bit deeper than this in explaining the economic rationale of outwork. In what senses, and for what reasons, was labour 'cheap' and 'abundant' in nineteenth-century England? Was it not so much the abundance of labour as the relative shortage of capital which may have given outwork its remarkable resilience? Or how far did hand-processes (and therefore in many cases home-working) survive simply because of the inability of contemporary technology to supersede them? And to what extent was the persistence of hand-techniques and outwork organization the result, not of the quantities of the respective necessary factors of production on the supply side, but rather of the nature of the market and of the rate of change on the demand side? In other words, did organization and techniques change slowly because they were not sufficiently stimulated in the direction of innovation by the market? Obviously, the relative importance of these possible elements in a total explanation will vary - perhaps drastically - from one outwork industry to another; and since the first part of the present study has shown how limited our present knowledge is of many aspects of these industries, it is clear that the time is not ripe for us to attempt a partial, let alone a comprehensive, 'theory' of the economics of outwork. Nevertheless, it should be possible, by looking more generally at aspects of the labour supply, the availability of capital and techniques, and problems of marketing and demand, to indicate some of the pitfalls and possibilities which future researchers into the individual industries are likely to encounter.

The Supply Side: Labour, Capital, and Technology

As we have seen, outwork was a means of achieving mass-production which often involved a minute subdivision of processes between different workers; but it differed from mass-production in the factory by being labour-, rather than capital-, intensive. Essentially, it required a great deal of simple and repetitive work which called for only basic skills, unsophisticated tools, and minimal training: quantity rather than quality was the keynote of its needs for labour. At its crudest, outwork was functioning well when, in the words of a Nottingham lace manufacturer in the 1860s, even 'in a busy time I could always find women who would offer to do a large piece of work at however short a notice'; and he went on, 'in spring and summer it is a common thing to see women leaving warehouses in the morning with large bundles of lace which they have to get finished by a fixed time, often very short, as the next day, but they always get it done somehow, no-one knows how'.[4] This over-riding need for limitless cheap low-grade labour is repeatedly stressed in both the evidence and the actual final reports of the successive official enquiries into the problems of different groups of outworkers: a London bootmaker, for example, told the Lords' Committee on sweating, rather pathetically, that 'if the manufacturer were not provided with so many men, and if so many working people were not taught this trade, I reckon that the boot line would be the best trade in the country'.[5]

The limited skill and the brief training required to be competent at most kinds of outwork cannot be sufficiently emphasized: it is true, of course, that most called for manual dexterity, that many demanded unremitting concentration, and that a few needed brute strength; and as such every industry had its examples of notoriously 'good' and expeditious workers who could turn out far more than the 'average' in an hour, and whose reward was immediately evident in their pay. But the basic talents demanded were commonly available in the human race, and their latency could be quickly realized: few people found the mysteries of stitching, treadling, and hammering beyond them; and if each of these humble arts has its elite of outstanding practitioners, they are also activities at which most people can soon show a crude competence. Thus it did not take a novice long to become a tolerable workman, and few potential recruits can have been deterred by fears that it would take them months to acquire the knack. Similarly, once acquired, many of these simple tricks could be applied in a number of different trades; and workers who had developed them might move from one occupation to another if necessity compelled or opportunity offered. In London, with its great variety of unskilled trades in the late nineteenth century, there were plenty of chances to shift from one job to another, as one woman trade-union organizer told the Royal Commission on labour:

> The women of the East End are not confined to any one trade. According to the seasons they have to vary their trades, and you will find, say, one or two women, perhaps, in a union such as mine, who have worked in half a dozen different trades or more.[6]

Even a trade like handloom weaving, which required careful co-ordination of hand, foot, and eye, did not take long to learn. Woollen weaving was generally said to be the most demanding branch: but even the witnesses before the Select Committee at the very beginning of the nineteenth century, who were anxious to retain apprenticeship in the industry, generally admitted that weaving on its own was but 'a very small part of the business', and that a seven-year training was justified rather in order to acquire that knowledge of the preparatory and finishing processes which every small master clothier 'who has cloth to carry to market' needed.[7] The simpler routines of plain weaving in the lighter fabrics such as cotton were even more easily acquired; and once started on the elementary types of work the weaver might, by practice and self-education, move into the more difficult branches of the trade in due course. It was said at Norwich in 1838, for example, that:

> When there is a great demand for goods, the men who have been working at less difficult fabrics are set to do the finer goods; and for the lower and coarser fabrics, men and women from any other employment can be put to the loom, and soon manage to do their work passably well. Hence it is that at times when there is a great demand for goods, if agricultural labourers be unemployed there is a great influx into the weaver's trade in the villages of Norfolk by persons of whom the regular weavers of Norwich make great complaints. These persons, it is true, are not completely master of all parts of their trade, and Mr. Athow [a manufacturer] calls them shuttlethrowers and not weavers: still, such parts as they cannot do themselves they get others to do for them, and they manage to do all the rest of their work.[8]

Outwork, then, did not as a rule need high-quality labour, and accordingly it had a large army of *potential* recruits at a time of rapidly growing population and highly imperfect regional labour markets. However, to convert the potential into the real, it was necessary that there should be no effective obstacles to the free movement of would-be workers into the various outwork occupations whenever employers needed more labour. Three possible barriers to unrestrained recruitment in the nineteenth century spring immediately to mind. The first is institutional: the existence of a trade union among the workers of a particular trade and the operation of a closed shop might make it impossible for non-members of the club to take up the craft. The second is legal: there might be some lawfully prescribed pattern for training different types of industrial workers, such as apprenticeship, which might – independently of any union closed shop – prevent any significant addition to the labour force in the medium term. And the third is locational: although potential recruits might exist in theory, in practice they might not be in the places where the employer needed them. In fact, however, it seems doubtful whether any of these possible obstacles significantly restricted the supply of outwork labour from the mid-eighteenth to the later nineteenth centuries, and their role can be quickly dealt with.

Firstly, it will be clear, from what has already been said and from the further discussion in the next chapter, that outwork labour was, characteristically, unorganized for collective bargaining with its employers, and that most groups at best managed to sustain only small, ephemeral, and highly localized trade unions. Given the wide spatial dispersal of the major outwork industries, and the often casual and temporary demand for (and supply of) labour, it is indeed surprising that collective bargaining was attempted at all in some cases. It is certainly no surprise to find that union successes were limited in their scope or duration and were largely confined to two groups: the workers in the highest-quality lines who really needed skill and training; and the urban workers in the major provincial centres of an industry, as distinct from their disorganized country cousins in the rural hinterlands. Indeed, the latent hostility between town and country which arose because the latter was liable to under-cut the wage-rates on which urban workers were trying to stand firm has already been encountered on several occasions: in the textile industries at Norwich, Coventry, and Macclesfield, and in the boot and shoe trades at Leicester and Northampton, for example. One of the few ways in which the organized townsmen could protect themselves lay in forcing their employers to different-iate sharply between the kinds of work done in the town and the out-districts respectively: and the unionized male chain-makers of Cradley, for example, seem to have done this very effectively around the beginning of the present century, when they produced in consequence that enormous disparity between their own earnings and those of the unorganized women workers in the villages, which led to the establishment of the trade board (see Chapter 3, p. 134). Indeed, fundamental to the trade boards and the minimum wages of the early twentieth century was the recognition that the remnants of the once numerous army of industrial outworkers constituted a 'special case', meriting an unusual degree of State protection, *precisely because* they were unable to help themselves as other workers did by establishing a trade union and by using the relevant tactics of collective bargaining. What was belatedly recognized in 1909 had by and large been equally true of most of the great horde of outworkers of sixty or seventy years before.

Secondly, as a universal and legally enforceable method of recruiting and training industrial labour, apprenticeship had to a great extent disappeared even before the Elizabethan legislation on which it theoretically rested was repealed in 1813. In the host of trades increasingly practising the subdivision of labour, in many new occupations which had sprung up since the sixteenth century, and in the unincorporated towns and villages where so many industries had come to be located, the notion that a boy needed seven years of strict training in order to grasp the 'mysteries' of a craft had long been discounted: and in an essentially 'new' industry, such as cotton weaving was in the late eighteenth century, the practice of apprenticeship seems to have been almost non-existent.[9] Elsewhere it was clearly in decay by the first decade of the nineteenth century: 'more than nine out of ten' were said not to have been legally apprenticed in the Yorkshire woollen industry in 1803;[10] two-thirds of the Midland framework knitters were described as unapprenticed 'colts' at a Parliamentary investigation of that industry nine years later;[11] and even at Coventry, an old corporate town where the properly apprenticed weaver obtained the Parliamentary franchise and other municipal rights and privileges when he became a freeman, short-term and 'half-pay' apprenticeships were brought in in the 'big purl time' at the end of the Napoleonic wars, when weavers came to be recruited from girls in the town and from labourers in the nearby villages, to whom the benefits of a regular apprenticeship would not in any case accrue.[12]

Thirdly, the locational factor seems, certainly for the first half of the nineteenth century, to have had little relevance. After all, the basic premise of outwork was that you took the work to the workers; and we have seen several examples of the distances over which merchants and manufacturers were prepared to operate via their middlemen in order to tap any reserves of suitable labour. When Yorkshire manufacturers were willing to utilize the women spinners of the Tweed and Gala valleys,[13] or London clothiers to have their shirts stitched in the Essex marshes or in Devon, it is clear that, to them, the advantage of abundant labour outweighed the transport costs, the delays, and the uncertainties which arose from operating over great distances. Indeed, if local supplies of suitable labour dried up, a common response of entrepreneurs in the out-work trades was simply to look for similar, but as yet unexploited, reserves of labour further afield: this, after all, was how outwork had first established itself in the textile industries of the countryside in the sixteenth and seventeenth centuries.[14] Only in the course of the nineteenth century did the pattern change, and outwork come to depend on cheap labour, not in the countryside, but in the rapidly growing urban agglomerations. This is a problem to which we must shortly return.

In the early nineteenth century, many outwork industries – weaving, framework knitting, shoemaking, and nailing – employed large numbers of adult men whom it is easy to think of as being essentially full-time 'specialists' at their particular job; and many continued to do so, if only in the sense that they attracted, some-times admittedly in a strictly temporary or casual manner, men unemployed and dispossessed from other trades and areas. But an essential feature of the outwork industries, which has emerged repeatedly from the descriptions of the various industries in the previous chapters, was the very high proportion of women and children that they normally employed: most of the needlework trades (except shoemaking) had, of course, been traditionally female-employing, but the general tendency was for the proportion of women to increase noticeably over time even in those industries where men had formerly been clearly dominant. Thus the pattern established back in the days when spinning had been the major outwork industry was reinforced, and not broken, during the acceleration of industrial growth from the late eighteenth century. In so far as women were employed in manufacturing industry (as opposed to services) in the nineteenth century, the bulk of them remained for long in an outwork environment: as the significance of outwork declined, the role of women within it increased; for as men moved out, women moved in. Accustomed to low pay, anxious for work which they could combine with domestic duties, lacking other ways of adding their mite to total family income, and generally incapable of collective self-defence, women became the key element in that persistent cheapness of labour which was one of the prime requirements of a viable outwork system.

The same is true of young children. Their economic value to their outworking parents as winders, stitchers, menders, bellows-blowers, and the like – so much admired by men like Defoe in the early eighteenth century – continued to be taken for granted and utilized until the combined effect of wider factory legislation and compulsory schooling effectively drove them out of the labour market in the last quarter of the nineteenth century. Until that time, it is possible that the proportion of children actually increased in some areas, and that children were replacing women there, just as elsewhere women were replacing men. The industries of the East and South Midlands appear to have a particularly bad record in this respect during the middle years of the nineteenth century: the prevalence of 'schools' in the straw and lace industries demonstrates the key role of children in the last days of those industries; and the enormous amount of stitching and finishing by young children in the lace and hosiery trades of Nottingham and Leicester is amply documented in the evidence of the two Royal Commissions on children's employment of the 1840s and the 1860s. Adult workers themselves were among the chief complainants about the abuse of child-labour in outwork, both out of humanity and because of the threat it posed to grown-up wage rates: and the fact that adults were not necessarily wholly insensitive to the exploitation of children in the mid-nineteenth century is shown, for example, by the testimony of a woman framework knitter from Bulwell, who told the assistant commissioner in the 1860s:

> I have seen a boy, twelve years old, come home from winding at 8 or 9 o'clock, and then set to stitch 'three dozen fingers', i.e. the fingers of three dozen pairs of coarse gloves. He works a frame too, sometimes, getting into his uncle's when he (the uncle) goes to dinner. This little boy is without a real home, and very much put upon where he is, having to do and go through all sorts of things. I have heard him ask, 'Am I big enough to be a sailor?'[15]

Even compulsory schooling and stricter workshop inspection did not entirely eradicate child-employment in the outwork industries, for the young could still be set to work out of school hours. Indeed, an inter-departmental Committee set up by the government to examine this question in 1899 reported that over 200,000 children were employed at home part-time. And when Miss Squire gave evidence to the Select Committee on homework a few years later, she described children as being at work before, between, and after school in the gloving industry of Somerset, in lace finishing at

Nottingham, in box-making, and in button-carding and similar trades in Birmingham.[16]

A further section of the population who were drawn into the net of outwork organization were the elderly. It is hardly surprising that, as outwork went into secular decline in many industries, their labour forces tended to age: few children were brought up to it, and the younger and more enterprising practitioners abandoned it more readily in favour of any reasonable alternatives; but the old, unable and often unwilling to change, were usually the last supporters. In a different way, however, homework could act as a final life-line before the workhouse to old people who might formerly have made their living elsewhere: indeed, it was often extolled precisely because it kept such people 'independent'. When in 1908 the setting up of the Select Committee on homework seemed to herald State inter- vention of some sort, the 'National Homeworkers League' came into being to 'protect the homeworkers from legislation which they consider decreases the amount of work and so lowers prices'. Its spokesman, Miss Vynne, proudly informed the Committee that she had recently seen 'an old couple, both in bed with rheumatism, who had a little parish relief, but who felt independent because they could earn the rest by glove-making', and also commended the case of 'a woman with only one capable hand ... who got a little parish relief. With her right hand she could just make enough in the gloving to keep out of the workhouse'.[17] So long as so many of the active and powerful in Victorian society – at *all* social levels – remained, behind a veneer of sentimentality, thoughtless of their young, domineering towards their wives, and heartless to the aged and crippled, it is not surprising that these weaker sections of the community became the chief victims of the monstrous possibilities of exploitation inherent in outwork.

With a labour force so heavily made up of women, children, and old people, it is apparent that many outworkers viewed their trade as something essentially part-time, casual, and supplementary to income coming into the household from other quarters. Such an attitude was not uncongenial to many employers, because if the supply of workers was often irregular, so too was the supply of work. Unfortunately the needs of entrepreneurs and workers in this respect seldom coincided: an employer's demand for extra labour did not necessarily come at the time when his potential workers either needed it or were able to offer their services; and no doubt

most outworkers, whether full- or part-time, would have preferred
work on a regular basis to rushed jobs at unpredictable intervals.
But it is clear that this sort of disharmony in the labour market
went against the interests of the wage earners far more often than it
did against those of the employers: there were always potential new
recruits ready to take up the work, and there were also retired
members of the force who could be pressed back into service. Thus
it can be suggested that in many trades the number of workers
actually employed at any one time was normally only a part of a
larger body of the *occasionally* employed; and that there was a
constant turnover among the active personnel, with one woman
coming in and another going out, according as their personal needs
or circumstances permitted or compelled them to do so.

The simple fact is that many women and children needed some
source of supplementary income to help boost total family earnings
and to ease their circumstances: and homework was *either* the only
kind of employment locally available *or* the only sort they could
conveniently do. The income may have seemed small in relation to
the time and effort involved, but it was a useful way of filling in
otherwise unprofitable time and it could be adjusted to other aspects
of the household routine. One commentator on the glove trade
noted in 1843:

> Although some persons devote themselves entirely to this occu-
> pation and make a great many pairs in the course of a week, yet,
> in the majority of cases the gloves are sewn at leisure hours and
> at odd times by the wives and children of the labouring men and
> small tradesmen: ... even where the gain of individuals is very
> small in a family, yet by their all working together and assisting
> with their contributions they make out a living.[18]

It is important, of course, to distinguish between 'part-time' and
'casual' employment in outwork. The 'part-timer', strictly, was one
who wanted a limited but regular amount of homework week by
week; the 'casual', on the other hand, might at certain times not
wish (or need) to work at all, whereas at others she would take as
much work as she could possibly get through. This latter process
was graphically described in the Midland hook-and-eye carding
trade to the homework Committee in 1907:

> A woman in a court, say, gets some of this stuff from a factory,
> and she works pretty constantly at it, and her neighbours know

she has it, and perhaps one day they are hard up for some reason, and a neighbour comes and says, 'Will you give me some hooks and eyes to do', and they give out so many cards; it is sublet like that. Some days a person may do it, and some days not.[19]

It is not difficult to imagine why housewives might suddenly find themselves 'hard up': a doctor's bill, a worn-out pair of shoes, or an out-of-work husband – these and many others were the kinds of domestic crises which impelled a woman to seek temporary employment. Commentators were especially prone to point out the inverse relationship between the woman's employment pattern and that of her husband: Miss Squire, a factory inspector, also told the homework Committee:

I find the employment of the wife in homework follows closely the periods of unemployment of her husband. It is in most cases a true index of the fluctuations of his work. The husband is out of work, and the wife at once goes round to the nearest place where she knows work is to be found. She wants it immediately for necessities, and she takes it at any price, and of any description that is offered.[20]

Finally, part-time outwork could be taken up out of permanent, rather than short-lived, necessity, by the widow, the semi-invalid, or the spinster looking after ailing parents. Among outworkers these last were generally the poorest of all: often they received some pittance of out-relief from the Poor Law on the strict understanding that they tried to support themselves as far as possible: yet it was precisely such groups as these who found their earning capacity most restricted by their circumstances and their other necessary commitments.

Whether their role was casual or part-time, temporary or permanent, it seems that harsh necessity and the lack of alternatives were the spurs which drove many women, children, and old people to take such poorly paid tasks as outwork frequently involved. Nevertheless, we need to question just how severe that necessity was in all cases: a woman does not need to be on the breadline to feel that she would like a little more money in her purse, and it is reasonable to assume that some took outwork to buy 'extras' and luxuries rather than bare essentials – just as many married women workers do today, in fact. A Scottish wholesale clothier told the

Lords' Committee on sweating, for example, that his homeworkers were 'generally the wives of artisans and various other workmen, who have nothing to do at home during the absence of their husbands, and it is so much money earned, when otherwise they would have gone idle'.[21] Obviously it is not easy to determine the relative proportions of those working from choice and from necessity, but Bulkley's study of the London box-makers at the outbreak of the First World War concluded, from a sample of over 300 workers, that 'close upon one-third are entirely dependent upon their own earnings (or on outside help); just over one-third are partly dependent, the husband's and children's earnings being insufficient to support the family; while the same proportion are not dependent at all upon their exertions, but work "to pass the time, like", or "to make things more comfortable", or to obtain extras.'[22]

Finally the army of outworkers always contained some – men and women – who positively insisted on working at home, and categorically rejected shop or factory work even when it was available to them. Such a preference for homework might be motivated, for example, by the reluctance of strict parents to risk their children being contaminated by the 'immoral' atmosphere of a factory or large workshop. Nor was the 'superior' working man apprehensive merely for his children: one small master in the bespoke tailoring trade claimed that the best workmen would not sit in a 'common' workshop 'for the simple reason that workmen are, as a rule, intemperate, improvident, and the language is anything but refined and gentlemanly, and men of a high sensibility cannot put up with that kind of thing.'[23] Moreover, the heady notion of the 'independence' which an outworker enjoyed as master of his own time still attracted some, in spite of low pay and irregular employment. When discussing the effects of cyclical unemployment on the Coventry silk trade Joseph Fletcher noted in 1840 that 'some of the women get into service; but so soon as trade improves, they too commonly disagree with their employers and return to the loom. Their education at home for service is indeed very bad ... and they all like the freedom from control which the ribbon loom affords them. This inducement ... is so strong, that in Coventry and its vicinity it is difficult to get good domestic servants' – this last being a complaint that more than one middle-class critic of outwork was to voice in the course of the century.[24]

Our examination of the make-up of the outwork labour force

has thus made it clear just what sorts of 'cheap labour' it depended on. But there are deeper demographic forces at work behind all this, and these too need to be considered in order to explain when, where, and why pockets of such labour came to be available: for underlying the problem of 'surplus' labour is the long and complicated story of population growth and migration during the late eighteenth and nineteenth centuries. Particularly important is the relationship between the growth and persistence of outwork organization, on the one hand, and the so-called 'population explosion' which accompanied the industrial revolution on the other. Obviously, if an abundance of the sort of labour just described was a prerequisite of outwork, it should follow that this kind of work would be likely to establish itself in places where local increases in population had outstripped the employment available in traditional occupations, and where in consequence wives, young people, and children were generally under-employed or largely unemployed: and such a development would be all the more likely if one result of population pressure on a local agrarian economy had been to increase the proportion of badly paid landless labourers or to reduce the average size and the economic viability of small peasant holdings. Seen in these terms, the expansion of rural outwork which characterized not only the late eighteenth and early nineteenth centuries, but also the sixteenth and early seventeenth, makes sense. Ignoring for the moment the problem of *why* population began to grow more rapidly in these periods, we can easily see that the under-employed and impoverished in overcrowded but still otherwise agrarian communities would not only welcome a new source of income, but would present particular attractions to town-based merchants and manufacturers anxious to escape the various vexations and restraints imposed on them by guilds of small masters or clubs of journeymen in the towns. That 'the wives and children of agricultural labourers' crop up so often among the various groups of industrial outworkers should cause us no surprise.

Yet, as so often in population history, it is difficult to disentangle cause and effect here. For if population growth encouraged outwork, it is quite likely that the presence of outwork locally was in itself a stimulus to population. At the moment it is impossible to answer the question 'which came first?', and we must be content with noting the snowball effects of this interaction. The main reason why a neutral stance must be taken is that the whole question of the causes of the 'population explosion' is still unresolved, and the even bigger problem of its economic consequences has been hardly tackled at all by economic historians. Nevertheless, there is growing evidence that the rise in numbers was at least partly the result of a real increase in human fertility in many parts of the country, and that this arose from a widespread tendency for people to marry earlier and to have larger families: and although the relative importance of this trend as against the permanent changes in mortality patterns which also seem to have occurred at the same time in the country at large is still hotly debated by economic historians – and part of the difficulty is that the *relative* significance of the two forces may have varied a good deal over time and space – there are few who would nowadays plump whole-heartedly for a single-cause explanation. The relevance of this long-standing debate to the question of the economics of outwork is simply this: among the areas where the rise in human fertility was most marked were those which were noted for the existence of outwork employment on a large scale.

This trend to earlier marriage and larger families has been best demonstrated in the case of the East Midland hosiery workers. It is some years now since J. D. Chambers showed, from a study of eighteenth-century parish registers in that area, that the 'industrial' villages had a lower average age of marriage and a larger number of baptisms per marriage than did the purely 'agricultural' ones: and he concluded that 'a differential birth rate' was 'a factor in the growth of the industrial population', and that 'the increase in the industrial population was partly self-generated through its higher birth-rate'. More recently, David Levine has made a detailed demographic study of one Midland knitting village, Shepshed, which fully confirms Chambers' generalizations: between the seventeenth century and the second quarter of the nineteenth century, the average age of marriage there for men fell from 29.4 to 24.1 years, and for women from 28.1 to 22.6 years; whilst the mean completed family size rose from 4.38 to 6.16 children. This was, indeed, a demographic revolution.[25]

As yet there has been too little work on other relevant areas to give full support to Chambers' thesis; but it is perhaps worth noting in passing that Colyton in Devon, where one of the best-known and best-attested increases in real fertility seems to have taken place during the eighteenth century, was itself one of the centres of

outwork in the lace industry at this time.[26] However the notion
that the arrival or expansion of outwork in rural communities
removed economic restraints and forms of social control which had
previously led to delayed marriages or hit-and-miss methods of
family limitation has been avidly seized upon by those indefatigable
protagonists of the 'birth-rate' school, H. J. Habakkuk and J. T.
Krause.[27] And outside Britain, there is evidence, notably in the
work of Rudolf Braun on the growth of textile industries in the
Swiss countryside at the end of the eighteenth century, that rural
outwork had liberating effects on marriage and family patterns by
giving relative youngsters 'the material prerequisites of marriage'.[28]
A good deal more work clearly needs to be done on the interaction
of population growth and economic change in the rural centres of
outwork industry, but it is beginning to seem as if Joseph Fletcher
was not too far wrong in his gloomy Malthusian interpretation of
the wretchedness of the rural silk weavers as compared with their
more affluent brothers in Coventry itself at the end of the 1830s,
when he argued that:

> It is obvious that the employments offered [in the villages] by
> the 'single-hand' branch to women and to children of both sexes,
> without any limitation of skill, removes the determent which an
> immediately lowered condition commonly presents to im-
> provident marriages and must keep the numbers in it full to an
> excess . . . ; [whereas conversely] . . . the supply of hands to the
> class of 'first hand' journeymen in the [city] engine trade is
> moderated by a system of regular apprenticeship and by the
> providence and character requisite to obtain looms and work.[29]

In so far as the growth of outwork was a rural phenomenon in the
eighteenth and early nineteenth centuries, its increasing hold on the
life of hitherto closed and socially regulated agrarian communities
must have presented a series of sharp challenges to traditional
customs, values, and disciplines; and it should not surprise us to
discover that, among other things, it reinforced tendencies towards
rapid population growth which may already have been at work in
the places where it now took root. In this way, the demand for
rural outworkers can be seen to have created its own supply.

The other demographic factor which we need to fit into the story
of the rise and fall of industrial outwork is migration: and here
again the interaction between the patterns of physical mobility

which emerged during the nineteenth century and the ebb and flow of outwork employment seem complex and even contradictory. The complexity arises because, in different ways and for different reasons, outwork seems to have relied on both immobile and highly migratory types of labour. The persistent pattern of migration in nineteenth-century England was from country to town – a process which by the last quarter of the century had transformed the typical Englishman from a villager into a townman: and as the balance of distribution of the whole population shifted in this way, so too did the location of the pockets of cheap labour. At the end of the eighteenth century, a merchant or manufacturer seeking suitable labour for his expanded outwork operations had gone out into the countryside: a hundred years later his successor looking for the same thing would have found it rather in the bursting working-class ghettos of some of the largest towns and cities. Yet if these two environments were vastly different in their physical attributes, the labour which they had to offer a potential employer was strikingly similar: for the wives of the East End dockers who manned London's 'sweated' trades in the 1890s had this in common with the agricultural labourers' wives who spun, wove, knitted, and sewed fifty or more years before – both lived in areas where the local economy provided low-paid work which employed men only. Denied a role in this local staple industry, but tied to their homes and families in a way which made employment outside their immediate vicinity impossible, women in this situation were essentially 'immobile': they had to be content with whatever work came to them, and it is hardly surprising that they seized on outwork if this was all that there was. Indeed, when one form of outwork failed in such an area, it is interesting to see how often it was speedily replaced by another: the widespread replacement of hand-spinning by hand-weaving, the frequent transfers from weaving one fabric to another, the substitution of lace for knitting at Nottingham – all are large-scale examples of the persistence of a tradition of homeworking once it had taken root in a particular community; and at a more modest level, the decline of hand lace-making in Devon and its replacement in some villages by brush-drawing at the very end of the nineteenth century is a case of the process still at work at a time when outwork was by and large an increasingly urban phenomenon.[30]

There is, of course, an obvious flaw in this kind of argument: for there were undoubtedly areas of the country where the staple trade provided little or no employment for women – colliery villages and steel and shipbuilding towns being good examples – but where outwork industries never took root. In other words, the existence of a large body of otherwise unemployed women was a necessary but not a sufficient condition for the presence of outwork. It is difficult to say just why some such areas were outwork centres and others were not; some of the factors may have been social, and have reflected marked differences in local cultural traditions and values. But in terms of the economic forces which regulated the *supply* of outwork labour, it could be that the crucial point was the level and regularity of men's earnings, because this would determine just how badly the women felt that they needed the extra money which outwork could bring; where husbands tended to be well paid on average – as they did in pit-villages and steel towns in comparison with agricultural districts and dock areas – their wives would not be under such acute pressure to resort to homework.

The 'immobility' of certain kinds of labour helped outwork to survive in other ways, too; nor did this merely stem from the fact that the local staple industry did not employ women. For one thing, a worker who had been following a particular kind of outwork from childhood might, after a good many years, fall victim to some occupational disease, and become unsuitable for any other kind of work: for example, Jedediah Strutt of Belper told the Royal Commission on children's employment in the 1840s that 'the effects of lace-running, chevening, tambouring, and embroidering of gloves are so injurious to the eyes and general health that they do not like to take them into the factory'.[31] Elderly workers, unwilling to move from the place where they had their roots and convinced that they were 'too old to change', were particularly 'immobile' and it is no surprise to find that descriptions of the last survivors of any outwork trade generally refer to very old people. And given that outworkers, whether old or young, were particularly prone to fall into poverty, it seems likely too that the imperfect institutional arrangements for dealing with the poor in the nineteenth century tended to keep these unfortunate people imprisoned and im-mobilized in their trade, and so prolonged the existence of outwork in some places: paradoxically, the old Poor Law before 1834 may in this respect have had the same effects by its alleged laxity as the amended Law did thereafter by its apparent harshness. It is possible

that the old Poor Law, by subsidizing industrial as well as agricultural wages in rural areas from the 1790s to the 1830s through child
allowances and the like, persuaded some of the country handloom
weavers in the Lancashire cotton industry, for example, to stick to
their doomed trade in the 1820s and 1830s instead of looking out
for something better rewarded.[32] Similarly, the incident of the
rheumatism-ridden couple who sewed gloves *in bed* in order to
prove their 'independence' – which was reported as late as 1908 –
suggests that fear of 'the House' as inculcated in the bleak deterrent
message of the new Poor Law made some poor old people go on
trying to eke out a living at the only 'trade' they could follow
when, had they been able to retire from gainful employment, that
particular sordid occupation might otherwise have disappeared.

In both rural and urban environments, therefore, workers could
for a variety of reasons be trapped in the net of outwork by their
immobility, which kept them at this miserably paid work for lack
of anything else; and so long as such pockets of immobile workers
existed, outwork had a chance of survival. Nonetheless, there was
one respect in which urban and rural labour forces differed, in that
the former offered another type of cheap labour which could feed
the appetite of the outwork industries: for the bottom of the *urban*
labour market was occupied by 'mobile' as well as by 'static'
elements. Among the very poorest inhabitants of the great cities in
the nineteenth century were the most recent immigrants, usually
countrymen attracted by the opportunity and the variety offered by
an urban existence. Although individual success stories are known,
we know far less about that larger number of first-generation
townsmen for whom the opportunities turned out to be illusions:
but what is clear is that the migrants with the least chance of
improving themselves by escaping from the bottomless pit of unskilled labour were those from different racial, cultural, or ethnic
backgrounds. In the first half of the nineteenth century this meant
the Irish: in the 1880s and 1890s it meant the immigrant Jews from
eastern Europe. As might be expected, both became noticeable
(albeit minority) elements in the outwork labour force.

The Royal Commission of 1836 on the state of the Irish poor in
Great Britain gives a remarkable picture of the place of the Irish
immigrant, even *before* the great famine, in the principal towns of
north-western England and western Scotland: and it is evident that
a trade like cotton handloom weaving still survived in Manchester

and Glasgow by that date because it could utilize the cheap labour of Irish immigrants, who were willing to take work which most of the natives rejected.[33] Likewise, the problem of 'sweating' in the London of the 1880s gained much of its publicity because of its association with the recent Jewish immigration. When John Burnett produced his first report on the subject for the Board of Trade he went so far as to claim that:

> . . . in these sweating dens nineteen-twentieths of the tailors must be Jews, large numbers of whom are as yet unable to speak the language of the country they work in . . . many of them arrive in London knowing no trade, in a state of pauperism, and depending on the well-known benevolence of their wealthier co-religionists for the means of subsistence and for assistance in obtaining employment. The readiness with which this has hither-to been obtained has undoubtedly tended to increase the flood of immigration and to develop the sweating system.[34]

In spite of the passions and prejudices which surrounded these immigrant groups in their day, however, it is important to keep their role in the history of outwork in its proper perspective: foreign immigrants were important only in the biggest cities, and were notably absent from smaller communities. Thus although Irishmen were prominent among the handloom weavers of Manchester in the 1830s, they would have been hard to find among their counterparts in Padiham or Todmorden: and as Hugh Cogan, a Glasgow cotton manufacturer, pointed out to the inquiry into the Irish poor in 1836, he employed equal numbers of handweavers (over 600 in each case) in Glasgow and in 'the country'; but whereas 'about half of those employed by us in town are Irish, of those in the country not a tenth are Irish'.[35]

It should now be clear just what kinds of cheap labour enabled outwork to survive as a form of capitalist industrial organization in the nineteenth century; and it only remains for us to examine briefly some of the ways in which the existence of 'surplus' labour made outwork a viable proposition. The essential point is that the periodic or normal excess of workers in the market tended to push down the piece-rates offered by employers. With a large casual and migratory element, and with a good proportion of its women workers trapped in the trade with no alternatives, it is clear that the supply of labour did not adjust easily to short-term changes in demand, especially when demand turned downwards. Such a recurrent and chronic over-supply was noted by Mr Austin, the assistant commissioner investigating the condition of the woollen weavers in the south-west, in his report of 1840: in a trade which had been in secular decline since the great slump of 1826, the weavers, he wrote, 'have not decreased so fast as the demand for their labour has'.[36] A situation of oversupply was particularly detrimental to the remaining full-time adult male workers in any trade which had increasingly been infiltrated by casual women and child workers: for as Richard Muggeridge noted, when he compared the results of his investigations of the handloom weavers and the framework knitters in the early 1840s, 'if men are willing or constrained to engage in such work, they descend to the level of those with whom they compete, and will be paid accordingly'.[37] As time went on, and the remaining outwork trades became more and more dominated by women workers, the whole situation simply became worse, because the women were less able to draw attention to their problems or to adopt any effective form of self-help. When their difficulties were finally exposed, towards the very end of the century, it is not surprising that the problems seemed insoluble even to so well-intentioned a body as the Lords' Select Committee on sweating, who concluded, in desperate confusion:

> It may be said that the inefficiency of many of the lower class of workers, early marriages, and the tendency of the residuum of the population in large towns to form a helpless community, together with a low standard of life and the excessive supply of unskilled labour, are the chief factors in producing sweating.[38]

Because the labour force was disorganized and divided, and because periodically, if not permanently, the excessive number of workers competed savagely for the available work, the history of piece-rates in most outwork industries is one of long-term decline. Such a decline often had nothing at all to do with competition between handworkers and machines, or between 'outdoor' and 'indoor' working: the competition of which it was the consequence was an inherent feature of 'pure' outwork. It is true, of course, that rivalry between handworkers and machines often characterized the last years of outwork; but this was little more than a final vicious twist of a spiral which had begun when the first urban manufacturer hired an agent to expand his operations in the countryside. Except in the final death throes of outwork, the problems of intermittent employment and low wages which faced the typical outworker arose, not because machines were replacing him, but because they were *not* replacing him. So long as outwork labour remained plentiful and its price fell ever lower, manufacturers had little incentive to turn to alternative means of production and every encouragement to go on relying on a 'system' which worked so obviously to their advantage. Indeed, contemporaries often believed that the very cheapness of hand-labour actually delayed the adoption of newly invented labour-saving machines, as we have seen: the slow progress of powerlooms in several branches of the textile industries in the 1830s and 1840s was frequently attributed to this; one manufacturer in the West Country cloth industry argued, for example, that 'he does not think that powerlooms will be introduced to any great extent because there is a surplus population, and therefore the price of handloom weaving will come down so as to render the powerlooms unnecessary', whilst another in Glasgow maintained that 'it principally has been the low rate of wages, for some years back, that has prevented the powerloom from making a considerable inroad on our trade'.[39]

It might be expected that competition for work would affect only the lowest and simplest branches of a trade, and that the downward pressure on wages would therefore be limited to the cheapest classes of goods: but in fact, once the process had begun, the effects of competition generally made themselves felt at all levels. For as the new recruit became increasingly competent at his work, he could move into the more complex branches of his 'craft' and start to under-cut the old-established workman there. Likewise, as the price of the cheapest mass-produced goods (whether made at the lowest levels of outwork or in the first wave of factories) fell steadily, many customers would no longer pay the widening differential price between these goods and those in the middle range, whose price might also fall in consequence.

Competition for work, then, was the factor which enabled employers to reduce piece-rates from time to time; and although the process might be reversed at a time when exceptional demand put the workers in a seller's market, such an event was likely to be short-lived. If the demand increased dramatically and the upward trend seemed likely to continue, many entrepreneurs would feel that it was now necessary to find a cheaper and more convenient way of getting the work done, and this would probably involve replacing the increasingly costly labour with capital; if the market soon fell again, on the other hand, the employer could revert to playing off one worker against another and offering lower piece-rates. In other words, when the rise in demand for labour was short-lived, the manufacturer's momentary inconvenience was small compared with the advantages of having an excess of workers afterwards. His erstwhile tormentors became his prisoners: it had been easy enough for them to get into the trade when times were good, but it was almost impossible to get out quickly when things worsened. At its worst, the process became, as one employer in the nail and chain trade put it in 1876:

> . . . a kind of auction reversed. On a Monday morning the contractors or mastermen assemble at the master's warehouse, when the master tells them what work he wants, and unless trade is very brisk he calls them in one by one, and tests them as to what prices they will make certain chains for, invariably giving the work to those who offer the lowest tender . . . and then they with their wives and children go to work day and night, as far as they dare, to make up for lost time.[40]

The worker's position was doubly vulnerable, because it was widely argued that, once piece-rates had slipped, outworkers tried to increase their output so as to keep up their total earnings: but by doing so they simply added to the very over-production which had caused the reduction in the first place. As a Bulwell framework knitter, George Chandler, told Muggeridge in 1844:

> . . . prices being so low, a man is obliged to do more than he would if he had a better price, consequently the more a man does the fuller the market gets of the article . . . . If they were to do less work, there would not be so much depression. There would be a regular steady demand for the article, and there would be no occasion for all those abridgements . . .[41]

The effect of competition on piece-rates is reflected in the sheer difficulty of ascertaining what the rate for a particular piece of outwork actually was at any time; apart from the element of diversity introduced by the size of the middleman's 'cut', the rates offered at their warehouses by different manufacturers might show marked divergences. Even when a list of prices was officially agreed between a union and the big employers, as for example in the Macclesfield silk trade, 'the price-list is not absolutely adhered to by the manufacturers': in this particular case:

> . . . some small firms wholly disregard it, and the larger ones only observe it when dealing with their indoor weavers. The price paid by these to undertakers and outdoor weavers is from 15 to 20 per cent lower than that paid to indoor weavers, while the smaller manufacturers pay from 30 to 40 per cent lower than to their indoor hands, who are already paid below the recognised scale.[42]

The confusion was even greater where no agreed list existed: and Mary MacArthur, secretary of the Women's Trade Union League, told the 1907 Committee on homework that:

> My experience is that in the unskilled women's trades there is no standard by which wages are computed – that there is very seldom any uniformity whatsoever either in the homework or in the factory work, and frequently in my interviews with employers I am informed that, as far as they know, they are paying higher rates than other people; if I can prove that their rates are really lower they will be pleased to raise them, or if I can manage to get the other employers to pay higher rates, to come up to their level, they will go one better.[43]

If cheap labour was the key to the viability of outwork it follows that outwork would disappear on a large scale once the pockets of labour vanished on which it had flourished. How far does the story of the decline of outwork bear this out? In trades strongly affected by sharp cyclical upswings or export booms, there were clearly times when employers could not get the labour they wanted except by paying more or by accepting the inconveniences of sending work further afield. It was in the boom of the early 1820s in cotton weaving that piece-rates rose to a remunerative level for the weavers for the last time; and in the comparable boom in the mid-1830s, not only did handloom weavers' rates increase, but manufacturers in both Manchester and Glasgow were having to send materials as far away as Ireland because they could not get them worked up locally.[44] On both occasions, it is not surprising to find that manufacturers turned to the powerloom in large numbers and thus signified that the end of handloom weaving in cotton was not far distant. In other words, when the rising cost of labour indicated that demand was outrunning supply, interest shifted towards methods of production which would soon supersede outwork altogether.

The same effect was produced when the supply of labour was dwindling although the demand for it was steady. This could happen for a number of reasons: as we have seen, with persistent migration towards the towns, which led to a decline in the absolute level of the population of many rural areas by the 1870s, the pockets of available labour in the countryside became much smaller, although their counterparts in the towns may have increased; this tendency was further reinforced because the natural increase of the population in the countryside was now lower than that in most towns and cities. Moreover, the supply of other types of potential outwork labour was being reduced by legal and institutional developments: the more society came to care for its most vulnerable members, the less need or opportunity would there be for them to take up casual homework. Once the hours and conditions of work in small workplaces were as strictly regulated as those in cotton factories; once children had to put in compulsory attendance at school; once the aged had freed from the stigma of accepting charity in 'the House' and had been given old age pensions; and once a minimum of wages had been fixed, either by trade union action or, for the last residual homeworkers in 1909, by government decree, then – and only then – would the labour market be rid of those whose necessities had in the past sustained one of the worst forms of exploitation which 'free' labour has ever known.

And yet the story is not quite so simple: because one finds – in the remoter parts of Nottinghamshire or Leicestershire in the 1840s, for example – that pockets of suitable workers *could* exist for years, waiting for work which never came. The supply of outwork *could* sometimes dry-up before the supply of outworkers. Outwork did not simply cease, therefore, when its supply of labour failed: and to provide a balanced explanation we need to look briefly at the relative availability of the factors of production other than labour which entrepreneurs had to juggle with in deciding how best to produce their goods, and, in a later section, at the ways in which their juggling was influenced, not merely by the supply of productive factors, but by the ways in which the markets for their goods changed.

In considering the relative abundance of labour and capital, we need to ask whether entrepreneurs in some circumstances had to stick to the outwork system because they lacked the resources to abandon a form of organization which they knew to be second-best in favour of a new type which would have embodied capital in some novel technology. Does a shortage of capital explain the long survival of industrial outwork? After all, it is well known that Britain's industrial structure in the nineteenth century was dominated by small independent firms; that investment continued to be mobilized through traditional, primitive, and essentially 'personal' channels from the private resources of the active members of small partnerships and family firms, or from ploughed-back profits; and that impersonal and institutional mechanisms for raising capital for home industry were surprisingly underdeveloped. Could it be that, in industries where many entrepreneurs seem to have lacked substantial resources and where fierce competition between a mass of small producers was likely to keep profit margins low, the long reliance on outwork methods merely reflected these notorious peculiarities in industrial organization and in the capital market? Or, to put the problem the other way round, would outwork have survived so long if the industries concerned had been dominated by a few big corporations, or if Victorian Britain had developed more complex institutional arrangements – investment banks, finance corporations, or even unit trusts – for channelling funds into industry at home?

It must be admitted at once that no definitive answer can be attempted here to questions which, in some cases, are highly hypothetical. Until we have fuller industrial histories of those sectors of the economy studied here, and above all until we have more accounts of individual firms in the outwork industries, there are simply not enough hard data to present to those 'new' economic historians who specialize in answering such counter-factual questions as these. Indeed, it could well be that the yield of untapped business records will turn out to be too meagre to allow these problems to be satisfactorily resolved – although this consideration is not likely to deter the enthusiastic future researcher. For the present we must be content with a few broad but unsubstantiated hypotheses which may serve as a starting point for others.

At the outset, it is important to remember that the replacement of outwork depended less on the availability of capital in the narrow sense than on the capacity of the current technology to produce new machines which could effectively and economically copy all the necessary movements of the human hand or match the watchfulness of the human eye. For how often is a viable new machine not taken up simply because those who might be interested in its adoption lack the necessary capital? How often, rather, are new machines 'ahead of their time', in the sense *either* that they are technically imperfect and unreliable in practical performance, *or* that their utilization would be worthwhile only if the demand for a particular industry's product were to grow faster than it actually is? In the early nineteenth century, when the machine-making industry was still in its infancy, execution often lagged behind intention. The first powerlooms, for instance, were not satisfactory because it took until the early 1820s to solve, by the slow process of trial and error, all the distinct technical problems involved in mechanizing the various parts of the art of weaving.[45] Not until the middle of the nineteenth century, when a specialized machine-making industry had come into existence, could the technical problems implicit in mechanizing certain basic hand processes such as stitching be effectively tackled.

Moreover, we need to bear in mind that the capital of an industrial enterprise goes beyond its machines to include workspace: but whereas in the outwork system this latter element was provided by the worker himself, in a factory system it had to be paid for directly by the employer. Anyone who takes work into his own home or workshop saves his employer the rent or ownership of premises, and also relieves him of the costs of heat and light. The former is particularly important, since the more it would cost an employer to build or hire suitable rooms the greater his incentive would be to go on putting his work out instead. With certain technologies, the entrepreneur has a choice between alternative systems, since machines or tools which do not call for the application of non-human power lend themselves to both domestic and large-workshop environments. In these cases, the level of factory rents or building costs may well have been the crucial determinant of the survival of outwork.

The introduction of the sewing machine provides a good illustration of this problem, for the high cost of floorspace in the centre of London was almost certainly a key factor in the long survival of subcontracting and homework in many of the stitching trades there. When H. W. Lord reported to the Royal Commission of the early 1860s on children's employment about the impact of the sewing machine on the needlework trades, and speculated on its likely future as a 'domestic' or a 'factory' machine, he concluded that:

> So far as I have been able to form any opinion, the rental of premises required for workrooms seems to be the element which ultimately determines this point, and consequently it is in the metropolis that the old system of giving out work to small employers and families has been longest retained, or earliest returned to.[46]

In fact, the high cost of building and the high level of rents probably helped outwork to survive in two ways: on the one hand it would deter employers, especially in seasonal trades, from sinking capital in large workshops or factories; and at the same time, because of the exceptional pressure that high house-rents placed on working-class budgets, it made any additional source of family income seem a boon, and thus increased the incentive of wives, children and other dependents to offer their services as outworkers, however low the wages. Thus if we wish to explain the continued viability of outwork in terms of some shortage of capital, we will certainly have to look further at the cost of providing alternative working accommodation for some different system of production.

On the other hand, it will probably be more difficult to show that outwork survived because entrepreneurs lacked the capital to buy new machines. For outwork itself often implied an increasing investment in fixed capital by the employers rather than by their workmen. Some homeworkers used remarkably expensive and sophisticated tools – the jacquard looms of Coventry, the various 'engines' in the Nottingham lace industry, the knitting frames of the East Midlands, and the sewing machine itself all spring to mind. In some cases, individual workers still managed to buy their own machines, as their forebears had done in simpler times; but many hired their equipment from a manufacturer, agent, or other rentier. Once a manufacturer had become involved in the provision of this kind of fixed capital, he was bound to face the problem of whether to keep the machines in his own workplace or to allow his workers to use them at home. Even where the machines in question were hand- or foot-powered, we can readily imagine that there would be some advantages of indoor operation, so long as the rent of floor-space, to which we have just referred, was not thought to be excessive. In any case, the employer might meet the extra cost by deducting 'loom-standing' or some such charge from his workers' wages; this certainly seems to have been common practice in weaving and knitting shops in the first half of the nineteenth century. As time went on, many employers of outworkers came to invest first in machines and then in workspace; and thus many of our industries contained an interesting hybrid at some stage in their development between the true domestic workshop and the steam-powered factory, in the shape of the *hand*-powered 'factory' or machine-shop. New practices were possible in this kind of 'half-way' environment: wages could be paid on a time- rather than a piece-basis, patterns could be kept secret, materials kept clean, and delivery dates met with greater certainty. It did not take Barrans, the leading wholesale clothiers in Leeds, long to realize the best way of using the new sewing machine: as early as 1864, their spokesman told an assistant Parliamentary commissioner that 'it is more profit-able for employers who have sewing machines to have their machine work done on the premises than by workpeople in their own homes'.[47] All such examples of the readiness of the interested parties to invest in complex but still hand-powered new machines, whether housed in factories or in domestic shops, do not suggest any shortage of capital at the appropriate points. Ultimately, of course, once a machine needed non-human power in order to be worked most efficiently, the entrepreneur had no alternative. In the absence of domestic power sources such as gas and electricity in the nine-teenth century, such machines had to be factory-housed, and the entrepreneur who wanted to use them had to be prepared to meet the cost of buildings and of power, as well as of the basic machines.

In spite of the apparent defects in the capital market of the nineteenth century, it would seem that the necessary resources were forthcoming whenever they were required for any of these additional developments or new purposes: but they would not be called for so long as sufficient cheap labour was available to keep the existing system going; so long as potential alternative techniques had not demonstrated their reliability; or so long as the growth in demand did not encounter supply constraints within the prevailing organization and technology. But where did this capital eventually come from? Obviously, some of it would come from new firms whose entrepreneurs came into the industry from outside. But when it came from within the industry, which of the existing groups – merchant-manufacturers, middlemen, or even wage-earners – provided it?

In most of our industries, by the time circumstances made the transfer of some process to the factory seem necessary, entrepreneurs currently active in the trade were already in fact providing some fixed capital in the form of buildings and machines. For, as we have seen, outwork and factory often co-existed and complemented each other in an industry, with one stage being done 'inside' the manufacturer's workshop with the aid of his machines, and the succeeding one being 'put out'. Thus yarn given out for weaving in the first half of the nineteenth century had often been spun on the frames, jennies, or mules housed in the factory of the manufacturer concerned. Similarly, at a later period much of the tailoring or shoe-making which was stitched or made up by homeworkers had first been cut out 'inside'. Furthermore, where costly and sophisticated hand-machines were introduced – as in framework knitting or in the industries which adopted the sewing machine in the mid-nineteenth century – the big manufacturer found it not only necessary but profitable to invest in such machines himself, even when they operated in the workers' homes rather than on his own premises. In short, his contribution already went far beyond the provision of 'circulating' capital, and he was obviously well placed to do more, if more was needed.

What about the existing middlemen in the outwork trades? In our ideal type of outwork, the putter-out was simply a manager employed by a big manufacturer: as John Biggs, the prominent Leicester hosier put it: 'The middleman . . . is selected as a man of character, whom we can trust with a larger amount of material. He is also a man of superior knowledge and skill, and selected as such; and it saves us a considerable amount of trouble in taking the work in, having to deal with one man instead of twenty or thirty.'[48] Yet Thomas Winters, a trade union organizer, speaking of the same industry a decade later, maintained that 'in these trades the employer *is* the middleman; there is no connexion at all between the real manufacturer and the veritable workman . . .' .[49] Obviously, Winters had a point: many a 'middleman' was in practice an entrepreneur and employer. In hosiery, for example, he might be agent for a number of manufacturers; he might own and let frames on his own account; he might even have his own large workshop. But, most important of all, he might – from time to time if not permanently – enter the market as a producer himself, obtaining his own materials and making goods either on speculation or to a direct wholesale order.

Indeed, there appears to have been a strong tendency for agents and middlemen in many of the outwork trades to gravitate into the ranks of independent producers; often they were neither managers for someone else nor entrepreneurs in their own right, but rather something between the two. The temptation to start producing for oneself must have been strong, when the opportunities (or perhaps in some cases the necessities) for doing so were so numerous. After all, under the outwork system there was usually no need to invest in tools and workspace: the workers already provided their own. All that was required was a stock of materials – obtained on credit, bought at knock-down prices during a glut from a bankrupt neighbour, or even embezzled – together with the hope of a quick sale. It is tempting, therefore, to echo John Burnett's comments in the 1880s about 'the ease with which men can become sweaters'; for he maintained that 'it is the desire of every man who works under the system to become as soon as possible a sweater of other people, and to get into the business on his own account'.[50]

But to make a start in outwork was one thing. To make a success and to accumulate enough capital to participate readily in the transition to factory production was quite a different matter. We have already seen the stratagems which the small struggling middleman-entrepreneur had to resort to in order to stay in business: in the popular view at least, it was he who led the way in reducing wage rates in order to undercut his bigger competitors. And if one consequence of cut-throat competition was the immiseration of the homeworkers in industry after industry, then another, in the more volatile trades at least, was a low level of profit margins for many small producers. This in turn would make it difficult for the smaller manufacturer to build up reserves which might be easily transformed into fixed capital in the shape of buildings, motive power, and machines at a later date. In short, the middleman might fulfil many of the functions of the true entrepreneur; but the sudden provision of large amounts of fixed capital was not likely to be within his capacity.

Clearly, whenever such investment was necessary, those large manufacturers who already had some of their work done 'inside' –

possibly with the aid of mechanical power – were in a much better position to provide it than were their agents or workpeople, as the example of the cotton industry in the 1820s shows. For the pioneer adopters of the powerloom were precisely those manufacturers with spinning mills, who merely added weaving sheds on to them and so created large integrated factories.[51] Lacking such a basis for easy expansion, the small manufacturer or middleman, who had previously operated with only a modest warehouse and/or a few hand-driven machines, would find the move to a real factory a much more daunting prospect. And as for the workers themselves, the lack of any viable domestic power source made it impossible even to contemplate running one of the most sophisticated machines at home, let alone to start up a whole factory of them: the attempts of the Coventry silk weavers in the 1850s to harness communal steam engines to the looms in their individual garret-workshops were interesting and ingenious, but they appear to have been unique (see Chapter 1, p 64).

It looks, therefore, as if it was in those industries where some of the manufacturers were already conducting operations partly on an outwork and partly on a factory basis – in cotton in the early 1820s, or in shoemaking half a century later, for example – and where it was a matter of extending an existing factory to bring more of the processes inside, that the new capital came from the group most obviously able to provide it. In a big city, the smaller middleman-entrepreneur would find it especially difficult to make the transition; but the small man in the provinces was probably rather better placed to effect the change eventually. For by contrast with the metropolitan employer, the entrepreneur in a more rural environment – in the villages of Nottinghamshire, Leicestershire, or Northamptonshire, or in the upland textile townships of Lancashire or Yorkshire, for example – at least had the benefits of cheap land and low rents when he contemplated entering the factory business. Thus we might reasonably hazard the guess that the self-made millowner of legend, who had fought his way up from the ranks of middlemen or wage-earners, or had even come from outside the industry, would be a more common phenomenon in the smaller communities on the fringes of the manufacturing districts than in the big cities which formed their centres; he would be encountered in Padiham or Hinckley, in other words, rather than in Manchester or Leicester.[52] Of course, such a man had by no means enjoyed an

easy ride: small communities like these had been seriously impoverished as declining outwork centres in the first half of the
nineteenth century. Nevertheless, it was remarkable how, in later
decades, the smaller towns and villages of north-east Lancashire, for
example, pulled themselves up 'by their bootstraps', and with very
limited local resources managed to provide themselves with cotton-
weaving mills: some were joint-stock ventures with a lot of small
shareholders; others were family partnerships; many began by renting space in cooperatively built factories on a 'room and power'
basis. Perhaps the secret of their ultimate success in the late nineteenth century was that, whereas outwork had needed cheap labour,
a factory system also needed cheap land; and the smaller communities on the edges of the textile and clothing regions were in fact
able to provide both.

All in all, then, there seems little at present to suggest that
outwork survived because of a shortage of capital or a failure of
technology. When a new injection of fixed capital was obviously
necessary, it was forthcoming; and if such investment was not
undertaken at some particular date, it was because actual and
potential entrepreneurs did not then deem it to be necessary. They
stuck with the existing, predominantly labour-intensive, system
which they knew, *either* until such time as the supply of suitable
labour dried up, *or* until demand changes encouraged pioneering
innovators to break with the past in order to take advantage of a
rising market. Once a few adventurous spirits had successfully
transformed the technical and organizational bases of their enterprises, those competitors who wished to stay in business would
sooner or later have to follow their example. We have already
examined some of the factors which led to the disappearance of
suitable labour from much of the country by the end of the
nineteenth century: we must now consider how the viability of
outwork was further weakened by changes in demand which were
taking place over much the same period.

The Influence of Demand

If 'the division of labour is limited by the extent of the market',
then the continued viability of outwork as a means of satisfying
demand for a particular product obviously depended on the nature
of the market and on the extent to which it changed over time.

Certain market situations might lend themselves ideally to production on an outwork basis: but any decisive alteration in the pattern of demand might well expose the inadequacies of outwork and force its replacement by some new system of production. It is important, therefore, to discover what kinds of markets were most compatible with outwork and to consider the effects that changes in demand might have on industries where outwork had hitherto been important. Before we can do this, however, we need to remember the difficulties which entrepreneurs had in the nineteenth century in assessing the markets they catered for. In an age of slow communications and no consumer research, how much did manufacturers really know about market conditions, and how far, in any case, was their behaviour actually determined by what they knew?

The individual entrepreneur who had to decide 'how much' and 'what sort' was often making up his mind without the benefit of direct contact with the consumers. The smaller the scale of his operations, then the more he depended for his outlets on the good offices of the great merchant and the less he was likely to know about conditions at the other end of the long chain of production, distribution, and consumption. As assistant commissioner Chapman said of the small Yorkshire woollen manufacturers in the late 1830s:

> They are completely ignorant of the circumstances affecting distant markets; and in adapting their supply to the demand they are guided solely by the state of the market on the last market day, and not by any enlarged prospective view. In the event of a slack market, they will refuse a warp perhaps to one weaver; a second dull market day, and a second weaver will be refused work, and so they go on until their production is confined to their own families. In the event of a brisk demand, they, being ignorant, are apt to be over-sanguine, and they work on until the consequence is a great aggravation of the subsequent depression. The only check upon this is the intelligence of the Leeds merchants; but they again are less cognisant of the circumstances affecting supply and demand than the merchants of great shipping markets . . . [53]

Indeed, the small producer in outwork – especially the 'middleman-entrepreneur' or the 'workman-entrepreneur' – was often encouraged or compelled to produce ahead of demand or on speculation: in other words, he made his goods without any guarantee of a

sale and with scant consideration for the state of the market. It was
said of the Luton straw-hat makers in the 1890s, for instance, that
'the majority . . . are small men producing on the chance of selling
their goods afterwards. They make a few special shapes, and when
these are in demand they obtain good prices; when they are no
longer asked for, the small maker goes on making them, and is
obliged to sell them at a low price to the merchant, who can afford
to keep them in stock until they are again wanted.'[54] The gap
between production and sale in such common items as boots and
shoes actually gave rise to a group of 'factors' or wholesale merchants
who, as well as giving orders to the big producers, also bought up the
stocks of small masters at low prices, taking advantage of the latter's
needs for a quick sale and their inability to hold stock. Such factors
either kept warehouses to which retailers resorted for their requirements, or sent out their own travellers and agents to retail shops in
the country.[55] The line of communication between producer and
consumer was thus a tortuous one: and it could take a long time for
a message to be conveyed from end to end. In the short run,
therefore, production was slow to adjust to changes in the market;
and because of these lags, most outwork industries were liable to
gluts, to sharp price falls, to cut-throat competition between producers, and to sudden swift deterioration in the conditions of their
workers whenever a drop in demand belatedly made itself felt.
These fundamental inefficiencies in producing for the mass market
during the nineteenth century need to be borne in mind during the
discussion below.

It is worth remembering, too, that outwork and factory were not
the only means by which the demand for common personal and
household consumer goods was supplied. The demand for clothing,
for example, reflected the diverse needs and tastes of the whole
range of social classes and income groups of nineteenth-century
England: and although outwork production was suitable for supplying some of these needs, it could not meet them all. At one
extreme, the well-to-do had their clothes made to individual order
and personal specification by skilled 'bespoke' craftsmen: at the
other, the very poor might rely on garments which were 'home-
made' or at least 'home-adapted' by the needles of their own
womenfolk. Under these conditions, a vital element in changing
demand over the long term was the increased 'mass-production'
element in the total domestic consumer market, as the share of both

luxury 'bespoke' and more particularly of low grade 'subsistence-sector' production fell. Our knowledge of the details of this lengthy process is at present scanty, and will only be filled out when historians have undertaken major studies of each of the great consumer goods industries: but for the student of outwork the basic point is clear. As the possibilities of mass-production increased, it was as likely – at any rate in the initial stages of the process – that these opportunities would be met by the expansion of outwork as by the building of factories: everything would depend, in fact, on the speed with which the market grew and on the relative abundance of the necessary factors of labour, capital, and techniques. Indeed, the rise of mass-production in response to long-term changes in demand was one of the chief factors in the long persistence of outwork production in the nineteenth century.

Of course, there was one perennial feature of the market for common consumer goods of which producers could not be unaware: customers tended to make their purchases at particular seasons of the year. The clothing trades, again, illustrate this point to perfection. Thanks to the vagaries of the English climate, consumers usually feel the need to buy lighter clothes when they become aware that summer is upon them, and to change back into warmer and heavier garments by the time that November and December are heralding the onset of winter. Thus the various clothing trades – and, at one remove, some of the minor textile industries – faced a regular and predictable seasonal pattern of fluctuating demand: William Biggs described the situation in the 1860s of the Leicester hosiery industry, which specialized largely in woollen and worsted knitwear in contrast with neighbouring Nottingham, which concentrated on cotton, as follows:

> The Leicester goods being thus in great part for the winter use, the busiest time is the second half of the year. But the Australian season of a month or two follows, and the goods for that market are of the same class as those for the home .... In spring and summer there is a demand for Canada .... [56]

Seasonality was not unique to textiles and clothing, for many of the multitude of London's 'sweated' trades were notorious for their alternation of slack and brisk seasons.[57] Box-making – one of the newer of these trades in the late nineteenth century – was a good example, for wholesalers and manufacturers who wanted special packaging for their goods usually made exceptional demands on the box-makers in anticipation of the Christmas rush.[58] The 'seasons' of different trades did not necessarily coincide, of course; so that an energetic and versatile worker in a place like London, with many such trades, had the opportunity to shift from one to another as the demand for labour alternately quickened or slackened. But in a smaller place, where only one kind of outwork was habitually available, the 'slack season' meant a dearth of work, and a loss of earnings.

Since 'seasons' in trade were as predictable as the year's weather, it is at first sight surprising that manufacturers did not try to spread their anticipated total production over the whole twelve months, instead of having at one point suddenly to expand their organizations in order to match peak demand and at another to slim them down again. But the logic behind their actions was clear and simple: as a Nottingham lace manufacturer said in 1863, 'The principle of the business is to keep as little stock as possible, as if manufacturers finish by anticipation they sink their capital in wages, instead of keeping it productive in their own hands.'[59] From the manufacturer's point of view, in fact, outwork organization was ideally suited to seasonal trades, so long as the requisite labour could be assumed to be forthcoming at the proper times; it allowed him to avoid having empty workrooms or idle machines when trade was dull, and to keep stocks and inventories low at all times, whilst all the risks, not merely of unemployed labour but also of unused capital in the shape of workspace and tools, were carried by the workforce.

If outwork suited trades with regular seasonal fluctuations in demand, it was equally welcome to those entrepreneurs in industries liable to be afflicted by the capricous shifts of 'fashion', especially in women's clothing. The lace industry was an outstanding example of a branch of textiles highly susceptible to sudden changes of this sort. As a Nottingham manufacturer explained to the homework Committee of 1908:

> One year a style of lace will be in demand which will give employment to every available worker, and another season a totally different class of goods would form the prevailing fashion which would give very little employment to the home workers. The styles of lace vary so considerably that one web may give

employment to home workers amounting to £3 or £4, whilst an equally large and valuable web might only give employment to the value of 3s or 4s. In fact, it is quite possible for a manufacturer to do an equal amount of business in two successive years, and yet in one of the years to pay two-thirds less for drawing, clipping, and scalloping than in the other year.[60]

Lace is perhaps an extreme case of an industry where demand could change suddenly and unpredictably; but to a lesser degree, 'fashion' influenced the fortunes of others and thus affected the viability of outwork production in them. Hosiery is a good case which illustrates the effects of more gradual and long-term shifts in clothing fashions, for many of this industry's difficulties in the first half of the nineteenth century reflected the shift in demand away from high-class 'fully-fashioned' stockings towards low-grade 'cut-ups' as hose became an under-, rather than an outer, garment. And the Scottish tweed industry is another instance of a trade which blossomed dramatically in the second and third quarters of the nineteenth century thanks to the popularization of all things 'Scotch' among the English well-to-do by Sir Walter Scott and Queen Victoria, but in which saturation of the market soon manifested itself.[61] In industries vulnerable to both short- and long-term changes in fashion, therefore, outwork offered the same advantages to the manufacturer as it did in the more predictable 'seasonal' trades: he could readily extricate himself from some of the worst effects of declining demand, and throw much of the burden of readjustment on to his long-suffering workers.

But only a relatively small number of the great outwork trades were affected by changes in demand arising either seasonally or from the fickle dictates of fashion; in most cases, it is to the longer-term shifts in the market that we must look for some explanation of outwork's survival and ultimate disappearance. Consumer goods industries were, of course, liable to be affected by the overall cyclical pattern of economic growth which asserted itself during the first half of the nineteenth century. Whenever the nine-to-ten year business cycle moved into its downswing, such industries were likely to experience bouts of intense price competition between producers, with lower wages and profit margins, and ultimately an increase in unemployment. In the earlier part of the century, too, when Britain relied essentially on home-produced food, it was generally believed that consumer demand for manufactures fell sharply in years when harvests were poor and food expensive. As Samuel Holmes, a Derby framework knitter, told commissioner Muggeridge two years before the repeal of the Corn Laws:

> I think that a greater demand for labour would alter our condition in a very great measure. I always find that when provisions are cheap I am always better off in all circumstances. I can not only buy my provisions cheaper, but I am employed better, and of course I can employ somebody else. I can buy clothing and employ my neighbours, the shoemaker and tailor. I wish I could employ them more than I do.[62]

Just as outwork relieved the manufacturer who was vulnerable to seasonal or fashion-induced changes in demand of some of the risks associated with a falling market, so it did on a longer-term basis entrepreneurs liable to be adversely affected in a cyclical downswing. In particular, where growth in demand in the upswing of a particular cycle has been fairly modest, or where there was no discernible secular upward movement in the market over a period of two or three successive cycles, a manufacturer would have had little incentive to replace outwork by some different form of production, since the 'benefits' of outwork would still have been self-evident to him: the technical and organizational stagnation of the Midland hosiery industry between 1815 and the 1850s, of which we have seen William Biggs' justification above, illustrates this theme very well.

However, the problem of the continued viability of outwork is best seen in those industries for which there was a long-term rise in demand, either at home or abroad, over our whole period. If demand grew in a series of swift, sharp, but irregular bursts, there would probably be some crucial point at which the prevailing outwork system would be stretched beyond its capacity and would be unable to supply the goods demanded: when this happened, the more active entrepreneurs in the industry concerned would begin to commit themselves to alternative methods of production which would probably involve investing in new machines, new or extended workplaces, and new sources of motive-power. But if, on the other hand, the increase in demand came in an altogether slower and steadier fashion, it might be possible to cope with it for a long time by simply extending or elaborating the outwork system, or by using some almost imperceptibly changing combination of outwork and factory methods.

What kinds of markets were liable to sudden and dramatic bursts of expansion in the nineteenth century, and what kinds were more likely to have a steadier long-term growth pattern? In this question lies one of the keys to understanding why outwork survived longer in some industries than in others. In suggesting an answer, the industries we have been considering probably need to be classified in two different (although to a large degree overlapping) ways: first they need to be divided into those which relied at least partly on the stimulus of foreign demand for their growth and those which were almost totally dependent on the home market; and secondly, a distinction has to be made between those industries which produced basic semi-manufactures, such as yarn and cloth, and those which made finished goods ready for direct sale to individual consumers, such as clothing or shoes.

Those mass-production industries which catered essentially for the British *domestic* market expanded and adapted their production in response to a number of different long-term developments. The high and *sustained* rate of population increase – between 1 and 1.5 per cent annually from the 1780s to the beginning of the twentieth century – would in itself have kept the sheer *size* of the home market for essential consumer goods growing steadily, even if there had been no changes in its *quality*. But important qualitative changes were also taking place. Some were inextricably involved with the general process of urbanization, which, *inter alia*, altered the locations of the most important domestic markets for consumer goods, speeded the decline of the 'home-made' or subsistence sector in the making of these items, and undoubtedly contributed to the creation of more uniform national standards in consumer tastes and material ambitions, so that new 'fashions' – in dress, household goods, and the like – soon spread throughout the country.

More important in qualitative terms, however, was the rise in the average real incomes of the urbanized working class: for only when the real purchasing power of the great bulk of England's population had grown sufficiently to leave them with an appreciable regular margin of resources which could be devoted to things other than the basic essentials of food, housing, and fuel could consumer goods industries such as mass-produced and ready-made clothing expand rapidly. Economic historians have conducted a long and often confused debate about what happened to the 'standard of living' in the first half of the nineteenth century, and appear to have concluded that it changed little: but after 1850, it is generally accepted that average real incomes began to grow, first in the 1860s and early 1870s, and then more dramatically in the 1880s and 1890s.[63] Not surprisingly, it was *precisely* in these periods that industries such as clothing or boots and shoes were transformed technically and organizationally: in both these cases, the years 1850-70 saw the adoption of the sewing machine and the establishment of elaborate combinations of factory and outwork production; whilst the last two decades of the century saw the almost complete transfer of all but the bespoke branches of these trades to the factory – except, of course, in London. During the first phase of growth, it was possible for the rising demand to be met largely by the expansion and greater sophistication of outwork: but with the more rapid growth of real spending power among the working class at the end of the century, outwork could no longer cope. By the late 1880s, it was beginning to be appreciated that one consequence of industrialization might be the emergence of the affluent working man. As Lloyd Williams, a Liverpool wholesale tailor, told the Lords' Committee on sweating:

> Our trade is certainly increasing .... I think working men are dressing better than they used to dress. They used to confine themselves principally to moleskin trousers; now they go in for the low-priced cloth trousers.[64]

With the dawning of what Rostow has called 'the age of high mass-consumption', we see the demise of outwork as a viable means of supplying the population's basic requirements in consumer goods.[65]

By contrast with those industries whose growth patterns were largely determined by domestic developments within Britain, those already producing for *export* as well – as the basic textile trades were doing long before the industrial revolution of the late eighteenth century – were open to different influences from foreign demand. Semi-manufactured items such as yarn and cloth, which foreigners could import and work up into finished products according to their own tastes and needs, were important in international trade, and had strong growth potential especially if Britain were to obtain a marked comparative advantage in their production. And this was precisely what she came to enjoy as a result of the great technical innovations which she pioneered, first in spinning in the last quarter of the eighteenth century, and then in weaving in the second quarter of the nineteenth. Vast overseas markets stood ready for these goods, and outwork production speedily gave way to factory spinning between 1780 and 1820 and to factory weaving between 1820 and 1860. But Britain did not enjoy a similar technical advantage, either then or later, in the production of finished consumer goods, such as clothing, for which there had in any case never been an international mass-market comparable to that for the basic textiles: and in so far as these industries *did* experience export growth in the late nineteenth century, it is significant that they found their best markets in the 'White' colonies where tastes were very similar to those back home.[66] Essentially, therefore, semi-manufactures were likely to move from outwork to factory production before finished products, because they were susceptible to demand generated – however irregularly – outside the more restricted confines of the home economy.

Two final points need to be made about the effects of changing demand on the survival or collapse of outwork. In the first place, we have so far confined out attention to the demands of private consumers; but it is worth recalling that *institutional* demand often both stimulated mass-production on an outwork basis and enabled it to persist in certain circumstances. More specifically, massive government demand in wartime for such items as uniforms and boots had considerable effect on the expansion of outwork in the textiles, clothing, and leather industries during the wars of the eighteenth century. It is true that this particular influence was less important during the hundred years of peace from 1815 to 1914, although we should not forget – as in the case of army underwear – that the rigid and unchanging military patterns and specifications could sometimes keep up a stable level of demand for particular products which continued to be supplied by traditional techniques and outwork methods. But if the contracts no longer flowed in from the British government, foreign governments might still oblige: and other civilian employers, both public and private, who increasingly insisted on putting their 'servants' into recognizable uniforms – as did railway companies and local authorities – were also important customers for the products of outwork.*

Secondly, in discussing the effects of demand changes on the

*For the effects of Government contracts on the boot and shoe industry for example, see Chapter 3, p. 107; for army underwear, see Chapter 2, p.97; for the link between local government contracts and 'sweating' at the end of the nineteenth century, see Chapter 5, p.243.

organization of mass-production, we have so far dealt with those products for which there was traditionally a considerable export demand or those which enjoyed a near monopoly of the home market. But of course there were a few mass-produced consumer goods industries where neither of these considerations applied and where, with the increased freedom of trade from the 1820s onwards, entrepreneurs in fact faced foreign competition in the British market and had to adjust to a secular *decline* in demand, rather than an increase. In the first half of the nineteenth century, the outstanding example was the silk industry, which, in addition to being vulnerable to the vagaries of 'fashion', encountered fierce French competition with the successive reductions of tariff protection in the early 1820s and again after the Cobden Treaty of 1860 (see Chapter 1, p.64). In such a situation, entrepreneurs were unlikely to feel much incentive to abandon outwork, although paradoxically the best chance of countering foreign competition probably lay in increased mechanization and factory organization. A very similar situation arose later in the nineteenth century in the boot and shoe industry, which began to feel the effects of superior American mechanization in the 1880s and early 1890s: in this case, the challenge of American imports was successfully met by the industry's complete mechanization at the turn of the century; and indeed, the boot and shoe industry went on to build up its own export markets, especially in colonial countries, in the years just before 1914.[67]

If we take an overall view of the economic viability of outwork as a 'system' for mass-producing various kinds of consumer goods, it becomes clear that, in the last resort, the changing size and nature of the market for those goods was the crucial factor. If demand for some particular item grew dramatically over a period of a year or two, the most important factor in outwork production on the supply side - labour - would probably not be forthcoming in sufficient quantity at a low enough price, not would it be sufficiently productive if it stuck to traditional technology. All these circumstances would combine to force some entrepreneurs towards technical innovation and new forms of organization, as they did in the major textile industries at different times between 1780 and 1860. But in industries with a more stable pattern of demand, or with only modest and irregular growth over long periods, the outwork system remained attractive to manufacturers for a good deal longer: certainly until the last quarter of the nineteenth century, they could usually expect to find the various kinds of 'cheap' labour which the system needed, and even in the 1900s there were still special forces at work in a place like London – with its high rents, its foreign immigrants, and its casual pool of unskilled, poorly paid, and under-employed *male* labour – which ensured a suitable supply of 'sweated' outworkers. Only in the 1880s and 1890s did things change: new opportunities were now presented to producers by the urban mass-market, but at the same time there was the attendant threat that cheap rival products from America might snatch them away if the relevant British industries did not mend their ways; moreover, compulsory schooling, slower population growth, and rising affluence itself, all helped to effect some reduction in the availability of cheap labour in many places. Both these developments made outwork generally unviable in such 'finished-product' industries as clothing or boots and shoes, and its survival into the twentieth century – except on a very small scale or in new industries – became the reflection of special circumstances prevailing in the capital- and labour-markets of particular localities.

But all this 'rational' economic explanation of outwork's survival and disappearance ignores an important part of the story. It assumes that an entrepreneur's attitudes were determined simply and solely by economic considerations; whereas in fact a manufacturer could never totally dismiss the views and interests of the workers whom his decisions would affect, nor could he neglect the possibility that his behaviour might be questioned by 'public opinion' and might even provoke public controversy. The problems associated with industrial outwork had a *political*, as well as an economic, dimension: what entrepreneurs might well on purely economic criteria have *wished* to do was often to some degree frustrated by the antagonisms of their labour force or by the outraged attentions of politicians. Before our survey of the place of industrial outwork in nineteenth-century Britain is complete, therefore, we must consider the part played by the collective activities of the outworkers themselves and by the changing concerns of the State in influencing both the survival of outwork and its decline.

Part Three
NARRATIVE

— 5 —
The Politics of Outwork

Today, the best-remembered feature of outwork is undoubtedly the material poverty and mental degradation which it imposed on those who came to be caught up in it. From the handloom weaver and framework knitter of the 1830s and 1840s to the nail-maker and sweated needlewoman of the 1880s and 1890s, the depressing story is almost unchanging. Whenever statements are made about rising standards of living during the industrial revolution, the outworkers are normally omitted from the list of beneficiaries and are regarded as the poorest of the poor. Moreover, it was easy to feel, fatalistically, that poverty was inevitable in this stratum of capitalist society: for if, as Darwinians taught, life – even in 'civilized' England – was a struggle for material survival, then contemporaries must always expect to encounter specimens of the unfit, the failed, and the almost extinct in their very midst. Such fatalism was widespread, both among outworkers themselves and among those public men who periodically found their consciences jolted by revelations of unimagined suffering and squalor such as those made by the Lords' Committee on sweating in the late 1880s. And one depressing consequence was a general feeling that the problems inherent in outwork were insoluble: workers could hope to gain nothing by collective action, whilst politicians saw any form of State intervention as ineffective or even counter-productive. Thus discussion of the perennial problems of outwork generated at worst apathy, and at best pessimism, in many people's minds.

And yet there were always some – if only a small minority – both within the ranks of the workers and among their better-off sympathizers, who would not accept the inevitability of poverty, and who were determined to fight for something better. Some groups of outworkers did try, against formidable odds, to defend and protect themselves by joint action: and theirs is a small but not dishonourable part in the story of trade unionism, popular radicalism and of other movements for mutuality and collective self-help in the nineteenth century. Similarly, there were always those among national politicians who, moved by the inability of many outworkers to help themselves, were prepared to put a special case for State intervention and public assistance to ameliorate 'intolerable' conditions: and as time went on their hand was strengthened by the sheer persistence of a 'system' which evidently could not simply be wished away, and which showed no inclination to die out altogether. These twin themes – of the outworkers' brave but generally unsuccessful attempts to help themselves out of their plight and of the politicians' efforts to treat their problems as an exceptional case – recur repeatedly, though rarely obtrusively, in the political history of nineteenth-century England: and no general essay on outwork would be complete without some account of them.

Self Help

Trade Unionism

According to the Webbs' classic history of trade unionism in the nineteenth century, 'the rise of permanent trade combinations is to be ascribed, in the final analysis, to the definite separation between the functions of the capitalist entrepreneur and the manual worker, between, that is to say, the direction of industrial operations and their execution'.[1] But if this was a necessary condition, it was hardly a sufficient one: for most outwork industries revealed precisely this separation of functions, yet very few groups of outworkers were able to establish trade unions, and many, indeed, seem hardly to have tried. Given that so many outwork industries relied heavily on the often casual labour of women, children, and immigrants, it is not surprising either that many of these groups made no effort to organize themselves, or that they received relatively little sympathy from such male trade unionists as there might be in the skilled branches of the same or similar industries. Indeed, as the remaining outwork industries came to rely increasingly on this kind of labour in the later nineteenth century, it became even *less* likely that effective collective bargaining machinery would be established: for outside the factory textile industries, women were hardly unionized at all before the very end of the century. Thus an attempt in 1892 to unionize the workers in the straw-hat industry at Luton encountered 'a great deal of apathy on the part of the people': whilst efforts to organize women in lace and hosiery to resist the arbitrary exactions of middlewomen or 'mistresses' who channelled the work to them seem to have quickly collapsed.[2] Immigrant workers in the 'sweated' trades of the late nineteenth century seem to have been equally unorganizable; for example, attempts to form separate unions for Jewish tailors and shoemakers in both London and Leeds appear to have failed.[3] Even native male workers often found the effort of carrying through a successful strike beyond them: to take one instance, the unorganized country silk weavers of the loom-shops of Bedworth, near Coventry, struck for a week in 1838 against a cut in piece-rates; in the short run they gained their point, yet 'though out for so short a time, the married men with families were much put about, and became afraid of any future strike', so that when a further reduction was demanded for loom-rent a few months later, it was 'not resisted because of the horror which so many of the men had of the inconveniences which they had previously suffered'.[4]

Yet although many outworkers never enjoyed the benefits of collective bargaining to improve their position, some of them certainly played a prominent part in early trade union history. The Webbs went so far as to claim that 'the pioneers of the trade union movement [in the eighteenth century] were not the trade clubs of the town artisans, but the extensive combinations of the west of England woollen workers and the Midland framework knitters'.[5] Undoubtedly during the period before 1825, when collective bargaining was under the ban of anti-combination legislation, the textile industries – still predominantly outwork in organization – experienced a high level of organized activity by their wage-earners, as Professor Aspinall's account of unions in the first quarter of the nineteenth century clearly indicates.[6] But we should not exaggerate the scale of this activity, since large groups of workers in these industries – notably the hordes of domestic spinners – were conspicuously unorganized, whilst some of those who did organize were workshop operatives, rather than true outworkers. The shearmen and croppers of the woollen industry, for example – whose attempts to revive protective mercantilist legislation in the first decade of the nineteenth century and whose subsequent involvement in Luddism has been often recounted – were workshop-based craftsmen rather than outworkers: and the same was true to some extent of the wool-combers of the Yorkshire worsted industry, whose union was broken after a major strike in 1825. But various groups of handloom weavers, who undoubtedly *were* outworkers, made vigorous attempts at collective action: and although, as we shall see, these tended to be most successful in the skilled branches or among the weavers of one particular town, there were nonetheless occasions when vast areas were disturbed by massive strikes. The Lancashire cotton weavers struck on a county scale in 1808 and again in 1818, whilst their fellows in Scotland organized a nationwide stoppage in 1812.[7] Similarly, in the hectic burst of trade union activity of the early 1830s, both factory and outworkers in the various textile trades of Yorkshire seem to have been involved in the attempts to create bigger 'general unions'.[8] However, the weavers' efforts did not succeed in keeping outwork alive (let alone prosperous) in the major branches of the northern textile industries after the 1830s. And in this sense, the disappearance of outwork implied a weakening of trade unionism as a whole. It is misleading to tell the story of trade union development in the nineteenth century as if it were a chronicle of continually increasing strength and widening scope; for in so far as *some* outworkers had tried to keep up unions, the elimination of outwork actually meant a *decline* in union numbers and effectiveness until such time as new unions had emerged in the factory trades which replaced it.

After 1825, trade unions operated in a less restrictive legal atmosphere and their activities were more open, and are better documented. In examining the contribution of outworkers to trade union development after that date, three topics seem to call for particular treatment: in the first place, it is worth looking at those groups which appear to have been successful in keeping up organized collective bargaining for lengthy periods; secondly, it will be useful to consider those groups which, in spite of repeated efforts at organization, either failed to create permanent institutions or at any rate had to accept industrial relations on their employers' terms; and thirdly, it is necessary to examine the rather special cases such as shoemaking and tailoring where there existed a minority of organized 'craftsmen' in the 'bespoke' branch, and a disorganized majority in the mass-production section, and where relations between these two groups could throw some light on the notions of 'working class solidarity' and the 'aristocracy of labour' in nineteenth-century Britain.

There is, of course, an important difference between the first two topics mentioned above and the third. For the most part, when examining outworkers' trade unions we are looking at organizations which sought stubbornly to keep outworking alive and to make it more prosperous and secure – a task which, in the end, generally proved to be hopeless as changing circumstances led entrepreneurs to abandon the old 'system'. But in the case of the organized groups of skilled workers in industries which also had a large substratum of outworkers, a more far-sighted attitude sometimes emerged: instead of fighting fruitlessly to keep their old trade alive and unchanging in the face of harsh economic reality, trade unionists recognized the inevitability of technical and organizational change in their industry, and sought rather to come to terms with it and to exercise a decisive say in the process of transformation.

Of the larger bodies of outworkers who sought to defend their jobs and their material rewards in the middle decades of the nineteenth century, the handloom weavers in some of the lesser and more isolated textile centres provide perhaps the best example of reasonably successful collective bargaining over a lengthy period. Whenever a particular trade was confined to a single town and its hinterland, and where the products of the district were fairly distinctive, the chances of putting effective pressure on the local manufacturers to keep up wages were good: for in these circumstances, the manufacturers were in no position to play off the workers in one town against those in another, and the weavers themselves did not have to worry about securing concerted action with their brethren in other places. Thus weavers' unions could be expected to have more success in such places as Norwich, Coventry, and Barnsley than in the bigger and more widely diffused cotton and woollen industries of Lancashire and Yorkshire – although it should be noted that even in the latter there could be small but effective local combinations in some of the 'fancy' skilled lines.

These 'one-town' weavers' unions had one over-riding aim: they tried to make all the local employers adhere to a uniform 'list' of piece-rates for the different classes of woven goods, and they sought to ensure that no weaver accepted, or no manufacturer offered, work 'below the list'. This task was generally made more difficult by the existence in the countryside beyond the town in question of a body of unorganized workers who had perhaps less group-consciousness than their urban counterparts, who were likely to be desperately poor, and who in consequence had a persistent tendency to take work 'under the list'. The tactics of the Norwich weavers' union which faced this situation in the 1830s were described to the Royal Commission on the handloom weavers by one manufacturer, who claimed that the committee of the union:

> ... chiefly direct their efforts to prevent any weavers in Norwich from working below the list prices and to prevent any goods being sent out of Norwich to be wove in the country. One of the methods adopted is to wait upon the weavers, as soon as they hear of any being employed below what they consider the list price, and to dissuade them from continuing their work. They also wait on the manufacturer, and in addition send him an admonitory letter; further, they set watch round his house to see who goes out and in; work is also cut and destroyed.[9]

Another manufacturer complained:

> Whenever I went out they sent someone to follow me to see to what places I went and with whom I transacted business. One day they followed a cart of mine, going with goods about the city ... Next Friday they followed a cart five miles out into the country ... I have been obliged to send out my work by night, and that with considerable risk.[10]

The secretary of the union proposed that the best solution to this problem would be to differentiate between the classes of work to be done in the town and in the country: for he believed that the countrymen 'might be made useful and contented producers of fabrics that do not yield sufficient remuneration for city work-men'.[11]

One of the best-documented handloom weavers' unions is that of the Coventry silk weavers.[12] From 1813 onwards, the Coventry trade saw a succession of 'lists' and a variety of strategies to prevent the less scrupulous manufacturers from evading them: in 1819, for example, the weavers' committee, with the support of sympathetic employers, raised a fund of £1,600 from which to support any weaver unable to obtain work at 'list' prices, but were frustrated when their scheme was declared to be contrary to the Combination Act in 1822. On occasions, the 'list' was revised by general consent, and the weavers accepted reductions if 'the state of the trade' manifestly demanded it: but at other times, when a particular 'list' had been seriously undermined by the repeated evasions of manufacturers, they had to resort to strike action to restore uniformity. Thus there were major strikes in 1822 and 1831 – the latter, ominously, including an attack on Beck's new powerloom factory. But, as Joseph Fletcher discovered when he visited the town in the late 1830s, the weavers relied particularly on 'moral persuasion' to bring erring manufacturers to heel. They were much given to calling on the Mayor to summon a 'general town meeting' at which 'good' manufacturers and other local worthies unconnected with the trade would make public professions of sympathy and support for the weavers' case.* Fletcher was greatly impressed by the good feeling between masters and men which this pattern of industrial relations seemed to imply, although he was obviously unhappy that proceedings of this kind were 'wholly unrecognised by economical science', for they implied that 'moral' considerations replaced market forces: as he rightly saw, the underlying object of the Coventry 'system' was:

> . . . to fix a standard of comforts for the population *at its base* below which it was esteemed wrong to descend, although trade *might* possibly be extended by reducing lower the subsistence of the workmen.[13]

Nevertheless, even when backed by 'public opinion', the Coventry weavers had a hard task to maintain 'list' prices. It was always more difficult in the 'single-hand' trade of the countryside than in the 'engine trade' of the city, but by mid-century the increasing use of the powerloom was threatening the whole pattern of industrial relations and the old notion of uniform 'lists' of piece-rates. The weavers fought back doggedly, as we have seen, by trying to bring steam-power to their domestic loomshops, and they won a final pyrrhic victory in the strike of 1858; but this was quickly nullified by the great increase in competition from French silks which followed the Cobden treaty of 1860.[14]

'One-town' unions with basically similar aims and tactics existed at Barnsley, with its linen industry, and at Macclesfield, another silk centre. The former seems to have remained active until the 1830s, when it was reported that 'their [the weavers'] dwellings present an appearance of comfort much superior to that of weavers in other places . . . In their persons, clothing, and the appearance of their children, the Barnsley weavers contrast favourably with the same class of persons at Leeds and elsewhere'.[15] The Macclesfield union

---

*It should be remembered that the Coventry weavers, as freemen and Parliamentary voters, were in an unusually strong position to turn to the civic establishment for support.

survived throughout the later nineteenth century, assisted by the creation in 1855 of one of the very earliest Conciliation Boards: but it seems likely that the agreed list of prices applied only to the 'indoor' handloom weavers of the 'factories' in Macclesfield itself, and under-cutting remained rife in the other sections of the trade.[16]

By contrast with the various groups of weavers, the nailers of the West Midlands are a good example of those outworkers who made sporadic efforts to protect themselves by collective action, but who failed to create a permanent or effective organizational structure for this purpose. Like the weavers and others, the nailers sought to ensure the uniform observance of an agreed 'list' of prices for the various classes of nails: but in the face of the ubiquitous 'fogger' and of the self-employed nailer, it was particularly difficult to detect and prevent under-cutting. Both general and local strikes took place on occasions: the former could be successful at a time of rising trade, as in 1872, but could fail disastrously and destroy any embryonic union in an economic downturn, as in 1876,[17] (see also Chapter 3, p.130). No permanent union or pattern of collective bargaining seems to have emerged, however: and William Price, who led the Halesowen Spike Nail-makers union between 1887 and 1890, lamented to the Royal Commission on labour that 'I never knew the nail-makers hold together so long as for the three years I held them together. I never knew them hold together above three weeks before. They fall out, suspicious of each other, and go and undersell each other'.[18] By the early 1890s, indeed, both manufacturers and workmen declared themselves anxious to set up a permanent Conciliation Board, although an earlier attempt to do so in 1880 had failed.[19]

One important group of outworkers who, after repeated failures to maintain effective unions, *did* eventually create a long-lived conciliation machinery, were the hosiery workers of the Midlands: and in view of the fashion for arbitration and conciliation in some areas of British industrial relations – a fashion often said to have been set by A. J. Mundella in the hosiery industry – it is worth looking at the framework knitters' record in a little more detail.[20] After Luddism died down, the framework knitters had shown vigour and versatility in their attempts to act in concert both politically, in their efforts to have 'cut-ups' banned by Parliament, and industrially, by trying to keep up piece-rates; following an extensive strike in 1819, there was even an ambitious attempt – which won sympathy from the general public and from the 'good' manufacturers – to establish a union which would build up a large unemployment fund. Most of the major urban centres of the industry experienced repeated strikes to obtain new statements of piece-rates in the 1820s: Leicester, for example, did so in 1824, 1825, and 1830. But by the 1830s, although strikes continued to take place, they tended to be local and to be confined to the workers in one particular branch of the trade: in the words of Professor Church, 'ad hoc societies were formed for specific campaigns when trade was favourable. In the event of success their existence was prolonged in order to defend any ground gained, but the lives of such societies were as temporary as the gains they secured. Subscriptions, if paid at all, were minimal . . .'[21] As the industry continued to stagnate, however, the chances of success grew dim, and repeated failure bred hopelessness and apathy: as one country knitter from Leicestershire told commissioner Muggeridge in the mid-1840s:

> . . . union without means is of very little use . . . Union in our district seems dead; the men have no heart, no spirit, and many of them have no means to subscribe and get a fund. We have had a strong try at it this last winter, but it was a complete failure with us.[22]

In 1860, however, the situation was transformed when, under the inspiration of A. J. Mundella – then one of the pioneers of the factory system in hosiery, but later a Liberal MP and cabinet minster – a permanent Board of Conciliation was set up in Nottingham: a similar board was established in Leicester in 1866.[23] The idea was by no means new in 1860: Muggeridge heard several proposals on these lines in 1844.[24] But Mundella's board survived – albeit with difficulty in its latter days – for almost a quarter of a century, and it was often hailed as a model of good industrial relations. For it gave equal representation to masters and men, and recognized the existence of the various sectional unions, which united in 1866. Initially, it sought to reach joint agreement by amicable discussion, without resort to an umpire or outside arbitrator. The knitters for their part seem to have been happy to rely on the board, rather than on their under-financed union, to resolve their problems, even though they were in effect accepting a pattern of industrial relations on their employers' terms. However, in the 1870s, with the growing mechanization of the industry and the differing interests of the factory and the hand-knitters, some groups of workers withdrew from the Board, and pursued independent objectives. Similarly, manufacturers chose increasingly to take their work and their factories into the smaller towns and villages outside Nottingham, where the unions were weak, and where it was easy to pay below the 'list'. The Board seems, therefore, to have become relatively ineffective some time before its final dissolution in 1884.

Nevertheless, the notion of conciliation and arbitration – popularized if not pioneered in hosiery – has been called 'the gospel of a generation'.[25] In its recognition of the positive value of trade unions and of the equality of masters and men in negotiations, it marked an important stage in the development of a formal structure of industrial relations in England: it also helped to symbolize the developing political alliance between organized working men and the popular Liberal party in the third quarter of the nineteenth century. Thus the problems of this particular group of outworkers helped to give rise to that important but now neglected strand in English labour history known as 'Lib-Lab-ism.'

The third aspect of trade union history which has a bearing on the outwork industries is rather different: instead of asking 'what did outworkers do about forming trade unions?', we need to consider how trade unionists reacted to outwork. In a general sense, the answer is clear – the habitual poverty of most outworkers was a living reminder of the fate of unorganized labour in a capitalist system, and was a constant spur to other groups in their own attempts at collective self-defence. But the problem is especially interesting in such complex industries as tailoring and shoemaking, where outwork production of ready-made articles co-existed with high-class 'bespoke' craftsmanship at the 'quality' end of the trade. In this situation, the relatively small number of artisans in the bespoke trade were organized in societies to defend their wages and to preserve the 'customs of the trade', but the much more numerous body of outworkers in the lower branches of the industry were not. This problem was acute in tailoring, where it was further complicated by the fact that outwork existed *inside* the bespoke trade, as well as outside it. As one West End master tailor in the bespoke trade told the 1843 Royal Commission on children's employment:

It is the custom in the trade for the journeymen to work at their own houses or at the shops of the masters when they have accommodation: in the former case there are no stipulated hours of work; in the latter case the regular hours are from 6 am to 7 pm; these hours, being regulated by a society, are not exceeded. Two hours are allowed for meals. When the men are at home in the busy season, they may sometimes work very long hours in order to complete a sudden order.[26]

Local unions of bespoke tailors seem to have existed in London and in the major provincial cities by the mid-nineteenth century, and they united into an Amalgamated Society in 1866. Their objective was always to secure an agreed 'log' or list of piece-rates for all 'first-class' bespoke work. The principle underlying the log was that an average tailor would need a certain length of time to complete a particular job, and that therefore the piece-rate for that job should be such as to give him a standard hourly income – the standard being the locally accepted conventional figure for what a craftsman ought to earn: any workman who could complete the job in under the average time would, of course, benefit from this system.[27] In detail, there seem to have been considerable variations between the logs of different localities, and it should be remembered that they covered only bespoke work: the Amalgamated Society made no attempt to incorporate workers in the cheap mass-production trade, who were the real victims of 'sweating', because, as its secretary George Keir indignantly told the Lords' Committee on that subject in 1889:

> The men who are employed by the slop shops or ready-made shops, and wholesale shops or warehouses are usually men who have degraded themselves, ... have gone down to a low position, and consequently have merged into that state that they do not care to belong to any society, and they do not care for themselves, almost.[28]

Thus the Society was small and exclusive, representing only the 'aristocracy' of the trade: and at the time of the Royal Commission on labour in the early 1890s it was said to have a national membership of 19,000 – a mere one-tenth of the total labour force in the different branches of tailoring.[29]

But if the Amalgamated Society of Tailors tried to ignore the ready-made trade, it could not avoid the problems arising out of the existence of outwork in the bespoke trade. So long as the 'customs of the trade' allowed 'first-class' men to work at home, there was the possibility that log prices would be undercut. One London master tailor explained how the process worked to the Lords' Committee on sweating:

> If I were to give a man a certain garment and he took it upstairs [to the workroom], and it was less that he received for that particular garment than we were in the habit of paying, they would not allow him to make it for that price; he would bring it down again, and I would have to give it outside for somebody else to make, if I wanted it made for that lower figure . . . [30]

Increasingly, many branches of the Society recognized the dangers, and sought to abolish outwork; and a strike on this issue in Liverpool in 1892 widened into a national dispute between the Society and the Master Tailors' Association which attracted the attention of the Royal Commission on labour. The Master Tailors objected that the Society 'oppose in one town what they allow in another, that is outwork, properly supervised outwork'.[31] On the other hand, Keir, the Society's secretary, protested that the masters wished to re-introduce outwork whenever it suited them and argued that:

> It would mean the utter degradation of the trade throughout the whole of the kingdom. Many of our branches look upon out-working as a deadly wrong and have denounced it as the father of the sweating system . . . We will not again be driven back to such abject slavery. We will not turn our homes into factories to enrich our employers, and above all we will not be isolated. We will work together on the shop board where every member knows his fellow member is working with him, and not under-selling his labour.[32]

After a lock-out in several centres, the specific dispute at Liverpool was referred to arbitration. Clearly, the high-class tailors were fighting an uphill battle in the late nineteenth century: and, as the Webbs scathingly remarked, they 'had succeeded neither in con-trolling the new machine industry, nor in upholding the standard earnings of the handworkers'.[33] But in their narrow-minded way, they too were eventually forced to see that outwork was a threat to the standards of even the 'aristocrats' of the labour world: wherever the pernicious system could be utilized, the workers sooner or later felt its baleful consequence.

The boot and shoe industry experienced similar problems in the later nineteenth century, but the situation there was more complicated. For in addition to an urban 'bespoke' branch of high-class shoemaking where, in the case of London, the craftsmen sought to impose agreed lists of piece rates on the 'first and second class houses' in the trade, there had long been a substantial mass-production industry in such provincial centres as Northampton even before the onset of mechanization in the 1850s. The workers in the Northampton branch had their own local traditions of collective organization which eventually coalesced in the National Society of Cordwainers in the 1860s. For these handworkers in the established centres of the mass-production industry, the persistent problem in the second half of the nineteenth century was the steady march of mechanization and the gradual diversion of one process after another into the factory environment. How did they react to the introduction of machinery?

A series of protracted disputes at Northampton in the late 1850s clearly demonstrated the hostility which the threat to produce machine-closed uppers on sewing machines housed in factories quickly aroused.[34] The workmen established a Boot and Shoe-makers Mutual Protection Society, which replied to the seductive arguments of the employers about the advantages of factory work with a broadsheet which said:

> Shopmates! Once within the infernal walls, once the damnable system is established, and your social degradation is secured for another generation, and you will leave your poor offspring a legacy for which they will curse your memory; and you will place them . . . so firmly in the grip of the employers that it will require almost superhuman effort to extricate them from their degrading thraldom and raise them in the social scale.[35]

Nevertheless, mechanization proved irresistable, and the Amalgamated Society of Cordwainers, refounded in 1862, was determined to come to terms with it, rather than resist it. This they tried to do by organizing the new groups of factory and machine workers within their own ranks. But their attempt was short-lived and unsuccessful: 'as has often happened when the national leaders have tried to open the ranks of a craft union, many branches quietly ignored this advice, convinced that they should fight change, rather than accept it. The Association's recent recruits . . . grew restive at continued domination by the craftsmen, and in 1874 they broke away', forming their own National Union of Boot and Shoe Operatives.[36] In terms of membership, the newer union flourished as the old declined, but it too had to come to terms both with the continuing problem of mechanization and with the persistence of outwork in the non-unionized rural hinterlands of the provincial urban centres of the industry and in the sweating dens of London.[37] Like the tailors, the National Union had by the 1890s come to the conclusion that the latter problem would only be satisfactorily solved if outwork were banned altogether. After a strike on the issue in London in 1890, the manufacturers agreed to bring in 'indoor' working as quickly as practicable, provided the workers accepted an Arbitration Board; and indoor working came to be accepted as the rule in Leicester in 1891 and Northampton in 1894.[38] But the problem of outwork was soon submerged in the wider question of mechanization which culminated in the national lock-out of 1895, involving most of the industry's principal centres. The employers' resounding victory precipitated the almost complete mechanization of the industry around 1900, and this inevitably killed the 'outwork' issue.

Thus, although outwork organization seems on the face of things to offer little opportunity for collective bargaining to develop, there are nevertheless several points where the history of the decline of outwork impinges on the story of trade unionism in the nineteenth century. The outwork industries contributed significantly to the continuing activities of unions in the days of the Combination Acts: in their insistence on securing agreed local 'lists' of piece-rates, groups of outworkers helped – along with the more 'enlightened' manufacturers of the 1850s and 1860s – to establish the tradition of Boards of Conciliation and Arbitration, which marked an important stage in the general acceptance of trade unions in English society: and even exclusive craft societies, who often seemed oblivious of the fate of their poorer, unskilled brethren, found that they could not ignore the problems inherent in outwork, and in the end were driven to press for its abolition. At the beginning of the nineteenth century, 'outwork' had been idealized because it brought a workman 'independence'; by the end, it was universally condemned – even by the leaders of organized labour – because it brought him insecurity and poverty. Once trade unionists themselves had rejected outwork, its days were numbered, and it is not surprising to find trade union leaders active in the final campaign against 'sweating' in the early 1900s (see pp.234-5).

Radical Politics

If outworkers played a not insignificant part in nineteenth-century trade union history, their contributions to the story of radical politics are also worth noting. Especially in the first half of the nineteenth century, when the outwork industries were still to a considerable extent male-employing and when successive groups of outworkers turned to the State for help without success, it is not surprising to discover clear links between outworkers and the various radical movements seeking Parliamentary reform. It was obvious and logical for the workers to attribute the indifference, ignorance, and negligence of Parliament to its unrepresentative nature: and it was natural to believe that 'things would be different' if they themselves had political rights and if privilege were replaced by equality. Yet it would be wrong to assume that the outworkers turned radical simply because of the economic hardships they suffered at this time. In reality, the outworkers' whole way of life, together with the nature and values of the village communities to which so many of them still belonged, were both inclined to push them into a naturally 'radical' stance.

In *The Making of the English Working Class* (1963), Edward Thompson demonstrated the deep roots which nurtured popular radicalism in the early nineteenth century, especially among the textile communities of the Pennines. His work clearly shows that the upland spinning and weaving villages in both Lancashire and Yorkshire had a well-justified reputation for individuality and independence in their political and their religious life by the late eighteenth century. In part, this sprang from the 'free' economic circumstances of the small hill-farmer and his family, who combined textile outwork with their agricultural pursuits. But it derived also from the fact that the Pennines, so long regarded as remote and impoverished, had never fully been subjected to the usual patterns of social and political control which kept the humble poor in their places in lowland England. That is to say, the influence at village level of a resident aristocracy or gentry and of the Established Church had never been strong, and it was not notably strengthened when, in the late seventeenth and eighteenth centuries, these once unimportant areas began to feel a quickening of economic life and an increase in general prosperity. Freed from the traditional disciplines exercised by his social superiors, and lacking the immediate presence of both employer and customer, the intelligent small farmer and village outworker of the now thriving uplands was able to work out his own political and religious values. He may not have had the Parliamentary franchise: but within his township he and his fellows administered the Poor Law as they thought best; and in the chapel he saw to it that his young were brought up to serious Bible-reading and God-fearing ways. Largely self-educated, and calling no man 'master', he was at once an individualist and a latent radical. It only required the collapse of the local economy, or the strict intervention of the central authorities in Poor Law matters, or an aggressive intrusion of revived Anglicanism – all of which happened in the second quarter of the nineteenth century – to bring this radicalism into the open. Here, very simply, lies the explanation of the northern outworker's reputation as the 'backbone' of the Parliamentary reform movement from the days of 'Orator' Hunt to the time of the People's Charter.

Other 'rural' areas with well-established outwork industries often showed some of the same characteristics as the Pennine textile villages, and seem to have been similarly inclined to radicalism: for example, the woollen district of mid-Wales, another remote region, relatively free from the normal English methods of social control, and having a marked cultural identity, especially in terms of language and religion. Here, the Newtown weavers were noted radicals, and their brothers at Llanidloes were actually responsible for one of the few 'Chartist uprisings', taking control of the town for several days in the spring of 1839.[39] Likewise, some of the framework knitting villages of the Midlands had a vigorous tradition of involvement in radical movements in the early decades of the nineteenth century – as indicated by their participation in Jeremiah Brandreth's ill-fated 'Pentridge rising' in 1817, and by their later enthusiasm for the Charter.[40]

Outwork was not a wholly 'village' phenomenon in the early nineteenth century, however: the urban outworker – also relatively 'free' from the control of his superiors – might also be caught up in the radical movement, although his motives and his responses might well be more complicated than those of his country cousin. Thus the urban framework knitters of Nottingham and Leicester, like their rural equivalents, were noted reformers in the decades after 1815.[41] However in the more complex social and economic structure of a major provincial town - even where one single manufacturing industry predominate - it is much less easy to equate radicalism with a particular occupational group; for there, political reform movements won support from many different segments of society, and it does not follow, simply because weavers or knitters were the largest single group in the population of, say, Bolton or Nottingham, that they *necessarily* dominated either the radical leadership, or the rank and file. Indeed, it does not follow that they provided support in proportion to their numbers in the local population, at all; and it could well be that urban outworkers were sometimes less prominent in this sense than were small shop-keepers or genuine artisans. In some instances, groups of urban outworkers seem indeed to have been characterized by political apathy - an accusation brought against the Spitalfields silk-weavers, for example.[42] At one major urban centre, Coventry, there already existed a wide freeman franchise for which weavers were eligible, and consequently there was, in the words of the town's historian, 'no Chartism',[43] whilst in the notorious case of Sudbury, an East Anglian Parliamentary borough disfranchised for corruption after the general election of 1841, local handloom weavers were among the known recipients and distributors of bribes.[44] All these examples should make us wary of assuming that dissatisfaction with the post-1832 political system was absolutely universal among industrial outworkers.[45]

Nevertheless, as a broad generalization the identification makes sense: and it is during the Chartist years that the radical outworker's activities are best documented, and when the various cultural traditions and economic influences to which he was subject were likely to be pushing him into active support for political change. Many historians have drawn attention to Chartism's strength in areas where outwork industry was still well entrenched and where adult men continued to be an important element in the labour force. The well-known local examples in Asa Briggs' collection of *Chartist Studies* illustrate the theme very clearly: of Somerset and Wiltshire, for example, we are told that 'where Chartism was present in these counties, cloth was usually being manufactured'; whilst of Leicester we read that 'framework knitters . . . provided the main dynamic of Chartism as a mass movement in the area'.[46]

Generalizing from these local studies, Professor Briggs has identified 'old centres of decaying or contracting industry' as being – along with new and expanding single-industry towns – the hotbeds of the movement: the outworkers were one of the three 'key groups' in Chartist politics; and they tended to follow those 'physical force' leaders 'who knew how to use, and were willing to use, militant headstrong language'. More recent historians of the movement have continued to bear out the traditional interpretation. Dorothy Thompson, who regards the 'industral townships which were the typical manufacturing centres of the nineteenth century' as the main Chartist strongholds, warns against making too sharp a distinction between the involvement of factory hands and 'domestic' workers, but nonetheless notes that 'the handloom weavers in particular seem to stand out as local speakers and organisers':[48] whilst J. T. Ward's recent narrative of the movement makes frequent mention of the role of outworkers in a large number of places.[49]

The radicalism of the outworker seems, then, to have flowered at its fullest in the Chartist movement of the 1830s and 1840s. However, as outwork became confined to a diminishing number of industries after mid-century and as many of the remaining outwork trades came to rely more and more on female labour, so the direct links between outwork and radical politics were weakened, and the mainstream of political 'labour history' must be pursued elsewhere. But did the association leave any permanent legacy to British political life in the later years of the nineteenth century? It is difficult to generalize here: but on the whole, it seems likeliest that the egalitarian, but essentially individualist, values which drew out-workers to Parliamentary reform between 1800 and 1850 were subsequently well catered for in the popular, radical wing of the Gladstonian Liberal party as it emerged in the third quarter of the century.[50] The characteristic religious nonconformity of many of the smaller outworking communities was another factor pulling in the same direction. Thus, after the Reform Acts of 1867 and 1884 had extended the Parliamentary franchise to increasing numbers of working men, many of the old outwork districts showed a marked tendency to vote Liberal. Although outwork as such was either dead or dying in these places, many of the new voters of the 1870s and 1880s, who had cut their political teeth in the Chartist years, would have had personal experience of it, or at any rate would have grown up when the memory of those hard but stirring times was still very fresh. Thus the county constituencies in the old weaving areas on both sides of the Pennines were staunchly Liberal until the very end of the century - the divisions in north-east Lancashire (Clitheroe, Rossendale, and Accrington) showing a marked contrast with many of the Lancashire boroughs, where popular Conservatism became well established, for example. A similarly solid Liberalism appeared in many constituencies of the East Midlands, in Leicester and its environs, for example, and in and around Northampton, whose shoemakers - perhaps the last remaining substantial group of male outworkers in the final decades of the century - consistently voted for the advanced radicals (but avowed anti-socialists) Bradlaugh and Labouchere in the 1880s.[51] Obviously, the 'radical outworker' tradition does not offer a sufficient explanation of the growth of popular Liberalism in these areas: but there can be little doubt that it made an important contribution. This political legacy of outwork complements the modest but significant part played by outworkers' trade unions in the movement towards conciliation and arbitration in the 1860s. Together, they helped to build up that dedicated working-class Liberalism and that pragmatic, collaborationist trade unionism which Socialists found such difficulty in dislodging in the early years of the twentieth century.

Other Forms of 'Self-Help'

In addition to trade unionism and radical politics, two other forms of 'self-help' which attracted groups of outworkers at times also deserve a brief mention, although they differ enormously from one another. The first of these - machine-breaking - was characteristic of the early decades of the nineteenth century, and was in some ways an adjunct to, or an embryonic form of, trade unionism - 'collective bargaining by riot', as E. J. Hobsbawm has called it. In fact, as Hobsbawm has shown, the motives of the various groups of machine-breakers, and the results they obtained, differed considerably: they were not invariably acting against 'new' machines which spelled technological unemployment, for in some cases they were using the threat to their employer's property simply as a means of strengthening their bargaining position about wages or some other trade matter.[52] Nevertheless, some groups of industrial outworkers - as well as such essentially 'workshop-based' groups of skilled operatives as the shearmen and croppers of the woollen industry - undoubtedly indulged in 'technological' machine breaking, especially during the classic Luddite period of the first quarter of the nineteenth century: an evident lack of Parliamentary sympathy, together with the legal restraints on open trade union activity (even where trade conditions made this feasible), forced such workers as handloom weavers and framework knitters to seek remedies in secret and violent methods.[53] The Midland framework knitters, who were the most active Luddites between 1811 and 1816, were certainly motivated in part by hostility to the new 'wide' frames on which the cheap and 'spurious' cut-up goods were made, although some of their activities also arose out of opposition to high frame rents and from a desire to push up wages.[54] Also in the Midlands, the night-time attack on Heathcoat's new lace machines at Lough-borough in June 1816 – which led to the removal of the factory to Tiverton – was another well-known incident possibly inspired by 'technological' considerations: in what Felkin described as 'one of the most deplorable of these memorable affairs', 55 frames, worth between £8,000 and £10,000, were destroyed, and in the aftermath eight men were executed for their part in the raid.[55]

Midlands Luddism in the Regency years tended to be a secret affair, carried on at dead of night by small groups of men with blackened faces, although it must have been widely connived at and condoned by the local community. Altogether more open and large-scale were the various attacks on powerlooms by large crowds of handloom weavers acting in broad daylight. Between the destruction of Grimshaw's Manchester factory in 1792, where Cartwright's new patent looms were being used to weave cotton, and the attack on Beck's factory in Coventry some forty years later when steam-power was being applied to silk weaving, there were several notable acts of sabotage against this new and dangerous machine. The most spectacular came in the severe economic depression of 1826, when for three days rampaging crowds of unemployed handloom weavers attacked powerloom factories throughout Rossendale and north-east Lancashire.[56] It is easy to understand and sympathize with the hopelessness and frustration which provoked these occasional mass outbursts, and in a few instances the tactic seems to have delayed mechanization for a time. The West of England cloth trade, for example, was generally slow to adopt new machines in the late eighteenth and early nineteenth centuries, the flying shuttle being still objected to as late as 1822. In part, this can be explained by the relatively modest growth of the market for its particular kinds of products, but it no doubt also reflected the long-standing opposition of the workers there to new machinery, since both factors would tend to make the local entrepreneurs reluctant to innovate. On the other hand, there is nothing to suggest that the spectacular loom-smashing in the cotton-weaving districts of 1826 instilled a dread of innovation into the manufacturers there: convinced of its necessity and satisfied of its technical viability, they continued to switch to the powerloom as soon as the industry's markets resumed their brisk growth.[57] Thus, if machine-breaking could help to retard the 'march of the machine' in the more stagnant branches of industry, it is unlikely that it did so in the more dynamic sectors: it only worked, in other words, where slothful entrepreneurs already had sound economic reasons for leaving things as they were.

The other form of collective self-help which occasionally attracted outworkers (as well as other groups) – cooperative production – was altogether different. Frequently advocated and occasionally tried in the second half of the nineteenth century, it appeared (at any rate to the well-to-do, who often encouraged it) to be everything that Luddism was not: that is, it was 'sensible', peaceful, forward-looking, and 'moral'. Among its earliest advocates in the 1850s were the small group of Christian Socialists which included Charles Kingsley, F. D. Maurice, and J. M. Ludlow. Inspired especially by the plight of the 'slop' workers in the tailoring trade, to which Kingsley drew attention in his novel *Alton Locke*, they established a Society for Promoting Working Men's Associations – such associations being essentially *producers'* cooperatives, as distinct from the consumers' cooperatives which were becoming increasingly popular after the 'Rochdale pioneers' of 1844. The logic behind the cooperatives was straightforward: if provided with the necessary tools and premises and assured of a ready market for their goods by wealthy sympathisers, groups of working men could work as their own masters, free from the competitive pressures and the penny-pinching tyrannies inflicted on them by 'sweaters', subcontractors, and other middlemen. A number of these associations were in fact set up, especially in London, in the early 1850s. They covered a variety of trades, including building and engineering, as well as some – such as tailoring, needlework, and silk-weaving – in which outwork existed. But they appear to have had little practical success, and their well-wishers – often more interested in the moral than in the material benefits of cooperation – soon lost interest.[58]

Nevertheless, 'producers' cooperation' continued to be advocated as a plausible solution to the evils of competitive capitalism in general, and of the 'sweated' industries in particular, in the later nineteenth century. Some of the second generation of Christian Socialists still regarded it as the ideal means of creating Christian brotherhood in human society in the 1880s and 1890s, although their most recent historian has observed that, in general, 'their attention . . . was diverted from such direct modes of brotherly activity as cooperation by the growth of Fabian collectivism, State socialism and . . . by the I.L.P.'[59] One of its supporters, the Rev. James Munro, a Congregational minister from Bethnal Green, was actually able to tell the Lords' Committee on sweating in 1888 of his own part in recently promoting 'the Workwomen's Cooperative Association, Ltd'. With a capital of £3,000 subscribed by City philanthropists (led by Francis Peek) who refused to take any interest on their money, a clothing factory had been set up: working a ten-hour day, it initially employed 80 women at 'decent' rates of pay which ranged from 10 to 12 shillings per week for sewers and finishers up to 16 to 18 shillings for machinists. In addition, the company provided sewing machines (presumably for homeworkers) to be paid off by weekly instalments of 8d over three years – which was said to be 25% less than was normally charged by 'private' employers. Ultimately, it was hoped that the company would make enough profit over the years to pay back the initial capital and buy up the shares, which would then belong to the workers and 'the factories will then be converted into a cooperative association for the benefit of the workers only'.[60] Nevertheless, even this arrangement appears to have been unable to combine economic competitiveness with 'living' wages for the workers, according to another witness who had supported the venture.[61] And, in spite of the hopes of philanthropists, producers' cooperation rarely enjoyed commercial success, and never established itself on a large scale. As Boyaval, the historian of the fight against sweating, put it: 'La coopération manque, en effet, de capitaux, et ne possède que rarement les qualités techniques et commerciales requises pour lutter avantageusement contre la grande entreprise.'[62] Like the other forms of 'self-help', it provided no real solution to the outworker's problems: in the end, this could only come from State action.

State Aid

At best, the outworkers' efforts to solve their problems by various forms of collective self-help enjoyed only a temporary or local success; and when self-help failed, State aid was the last resort. Different groups of outworkers made many attempts to draw the attention of society at large to their particular problems, and to put pressure on the State to intervene and resolve their difficulties: and from the other side, there was a succession of well-to-do philanthropists and social reformers throughout the nineteenth century who at times took the initiative themselves in calling for public action to help outworkers. By the last years of the century, with outwork an increasingly marginal activity involving mainly women and children, the balance swung between these two forces: in the first half of the century, successive groups – the Yorkshire woollen workers, cotton handloom weavers, and Midlands framework knitters, for example – made their own vigorous attempts to pressurise the State into action; but by the 1880s, the initiative in calling for public intervention to remedy 'intolerable' abuses had passed from the workers themselves to their better-off sympathizers. Thus the emphasis shifted from what the workers concerned actually wanted, to what their social superiors thought that they *ought* to want, or what was 'good for them' – and this did not necessarily coincide with the outworkers' own perceptions of the problems.

But for all that, the workers' attempts to win legislation on their own behalf in the first half of the nineteenth century were seldom effective: whereas in the end, their last survivors were the beneficiaries of one of the most far-reaching, if now most neglected, of the social reforms handed out by the last great Liberal government before the First World War. Of course, the nature of the political system and the very language of political debate had changed enormously in the interim: working men were voteless 'outsiders' and their chances of influencing national politics were very limited before 1868; whereas they had at any rate to be occasionally placated and humoured after they had acquired the franchise in the later nineteenth century. Indeed, as we have seen, the outworkers played some part in bringing about those very political changes from which their successors ultimately if belatedly benefited: for when those who controlled the existing political system demonstrated their reluctance or their inability to deliver the desired legislation, it was natural for frustrated outworkers to add their voices to any cry for political reform which might be current. At all these points, therefore, the problems of industrial outwork impinged on national politics: we must now recount the story of the successive attempts to solve these problems by law, and examine some of the solutions which were proposed or attempted.

Agitations and Enquiries

With the variety of strains placed upon the economy in the first decade of the nineteenth century both by the long-term pressure of population growth and by the short-term fluctuations of war, it is not surprising that many groups of industrial outworkers sought Parliamentary help in solving the problems they were encountering at that time. In looking to the State in this way, they were, of course, keeping up a tradition of government regulation and protection long associated with 'mercantilism', and one which, as late as the 1770s, had still been sufficiently alive to give legislative backing to the regulation of wages in the silk industry of Spitalfields. At the beginning of the nineteenth century, there was much legislation on the statute book – especially in relation to the woollen industry – which claimed to maintain the standards of British workmanship, to uphold apprenticeship, to fix wages and prices, to forbid the use of techniques and tools deemed 'unsuitable', and – it must not be forgotten – to discourage wage-earners from resorting to collective action to solve their own problems. But much of it had long been unenforced, or had been undermined in detail by generations of legal interpretation. By no means all this legislation appealed to the workers. They wanted 'protection' on their own terms, and did not wish to perpetuate or encourage those forms of interference or restriction which they regarded as unnecessary; and by being selective in this way, they naturally weakened their case. However, there were other reasons for their failure to gain a sympathetic hearing in the early 1800s. In the first place, most of their major employers seem to have been anxious to see the old statutes removed, rather than reactivated or amplified; secondly, governments increasingly sided with employers on this issue as individual politicians developed that predilection for the doctrines of 'laissez-faire', which provided them with a perfect justification for no longer attempting to do all those grandiose things which pragmatic experience taught them that they could not in any case hope to do effectively; and thirdly, during wartime any popular expression of dissatisfaction – however worthy of sympathy and however 'respectably' supported and managed – inevitably aroused sinister suspicions of disloyalty and even rebellion in the minds of politicians who were frightened, ill-informed, and credulous.

The efforts of various groups of outworkers to gain something more than pious expressions of sympathy from Parliament in the first two decades of the nineteenth century were, therefore, conspicuously unsuccessful: but they certainly did not fail for want of trying. The pattern was first established in the woollen industry, where petitions and counter-petitions flowed in from the West Country and from Yorkshire about the enforcement of the old regulations in the aftermath of anti-machinery riots in Wiltshire and Somerset in 1802. The Commons' Select Committee set up to review the situation in 1806 heard perhaps the most fulsome of all defences of the classic 'domestic system' which characterized the Yorkshire branch of the industry in the eighteenth century. The inhabitants of Saddleworth, so it was informed, had:

> . . . resolved unanimously, that the domestic system is highly favourable to the cultivation of paternal, filial, and fraternal affections, the sources of domestic happiness, and to the generation of good, moral, and civil habits, the sources of public tranquillity: [and] that the factory system tends to the prevention of these affections and habits, and leads youth sooner into the strongest temptations . . .[63]

Nevertheless, even those workers who defended the 'status quo' expressed their willingness to see an end to *some* of the old legislation – such as the inoperative apprenticeship laws or the Acts requiring the cloth produced in certain areas to be inspected and approved by government officials, although they were anxious to retain (and even extend) the rest – such as the ban on certain labour-saving devices or the proposed restriction on the number and size of machines to be housed in any one workplace. Because of these contradictions, the Select Committee – although extolling the virtues of the 'domestic' system – had no difficulty in recommending the repeal of all regulatory legislation for the woollen industry, using arguments which were to become depressingly familiar to other groups of outworkers in the next few years:

> Considering the different principles of commerce which are now recognised, it cannot be necessary for your Committee to enter into any minute detail of the reasons on which they recommend to the House the repeal of the general mass of the above laws, as being at this day not only unnecessary, but, if enforced, utterly inexpedient, or rather extremely injurious. [64]

Furthermore, the Committee expressed deep concern at the dangerous tendencies implicit in the activities of the trade union or 'institution' which had organized the workers' petitions and masterminded their case.[65] Having thus been spurned by Parliament, it is not surprising that the most disgruntled and best organized group of woollen workers – the elite of workshop-based shearmen and croppers – took the law into their own hands in the Luddite outbreaks of 1812 (see p. 221).

At the very moment that the woollen workers were losing their battle for Parliamentary protection, the cotton weavers were starting their own. But their aim was different. Unlike wool, cotton was not regulated by a mass of ancient law, and the handloom weavers were not particularly worried about apprenticeship, government inspection, or – at this stage – labour-saving machinery. Rather, their concern was with the recent sharp decline in their earnings in the volatile conditions of wartime, and their demand was for legislation akin to the Spitalfields Act which would enable magistrates to intervene and fix legal minimum wages. Select Committees of the House of Commons considered their petitions in 1808 and again in 1811, and on both occasions came up with a blank refusal expressed in terms which clearly demonstrated the growing strength of 'laissez-faire' notions in Parliamentary circles. As the report of the first committee put it:

> . . . fixing a minimum for the price of labour in the cotton manufacture is wholly inadmissible in principle, incapable of being reduced to practice by any means which can possibly be devised, and if practicable would be productive of the most fatal consequences.[66]

In the second decade of the nineteenth century, the framework knitters of the Midlands counties, undeterred by these failures, also tried to secure Parliamentary solutions to some of their problems –

although it should be remembered that they, like their brethren in other trades, were still prepared to try self-help, too. They avoided the trap into which the cotton weavers had fallen, by eschewing any attempt to secure a legal minimum wage, although they were anxious that every manufacturer should be obliged to exhibit a full statement of the wages he was prepared to pay in some prominent place in his warehouse. However, they had two principal objectives: to ban the use of the new 'wide' frames and the manufacture of the 'fraudulent' cut-up work produced on them; and to abolish the practice, peculiar to this industry, of frame-renting. Although Select Committees duly inquired into their grievances in 1812 and 1819, no legislation was forthcoming: but the knitters were still prepared to revert to this tactic from time to time during the next two decades.[67]

The reform of Parliament in 1832 revived general hopes that government might yet be induced to step in and save struggling groups like the weavers and the knitters; but in practical terms, any such expectations went unfulfilled. Far from offering 'protection', the reformed Parliament undermined one of the few legislative props on which such workers had come to rely when it initiated its reform of the Poor Law in 1834.[68] But a good deal was discovered by Parliament - to the great benefit of later historians - about the condition of the weavers and knitters in the 1830s and 1840s, even though no significant action was taken. The handloom weavers were scrutinized by a Select Committee of the Commons in 1834-5 and by a Royal Commission in 1838-41, whilst a Royal Commission looked at the knitters in 1844-5. The Select Committee on the weavers actually recommended the introduction of statutory wage regulation; but since it was a partisan body stage-managed by John Fielden, John Maxwell and a handful of other MPs friendly to the weavers' cause, the Commons felt no obligation to follow its advice. The Royal Commission, headed by Nassau Senior and Samuel Jones Loyd, two of the leading exponents of the 'orthodox' economics of the day, conducted a more thorough investigation by sending assistant commissioners to gather information all over the country, but its result was a foregone conclusion: it did no more than recommend such general panaceas as lower taxation, free trade, and universal education so that the poor could learn the basic precepts of political economy and act upon them.[69] Three years later, the Commission on the framework knitters was conducted single-

handed by Richard Muggeridge, who had been one of the travelling assistants under the handloom weavers inquiry: it produced a
thousand pages of meaty evidence, but its only practical result was
an Act obliging manufacturers to give out a ticket with each piece
of work stating the price to be paid, in the hope that this would
prevent frauds by middlemen.[70] Ten years later, a further Select
Committee examined the specific problem of frame-rent in the
hosiery trade, and recommended – by a majority of one vote in
committee – that frame-rent be banned as a species of truck:[71] but
in the event, frame-rents were not abolished until after the more
general enquiry into truck by a Royal Commission in 1871.[72]

Although the record of detailed enquiry and subsequent inactivity
is a depressing aspect of the middle decades of the nineteenth
century, there was nevertheless one area in which progress was
gradually made towards protecting one particular section of the
outwork labour force. The general problem of the employment of
children – other than the very limited numbers who worked in
textile factories and whose hours and conditions were effectively
regulated by law after 1833 – engrossed the attention of two Royal
Commissions, in the early 1840s and the early 1860s: and much of
the evidence they collected dealt with the role of children in the
remaining outwork trades. By the time of the second enquiry, there
was a growing feeling that children employed *outside* the already
regulated factories ought to have the benefit of legal protection, too:
and alongside this was a further concern to improve their education,
if necessary by State intervention. If young children could be
prevented by law from working, then their education could be
better attended to – provided always that sufficient school places
were available and that parents were obliged to let their children fill
them. But it was pointless arguing that children should be forbidden
to work because they ought to be at school, when there were not
enough schools for them to go to and no compulsion to attend.
Regulating child labour and introducing compulsory universal
education were, therefore, different sides of the same coin: and it is
not surprising that the extension of the principle of State inspection
and regulation to workshops as well as to factories in 1867 was soon
followed by the Education Act of 1870. Both Acts served to remove
some of the worst abuses of child exploitation in such outwork
industries as straw-plaiting and lace-making: for the factory
inspector and the Board school headmaster between them succeeded

in closing down the appalling 'school/workshops' in the villages where these trades had lately flourished (see pp. 104, 120).

By the last two decades of the nineteenth century, the situation of industrial outworkers had changed in two important respects since the fruitless Parliamentary enquiries of the 1830s and 1840s. On the one hand, working men now carried some political weight nationally, and established politicians were beginning to find that some of the ideas deemed 'impossible' by political economy were perhaps expedient, and even practicable, after all. On the other hand, the number of outworkers had dwindled, and those who remained – predominantly women and foreign immigrants in the great urban slums – were still politically insignificant *and* at the same time less capable of drawing public attention to their problems than the vociferous village radicals of the textile and hosiery districts had been half a century earlier. The later enquiries which looked at outwork, therefore, tended largely to be initiated 'from above' and reflected the new values and perceptions of middle-class philanthropists and social reformers. The sudden burst of interest in 'sweating' in the late 1880s demonstrates this trend very clearly.

Overwork and low pay in insalubrious working conditions in such trades as tailoring and shoemaking was not 'discovered' for the first time in the 1880s, of course: Charles Kingsley and the early Christian Socialists had exposed the evil dens where 'cheap clothes and nasty' were made in the 1850s, and had tried to solve the problem by encouraging the setting-up of producers' cooperatives under well-to-do patronage. But the revival of interest in the problems which was provoked by two brief Board of Trade reports in 1887 and 1888 on the 'sweating system' in the East End of London and in Leeds never wholly died down, and led in time to the Trade Boards Act of 1909. These reports were the first significant results of the appointment, in 1886, of the Board of Trade's 'labour correspondent', John Burnett, who had led the Tyneside engineers in their successful strike for a nine-hour day in 1871 and who had later been secretary of the Amalgamated Society of Engineers. The first report was sufficient to stir the House of Lords into appointing a Select Committee under the Earl of Dunraven to enquire initially into sweating in the East End, although it later extended its scope to cover the whole country. Between August 1888 and May 1890, the Committee produced five reports containing evidence collected from nearly 300 witnesses in the course of

some seventy sittings. Many of the revelations were highly sensational, and their validity was hotly disputed. A great deal of
evidence about the East End appeared to have been drummed up in
a somewhat unscrupulous way by Arnold H. White, a radical
journalist who later became a rampant Imperialist; and there were
also claims that a very one-sided picture had been painted of
conditions in the nail and chain trades.[73] As with earlier enquiries,
the claims and counter-claims of the protagonists probably made it
impossible for conscientious but basically ignorant noblemen to
decide just how big the problem was, or whether anything could be
done about it. Certainly, the Lords' Committee lifted the lid off
something highly unpleasant: but its members seem to have become
either so confused or so dispirited by what they found that they
were unable to suggest any effective solutions to the 'sweating'
problem. Indeed, the pious concluding paragraph of their final
report was as pathetic a climax as could possibly be imagined:

> When legislation has reached the limit up to which it is effective,
> the real amelioration of conditions must be due to increased sense
> of responsibility in the employer and improved habits in the
> employed. We have reason to think that the present enquiry
> itself has not been without moral effect. And we believe that
> public attention and public judgement can effectively check
> operations in which little regard is shown to the welfare of
> workpeople and to the quality of production, and can also
> strongly second the zealous and judicious efforts now being made
> to encourage thrift, promote temperance, improve dwellings, and
> raise the tone of living.[74]

But if the Lords' Committee laboured mightily to produce so feeble
a mouse at least it provided what came to be the standard definition
of 'sweating'. 'Sweating' existed, their Lordships concluded,
wherever workers spent long hours in poor conditions for only low
wages – a highly impressionistic definition, admittedly, but, as the
French historian of the system, Paul Boyaval, put it, 'la langue
anglaise ne pouvait nous fournir vocable à la fois plus concis et plus
tristement suggestif'.[75] On this wide definition, it is important to
remember that 'sweating' was not exclusively a problem of outwork
or 'domestic' industries: but such industries almost invariably
satisfied all three criteria which the Lords had laid down. Further-

more, by making low pay the first of these criteria, the Lords' Committee had pointed a faltering finger towards the 'minimum wage' solution: long hours and poor working conditions might be tackled by more thorough registration, inspection, or licensing by local authorities or by factory inspectors; but the problem of wages needed a more drastic remedy.

Hard on the heels of the Lords' Committee came the more comprehensive and sober Royal Commission on labour, which dealt with sweating along with a large number of other topics relevant to the whole field of labour conditions and institutions in the early 1890s. The general tone of the evidence it collected was less sensational, and the Commissioners themselves were more diverse in origin and better informed about 'labour' questions in general, than had been the case with the Lords' Committee. Among its witnesses was Sidney Webb, who made what for him must have been a distinctly impassioned plea for a firm solution to the 'sweating' problem: arguing from the incalculable benefits which factory legislation had brought to the cotton workers of Lancashire, he maintained 'that it is of the highest public importance that the extension of the public control in the better organised industries should be accompanied by an extension of that control in the degraded industries'.[76] Both majority and minority reports of the Commissioners in 1894 responded by recommending a tightening-up of the law as regards the registration and inspection of all workplaces: the minority report – whose signatories included the improbable combination of William Abraham, James Mawdsley, and Tom Mann – actually went so far as to put 'the reform of the sweated trades' at the top of their list of 'the most pressing necessities of the industrial situation'.[77]

Yet outwork refused to die, and the wages of the sweated failed to improve: indeed, as we shall see, it was argued that the better regulation and enforcement of Factory and Workshop Acts – at any rate in London – actually *increased* the amount of homework, as this was less amenable to effective public control. Increasingly, the opponents of sweating switched their line of attack from the elaboration of factory and workshop law to more radical proposals to raise income by instituting a 'minimum wage' backed by legislation on the lines of that recently tried out by the new Labour parties in Australia. The whole notion of a 'national minimum' was becoming familiar to social reformers by the beginning of the twentieth century, backed up as it was by the findings of such social observers as Rowntree, who demonstrated that below a certain income level it was simply impossible for a household to acquire enough of the basic necessities of food, clothing, and housing to maintain its physical efficiency. Similarly, the real cost to society of pauperism, ill-health, widowhood, and crime was beginning to be calculated, and the long-term effects of the wastage of our human resources were causing concern to many who – not 'radical' in any accepted political sense – were nevertheless alarmed about the declining physical efficiency and economic competitiveness of the 'Imperial race'. Arguments of this kind were trenchantly expressed by Constance Smith in a passage which deserves quotation in full:

> The children of the hood and eye carders and the handkerchief drawers are doomed by the fact of a childhood and youth passed without training, without discipline, without adequate care, to just such an existence as that of their parents before them. The boys will become casual labourers if they do not become loafers. The girls will marry men like their brothers and supplement the meagre wages irregularly brought home by their husbands by working at sweated rates in some home piecework trade ... So the child goes forth to the industrial battle unequipped with the armour of knowledge or the weapons of skill; physically feeble and undeveloped, by reason of the overwork and underfeeding of his early years; intellectually backward, because bodily fatigue and a too precocious initiation into the round of mechanical toil has dulled wits that at the beginning were perhaps bright enough ... The moral wrecks to be found among the children of the sweated are frequently as much the products of the sweating system as their sickly, feeble-minded and defective brothers and sisters. Together they help to furnish recruits to the growing army of the unemployed and unemployable, to fill our work-houses, hospitals, asylums, and prisons.[78]

Moreover, organized labour was becoming more vociferous in calling for State aid for the unorganized: groups such as the shoemakers and the bespoke tailors had been trying to abolish outwork since the early 1890s, as we have seen; the TUC had itself been backing the demand for effective factory legislation to be applied to domestic workers since 1891;[79] and the small but determined band of women trade union organizers, led by Mary MacArthur, Gertrude Tuck-well, and Margaret Irwin, had come to realize the hopelessness of trying to raise many women's wages without legislation.

The call to 'do something' about the persistent problem of sweating, especially in the homework trades, was thus attracting the support of many sections of the articulate public: at a time of sharpening political differences, it offered one issue on which tariff reformers, imperialists, social radicals, trade unionists, and socialists could work together both inside and outside Parliament. And with the advent of the Liberal government late in 1905, pressure for action built up immediately.

In May 1906, the *Daily News* organised the first great 'anti-sweating exhibition' at the Queen's Hall, London, to demonstrate graphically the ubiquity of sweating and the evils associated with it. This was followed by the creation of the National Anti-Sweating League, which in October of the same year held a huge delegate conference at the London Guildhall for the representatives of in-terested organizations: taking the chair at the conference on succes-sive days were Sir Charles Dilke, the Liberal-imperialist social reformer, who had brought in an annual bill to establish trade boards since 1898; G. N. Barnes, one of the new Labour MPs; and Lord Dunraven, who had chaired the Lords' Select Committee of 1888. During the next twelve months, the League established branches and organized exhibitions in the provinces – an exhibition at Oxford in December 1907 being opened by no less a dignitary than Lord Milner, the prominent Imperialist – as well as keeping up its propaganda in London and its pressure on the government. Meanwhile, the government had not been idle: an all-party Committee, which reported in 1907 and again in 1908, had been set up to enquire into homework and into the possibility of establishing wage-fixing boards for the industries concerned. Private members' bills on the subject from Arthur Henderson in February 1907 and from G. Toulmin a year later kept up the pressure, and when the Select Committee reported finally in July 1908 it recommended wage-fixing boards for the most degraded of the 'sweated trades'. The Speech from the Throne in February 1909 promised action, and on the 24th March the government introduced its minimum wage legislation in the shape of the Trade Boards bill, which covered men's tailoring, cardboard box manufacture, lace finishing, and chain-making: brought in by Winston Churchill as President of the

Board of Trade, it encountered minimal oppositon, and passed into law in July.[80]

The ease with which the State was finally able to fix minimum wages shows just how broad the consensus had become – a point well illustrated from the names of those who backed the National Anti-Sweating League. In 1910, among its vice-presidents, headed by George Cadbury, were Dilke, Dunraven, Lord Gladstone, Keir Hardie, Canon Scott Holland, the Chief Rabbi, the Bishop of Ripon, the Webbs, and H. G. Wells: whilst its executive committee, chaired by A. G. Gardiner, included G. N. Barnes, Mary Mac-Arthur, Gertrude Tuckwell, Mrs Bernard Shaw, L. G. Chiozza Money, and (in 1911) Arthur Henderson, with J. J. Mallon, later Warden of Toynbee Hall, as secretary. Nor did the League fade away with the passing of the Trade Boards Act: it publicized the provisions of the legislation among the groups affected, tried to organize the workers who would sit as representatives on the wages boards, and generally acted as a watchdog on the early operations of the different boards. By 1913 it had gone further, and was calling for the extension of the minimum wage to more industries, including laundering, ladies' tailoring, shirt-making, and other making-up trades.[81]

As the League said in its report for 1910, 'to secure the passing of a measure such as the Trade Boards Act was a considerable achievement', although it is unclear just how much credit ought to go to the League, in view of the widespread acceptance of the need for something on these lines. But before looking at some of the details and the consequences of this and other measures, it is perhaps worth asking at this point just what the 'sweated' workers themselves thought about the wave of sympathy they received, or how they viewed the panaceas suggested on their behalf at the beginning of the present century. It seems clear that many women believed they *needed* homework, because there was no other way they could earn: and some of those who were in easier financial circumstances may even have derived some non-material personal satisfaction from doing it. Any legislative interference in homework inevitably aroused their suspicions, therefore: as Mrs Fray, of the Leicester Hosiery Seamers Association, had told the Royal Commission on the Factory and Workshop Acts back in 1876:

. . . our worthy treasurer wished us to attend and declare that there was no need for the stitchers to be interfered with on this occasion, as their work was done entirely at home.[82]

Indeed, the activities of the Anti-Sweating League and the Select Committee on homework in 1907 led to the formation of a rival 'National Home Workers League'. As an organization, it seems to have been small and short-lived, claiming only 3,000 members and an embryonic existence in about a dozen provincial towns.[83] But its secretary, Miss Vynne, gave forthright evidence to the Committee on homework in 1908, arguing that 'any worrying about home-work makes the masters stop giving it out. A Sweated Industries Exhibition in a town instantly means that two or three manu-facturers stop giving out work and the people suffer'. She also claimed that these displays gave a one-sided view of the quality of home-produced work: 'at Bristol they were exhibiting all the cheapest, worst, and most ill-paid work, that no woman would ever accept, except as a last resource'.[84] It is easy enough to feel that Miss Vynne overstated her case: her personal knowledge of homework seems to have been derived more from the glove trade of Yeovil than from the slop shops of the East End, and it was she, after all, who rejoiced to see old bed-ridden couples and one-handed widows maintaining their 'independence' by sewing (see p.165). Never-theless, until society had accepted that its weaker members should not *need* to try and support themselves, and until the poorest of the potential homeworkers had learned to accept the State's 'charity' without loss of self-respect, there would be those, even among the workers themselves, who would go on fawning over the hands which oppressed them but on which they felt utterly dependent.

Remedies and Solutions
As the problems facing particular groups of outworkers varied in detail, so, to some extent, did the range of nostrums for which they sought Parliamentary approval and public sympathy: the framework knitters, for instance, were naturally obsessed by the unique and serious problem of frame-renting. But in the main, the precarious position of *all* outworkers stemmed from similar economic circum-stances: generally, they suffered because they were unskilled, un-organized, and frequently too numerous in relation to the normal demand for their services; and this basic predicament was often aggravated at some point by the impact of new machines and new

methods of production on a particular trade. In theory, two crude solutions might present themselves to those facing these problems: drastic restrictions could be imposed on the size of the labour force; and new technology could be, if not banned, then at any rate strictly controlled by the State. In their efforts to protect themselves by self-help, many *organized* groups of workers have in the past attempted precisely such strategies: the earliest effective trade unions – among the skilled traditional artisans or the 'new' engineers, for example – often tried to restrict their numbers by controlling apprenticeship or by assisting migration among their membership when necessary; and they similarly had an abiding concern to control the impact of new techniques on the organization of their work and on their status and rewards. But although small groups of irreplaceable skilled trade unionists might hope for success through these tactics, it was a different story when large and unorganized bodies of unskilled outworkers attempted the same thing, as we have seen in recounting the patchy history of workers' organizations in the previous section. Apprenticeship, after all, was meaningless as a form of training in basically unskilled work, and either never existed in most outwork industries or at any rate failed to survive in them after the mid-eighteenth century. And although enraged handworkers were at times driven into bouts of machine-breaking which had a genuinely 'technological' basis, their efforts to retard the progress of 'the machine' in this way were rarely successful outside the short-term or local context.

Self-help, then, seldom made it possible for outworkers to control their own numbers or impede technical change. Nor was the State likely to offer assistance in either of these areas during the nine-teenth century. The repeal of the Elizabethan statute of apprentices in 1813 demonstrated clearly that no obstacles were to be put in the way of an individual who wished to practice any legitimate trade in so far as his talents would allow, and that the State was not prepared to restrict the general mobility of labour. Similarly, the prospects of retarding the 'march of the machine' by State inter-vention were equally unpromising, as the woollen workers and framework knitters found when they tried to have gig mills or 'wide' frames banned in the early decades of the century, and as the hand-loom weavers discovered when they half-heartedly proposed a tax on 'steam looms' in the 1830s[85]

There was, however, *one* feature of the labour market in the late nineteenth century which might provoke government action. If the oversupply of unskilled labour could be attributed to foreign immigration of a kind which might be thought 'undesirable' for political or cultural reasons, something positive might be achieved if the influx were banned. This was precisely the argument of Arnold White and his supporters before the Lords' Committee on sweating: whilst skilled and enterprising Englishmen were continually emigrating, the country was receiving a horde of immigrants (largely Jewish) of alien language and 'lower' culture, who flocked into the unskilled trades, forced down the wages paid to 'native' labour, and generally intensified the problems of sweating. To their credit, the Lords were unimpressed by the argument, pointing out that 'the evils complained of obtain in trades which do not appear to be affected by foreign immigration'.[86] Nevertheless, the damage had been done. The roots of working-class anti-semitism – especially in the East End of London – were given extra nourishment, and a campaign against 'pauper immigration' persisted through the 1890s, producing books with titles like *The Alien Invasion* (by W. H. Wilkins, 1892), or Arnold White's own *The Modern Jew* (1899), and eventually contributing to the more stringent regulations of the 1902 Aliens Act. But sweating and homework still went on, regardless.

If neither self-help nor State aid was capable of solving the outworkers' basic problems in the crude and obvious fashion, any remedy which needed the support of public opinion and the backing of legislation must of necessity be more modest, specific, and practical, and above all it must not offend against the generally accepted canons of political economy. Few proposals met these criteria in the mid-nineteenth century, but there were one or two which did. For example, throughout the period there was widespread opposition in political circles to wages being paid in 'truck' rather than in cash. Any group of workers who could show that the real value of their earnings was diminished *either* because they had to accept payment in arbitrarily priced goods *or* because it was locally 'understood' that they must patronize a particular shop in which their employer or his agent had an interest, was likely to get a sympathetic hearing. Legislation against truck was tightened up in 1831, but the practice persisted especially in nail-making and framework knitting where the workers were particularly dependent on the good offices of local middleman or 'foggers' in obtaining work or disposing of their surplus goods. The Royal Commission of 1871 still condemned trucking among the country workers in these two industries, and in the case of hosiery it further ruled that the still surviving practice of frame-renting constituted a species of truck. Basically, however, truck seems to have been a fairly minor and localized problem by the mid-nineteenth century, and both outwork and sweating managed to survive its gradual decline and disappearance.

Another acceptable approach, likely to win legislative support, lay in attacking some of the other frauds and abuses perpetrated by middlemen. If, for example, every piece of work given out were to carry a ticket showing the price which the *manufacturer* was paying, it would be easy for the worker to see exactly how large a deduction his agent was proposing to make for his services. An Act along these lines for the hosiery industry followed Muggeridge's Commission in 1845; but ten years later Muggeridge was himself lamenting that it had become a dead letter within a month because of 'a defect in the construction of the interpretation clause'.[87] But even if the Act had been properly drafted and the workers fully aware of its provisions, it is perhaps questionable whether they would have insisted on their rights: for their dependence on the 'bagman' was often such that they had to be prepared to connive at his malpractices for fear of losing work.

Piecemeal legislation could not cure the real abuses of outwork: and as in the second half of the century the State became more and more concerned at their persistence, two more fundamental (but basically different) lines of attack came to command growing support. The first sought to improve the working conditions of outworkers by extending the principle of factory and sanitary inspection to cover domestic workshops; the second – more revolutionary in its implications – tried to tackle the specific problem of low earnings by fixing a minimum level of wage-rates which employers were obliged to pay. Needless to say, the former and more cautious proposals won the earliest backing.

The history of the extension of effective factory regulation and inspection by the State from its limited beginnings in the textile factories after 1833 is long and complex. The practical problems of carrying the law into new fields were formidable, and the possibilities of evasion endless. No sooner was one legal loophole stopped up than another was discovered, and thus the law needed

continuous revision and amendment. Fortunately, the detailed in-
tricacies of factory and workshop legislation need not detain us too
long, for our interest can be confined to the impact of the 'law on
the 'true' outworker in his domestic workplace.[88]

The first attempts at the general regulation of hours and conditions in *all* kinds of workplaces followed from the findings of the
Royal Commission on children's employment in the mid-1860s,
and were embodied in the Factory Acts Extension Act and the
Workshops Regulation Act of 1867: the former covered all establishments which employed more than fifty workers, whilst the latter
applied to all workplaces - including domestic ones - which
employed forty-nine or less. The Workshops Act prohibited work
by children under eight years old, and laid down the maximum
daily working hours for the various categories of 'protected' persons
(older children, young people, and women), together with certain
health provisions: its enforcement lay initially with local sanitary
authorities, but their inability to fulfil the duties was soon manifest.
As a result, an amending Act of 1871 gave the actual supervision of
workshops to the factory inspectorate - although some of the
sanitary regulations remained the responsibility of the local
authorities. Even with these alterations, the regulations pertaining to
'factories' (as arbitrarily defined in 1867) remained generally more
stringent than those in 'workshops'; and a Royal Commission in
1876 recommended a new definition, which was not simply based
on the size of the workforce, in order to assimilate the two branches
of the law more fully. After the consolidating Factory Act of 1878,
any workplace with any form of *motive power* was a 'factory':
anything else was a 'workshop'. Unfortunately, so far as purely
'domestic' workshops were concerned, the 1878 Act was retrograde,
since any home-workplace where the master or mistress employed
either merely his or her own children *or* women workers exclusively,
could escape the more stringent sanitary provisions which applied in
the more 'public' workshops. In other words, outwork genuinely
done in 'home' surroundings was still less subject to regulation than
was subcontract work in a 'factory' or 'public' workshop, and was
in any case harder to control in practice because of the sheer number
of establishments involved. After the Lords' Committee on sweating
and the Royal Commission on labour, some attempt was made to
make the regulations affecting homeworkers still more effective:
employers were obliged to submit registers of their homeworkers to

the factory inspectors, and later to the more vigorous local authorities of the post-1888 era. But the practical difficulties of locating and inspecting so many private dwellings were still enormous, and the relatively unrestricted conditions of homework seem, at any rate in parts of London, to have actually given it a new lease of life at the turn of the century.[89] One possibility, which the Lords' Committee had specifically rejected, was to ban homework altogether; but this would have been both impracticable and un-fair.[90] But even if there had been enough well-informed factory inspectors and local health officials to ensure that the working conditions of homeworkers *were* properly inspected and regulated, the fundamental problem of their low earnings would not have been solved. For this, a completely different approach was required.

The idea that the State must intervene to fix the level of minimum wages for the otherwise defenceless victims of 'sweating' – of whom homeworkers formed perhaps the most important category by the beginning of the twentieth century – won only slow acceptance. For the well-to-do sympathizer, it raised a serious conflict between the heart and the head, with emotion pointing one way and 'reason' another: and many were driven to look for other remedies before they would accept wage fixing by law. One type of response was to form consumers' leagues pledged to producing 'white lists' of establishments which made and sold goods under 'good' (i.e. non-sweated) conditions.[91] But given the complexity of production and marketing in modern society, it was clearly im-possible for the consumer to be certain which goods, or parts of goods, had been made in 'satisfactory' conditions, and which had not: as Clementina Black put it:

> . . . [sweated work] in some shape or form, comes into every home in this country. Our potatoes and our flour are carried in sacks, although not perhaps to our doors; our eggs are sold to us in cardboard boxes; our garments are fastened with buttons or with hooks, or perchance with safety pins; the gentleman's collar and tie and the lady's waist-belt may probably be the handiwork of some half-starved homeworker whose life is being shortened by her poverty. Only ignorance can flatter itself . . . with the idea that none but cheap goods or cheap shops are tainted with sweating . . . The taint is everywhere; there is no dweller in this country, however well-intentioned, who can declare with

certainty that he has no share in this oppression of the poorest and most helpless among his compatriots.[92]

Whilst still reluctant to go the whole way in fixing wage levels, reformers in the 1880s and 1890s were at least prepared to concede that the State itself should set a good example by paying 'fair' wages for government contract work. Since 1880, army uniforms, for example, had been increasingly made in the government's own factory in Pimlico, but a quarter of the work was still contracted out; and army boots were still wholly supplied by private contractors in the Midlands.[93] Here at least was an area where public opinion could ensure that 'decency' prevailed. Yet the Lords' Committee on sweating heard disturbing evidence from Arnold White about the low earnings of outworkers in London's East End who were making army and navy uniforms; and in their final report, their Lordships spoke of 'grave irregularities' and stressed the need for 'greater vigilance' in the letting and supervision of public contracts.[94] Acting on the Committee's advice, the House of Commons on 13 February 1891 passed the famous 'fair wages' resolution, which read:

> RESOLVED: that in the opinion of this House it is the duty of the government in all government contracts to make provision against the evils recently disclosed before the Sweating Committee, to insert such conditions as may prevent the abuse arising from sub-letting, and to make every effort to secure the payment of such wages as are generally accepted as current in each trade for competent workmen.

Local as well as central authorities were inspired to insist on 'fair wages' clauses in all contracts which they made for materials and equipment. The new London County Council, for example, drew up a 'log' of net piece-rates to be paid on all tailoring contracts in 1890, and banned homework on council contracts four years later.[95]

At best, fair wages on public work could merely set an example to the private sector. But in practice, the concept proved difficult to operate even in the narrow confines of government contracts, as a Select Committee set up in 1908 to report on the effect, of the 1891 resolution soon discovered. After all, in non-unionized trades there was no such thing as a 'generally accepted' or 'current' wage to serve as a yardstick of 'fairness'. In fact, this Committee concluded that there were 'no widespread defects in the working of the Fair Wages Clause'.[96] But this limited approach to the problem of low earnings in the sweated trades was now being overtaken by events – in particular by the activities of the National Anti-Sweating League and of the Select Committee on homework which was sitting at the same time. From these two quarters an altogether more far-reaching proposal for 'fair' wages was now to emerge.

Undoubtedly, the Australian example did much to prepare the way for a more fundamental approach to the problems of low earnings in England. The Australian economy suffered severe recession in the early 1890s, and consequent political developments made the 'protection' of labour a key issue there; and in 1896, the State of Victoria established wage-fixing boards in six industries where wages were low.[97] Thus at the same time that the homework Committee was set up, the Liberal government in England des-patched a Board of Trade official, Ernest Aves, to see the Australian legislation in action and to report back. In the event, Aves was sceptical about what he saw, and claimed that conditions differed so much between England and Australia that it was impossible to say whether similar boards would be viable in the mother country; in particular, he pointed out that protective tariffs in Victoria created a situation much more conducive to experimental legislation.[98] The Committee politely brushed these objections aside, however; the members appear to have been more impressed by the favourable attitude of another Board of Trade official, G. R. Askwith, and a woman factory inspector, Miss R. E. Squire.[99] Most of all, perhaps, they saw the force of such arguments as those put by a woman trade union organizer, Margaret Irwin, to the Select Committee on the 'fair wages clause', which was sitting at about the same time: for she had been driven to confess that it was:

> . . . very difficult to organize women to such an extent that their trade unions can be any real protection to them in their work. Therefore, personally, I should be very glad to see the State step in and do for them what the Trade Unions have done for men.[100]

In its final report, the Committee on homework recommended wage boards in 'tailoring and the making of shirts, underclothing and babylinen, and the finishing processes of machine-made lace', on grounds which indicate just how far public opinion had moved

since the 1830s, when the handloom weavers had sought a minimum wage in vain:

> If it be said that there may be industries which cannot be carried
> on if such a standard of payment be enforced, it may be replied
> that this was said when the enactment of many of the provisions
> of the Factory and other similar acts were proposed, and public
> opinion supported Parliament in deciding that, if the prognostica-
> tion were an accurate one, it would be better that any trade,
> which could not exist if such a minimum of decent and humane
> conditions were insisted upon, should cease. Parliament, with the
> full approval of the nation, has practically so decided again and
> again, when enactments have been passed forbidding the carrying
> on of specified industries unless certain minimum conditions as to
> health, safety, and comfort were complied with. It is doubtful
> whether there is any more important condition of individual and
> general well-being than the possibility of obtaining an income
> sufficient to enable those who earn it to secure, at any rate, the
> necessaries of life.[101]

Not all advanced radicals and feminists were necessarily in favour of
the 'trade board' solution, however: two notable exceptions were the
Ramsay MacDonalds. Mrs MacDonald appeared as a witness before
the homework Committee in 1907 and, whilst not opposing wage
boards in principle, believed that it would be impossible to prevent
homeworkers from accepting work 'below the minimum'. She
argued that a wage board on its own would be useless without
'some licensing, something more definite than we have at present, to
check the homeworkers' – in other words, the minimum wage
would only be enforceable if it were also made an offence for
anyone to take homework without a factory inspector's licence.[102]
Indeed, the MacDonalds seemed anxious to make an end of homework altogether, and clearly saw no place for it in the coming
socialist millennium. As Mrs MacDonald told the Committee, if the
more fundamental problem of unemployment among adult men
were solved, there would be no need for their wives to resort to
homework; and if widows or wives with invalid husbands and
families were properly maintained by the State, they too would no
longer need to take whatever ill-paid work came their way.[103] It is
not surprising, therefore, to find that, towards the end of her
evidence, the Liberal reformer Charles Masterman asked her

whether she saw wage boards as merely a 'middle-class alternative to socialism' – a phrase which neatly summarizes the suspicions with which some socialists in the early twentieth century viewed many of the Liberal government's welfare policies.[104]

In the event, the experimental legislation of 1909 did not cover all the trades suggested in the Committee's final report: chains and cardboard boxes replaced shirts, knickers, and nappies. Even in this narrow range of industries, the implementation of the law took time, and the effect on earnings, as we have seen from the studies of Tawney and Bulkley, was seldom dramatic (see pp. 75, 135, 140). The annual reports of the Anti-Sweating League after 1909 spoke of evasions and difficulties in all four boards, and dwelt on the disparity in negotiating skill and experience between the workers' and the employers' representatives.[105] The tailoring trade – large-scale, dispersed, and responsible for a bewildering variety of products – proved especially difficult to regulate: for what exactly did 'tailoring' cover? In the end, as Tawney put it, 'the trade board marched through a pantechnicon of apparel . . . deciding that football knickerbockers are, but flannel singlets are not, tailoring; sweeping boys' sailor blouses into its net, but excluding certain kinds of smocks, asserting its claim to boys' collars when they form part of a jacket, and waiving it when they do not . . .'[106] To operate effectively throughout the country, this Board, which itself had 49 members (22 workers, 22 employers, and 5 appointed 'outsiders') had initially established seven district committees with a further membership of 169.[107] Having first met in December 1910, the Board did not manage to produce its basic recommendation for a standard 'time rate' until August 1912, and the new rate did not operate for a further six months: and even then, the onus was simply left with the employers to adjust their piece-rates so that the 'average' worker would be able to make the standard time-rates of $3\frac{1}{4}$d an hour for women and 6d for men. In Tawney's words:

> . . . the Board crawls to an agreement along a path of which the milestones are one sixteenth of a penny, and . . . its ultimate decision represents a compromise between the employers' instinct of what the trade will bear and the desire of the workers and the appointed members to establish a 'living wage' . . . The elements of economic strength, bluff, and skill in bargaining are not ruled out, but merely limited by the fact that the participation of both

parties in the work of the Trade Board does something to moralise economic relationships and that the ultimate decision rests with the appointed members whose duty it is to represent the public economic conscience.[108]

Although the initial trade board legislation of 1909 was modest in scope, and its introduction fraught with practical difficulties, it deserves more than the brief passing mention which it usually gets from historians of 'the origins of the Welfare State'. Its potential implications for the future of British industrial life were enormous, and even *before* 1914 the notion of a nationally negotiated minimum wage with Parliamentary backing had been successfully taken up by the coalminers who, by contrast with the sweated workers, were the best-organized and most numerous of adult male wage-earners. In due course, trade boards would appear in other underpaid industries, too: but fundamentally, statutory wage-fixing suggested the 'national minimum wage' – long beloved of liberal social reformers – as the next step, and it painted an inviting prospect of a world in which *all* relationships between wage-payers and wage-earners could be 'moralized' by the operation of 'the public economic conscience', to use Tawney's expression. More than anything else, it was a portent of that optimism with which Liberal England still viewed the practical possibility of achieving a harmonious social order where the weaknesses of private capitalism had been corrected by the intervention of a State which was at once efficient and humane. In the short run, both optimism and harmony were to be swept away – along with the Liberal party itself – by war and its aftermath. Nevertheless, the tentative introduction of 'justice' and of 'the public interest' into wage bargaining ought not to be forgotten by a generation still grappling with the problems of an incomes policy, with the need to protect the economic rights of women, and with the reconciliation of wealth-creation and welfare-diffusion. The introduction of trade boards heralded a far bolder break with the past than did many of the other Liberal reforms; and it is time some energetic young historian did fuller justice to the great campaign against 'sweating' than has been possible within the confines of the present study.

Conclusion

The survival of the traditional 'outwork' system as an important feature of industrial organization for at least a century after the dates usually taken to mark the beginning of Britain's 'industrial revolution' suggests a number of interesting problems for students of development economics or comparative industrialization to ponder. For the outwork system is usually regarded as a feature of the pre-industrial economies and rural societies of early modern Europe, whereas the industrial revolution is generally equated with factory production and the urbanization of the population. The process by which the pre-industrial form of organization was replaced by the modern has always formed an important topic in the study of economic history, and the strains and stresses associated with the displacement of outwork by the factory have received the regular (though not necessarily profound) attention of students and teachers. Can our present introductory survey of outwork's survival in nineteenth-century Britain shed any light on the broad question of the process of economic modernization? Does outwork help to explain the industrial revolutions of the past, and can it offer any lessons for the countries of the 'Third World' in the future?

Economic historians who are concerned to understand why modern industrialization began in Europe when it did, have recently been looking more closely at the heyday of the putting-out system in the eighteenth century, in an attempt to assess what this early form of industrialization – which has been termed 'proto-industrialization' – might have contributed to the acceleration of economic growth and the modernization of industry which much of Western Europe experienced in the course of the nineteenth century.[1] According to C. and R. Tilly, the 'protoindustrialization of the European countryside' was significant because it constituted 'one of the greatest differences between the industrialization of Western Europe and the developing countries of today'.[2] One of its great advantages was that 'labour previously unemployed or under-

248

employed during a part of the year was put to work on a more continuous basis', thus bringing about a marked increase in productivity.[3] Furthermore, this labour acquired new habits and values as a result of being employed in industry: it became 'a propertyless proletariat with certain specialized inherent skills, prone to migration . . . easy to upset and uproot, with a value system which differed from the traditional peasant one and was regarded as immoral by the standards of a property-holding and -inheriting peasant society'.[4] In other words, protoindustrialization reduced rural unemployment, increased productivity, and also created a labour force which would prove fairly adaptable to the demands and opportunities inherent in economic modernization. A second important aspect of protoindustry was that it 'created an accumulation of capital in the hands of merchant entrepreneurs, making possible the adoption of machine industry with its (relatively) higher capital costs', and that it 'helped to form an entrepreneurial class and entrepreneurial skills'.[5] In terms of both labour and capital, therefore, protoindustrialization 'tended to induce the passage to modern industry'.[6]

Nevertheless, protoindustry was not an unmixed blessing, as its discoverers admit. If it was a necessary factor in subsequent industrialization, it was not a sufficient one – 'there was nothing unavoidable or automatic in the passage from one phase to the next'.[7] Indeed, certain areas – East Anglia or the Cotswolds would be good English examples – conspicuously failed to transform their traditional protoindustries: in the course of the nineteenth century they became 'de-industrialized', and the mainstream of industrialization was diverted elsewhere. In addition, many have pointed out, on the debit side, that the putting-out system had potentially disastrous demographic consequences, in that it encouraged early marriages and large families, and so contributed to building up population pressures in societies relatively ill-equipped to cope with them* As such, it might delay or even prevent the onset of modern industrialization at a regional level, rather than expedite it.

What light does our present study throw on the currently fashionable notion of the protoindustrialization of Western Europe? If anything, it would appear to suggest that the new concept needs to be used with some caution, since a major feature of this study has been the repeated demonstration that any simple antithesis between 'outwork = pre-industrial = rural' on the one hand, and 'factory

---

* See Chapter 4, pp. 169-71.

= modern = urban' on the other, does not hold good for much of
the nineteenth century. Putting-out was no mere antiquarian survival: given the right economic conditions, it was still capable of
growth and expansion, and, far from being in rivalry with the
factory system, it could be effectively combined in harness with it. It
was still an important part of industry in the world's most
modernized economy, and if it had disappeared from some branches
of industry by 1850, it was more firmly entrenched than ever in
some others.

Furthermore, it is misleading to talk of protoindustrialization in
the context of the whole economy, although it may be meaningful
to do so with reference to particular industries or regions. Whatever
benefits protoindustrialization may have brought to the subsequent
transformation of industries such as textiles, they were clearly not
applicable elsewhere. We should not become so obsessed by the role
of 'industry in the countryside' down to the end of the eighteenth
century that we forget that certain key industries, vital to economic
modernization, were not dispersed on this pattern: mining, iron-
making, shipbuilding, and other producers' goods industries already
called for highly centralized and capitalized activity. To explain the
whole of the 'industrial revolution' as a *consequence* of protoindustrialization is obviously wrong, when outwork was a feature of
the 'industrial' as well as of the 'pre-industrial' world, and when not
all 'pre-industrial' manufacture was organized on outwork lines.

We might also question two of the main assumptions of the
protoindustrializers. Did the old system really produce an adaptable
labour force for the modern economy? And did it really contribute
significantly to the pool of modern capital and of modern capitalists? If the answer to both these questions is still broadly 'yes', then
it must be 'yes – with serious qualifications'. If, as we have
suggested, putting-out always relied predominantly on women
workers, it is hard to see how the attributes and values acquired by
casual, part-time, and unsupervised work in the home were of great
use in 'the rise of modern industry', for the indiscipline of homework contrasted strongly with one of the prime features of full-time
factory work. True, the outworker had learned to live an insecure
and ill-paid life, and this 'education' may have been important in
habituating people to the vagaries of private capitalism; and
similarly, some of the manual skills gained at home could be readily
adapted to certain factory machines. But if we take the great bulk

of women outworkers, it would seem most unlikely that their domestic by-occupation inculcated habits of regular disciplined working or encouraged a high degree of physical mobility; and many spinners in the last years of the eighteenth century, or needlewomen a hundred years later, must have ceased to use their 'skill' altogether once they stopped taking work into their homes.

As far as capital and capitalists are concerned, the legacy left by protoindustrialization must remain a matter of uncertainty until more is known in detail about the history of individual enterprises in the wide range of industries which employed outwork. Some of the capital accumulated, and some of the skills acquired, by merchants and their agents under the putting-out system clearly contributed to the modernization of the industries concerned, but it was not sufficient in itself to effect the transformation. In most cases, some capital came from outside the industry, whilst some capitalists within the outwork system – William Biggs in mid-nineteenth-century hosiery would be a good example (see Chapter 2, p. 90) – were singularly reluctant to apply their resources to technical and organizational innovation within their industries.

It would seem, therefore, that the grand concept of proto-industry, which is derived largely from the widespread existence of the putting-out system in textiles in Western Europe before the nineteenth century, it not necessarily so helpful in explaining the subsequent dramatic rise of modern industry as some of its inventors seem to imagine. It rather overlooks the fact that not all pre-nineteenth-century industries used outwork, and it tends to forget that outwork persisted, and in places expanded, well into the nineteenth century. And even if it played some part in the rise of class of capitalists and entrepreneurs who were to be actively engaged in the process of economic modernization, its contribution to the creation of the modern industrial labour force was probably of minor importance.

If the prior existence of the putting-out system before the late eighteenth century is of only limited use in explaining why the pace of economic growth quickened in Western Europe during the nineteenth, can outwork – labour-intensive as it was – offer any possibilities to those present-day societies, rich in manpower but poor in capital, which are trying to increase output and real incomes in the face of continued population pressure? According to E. F. Schumacher, the problem of many 'Third World' countries is to harness the work potential of their millions of poverty-stricken, unemployed villagers; and in his widely-read book, *Small is Beautiful* (1973), he elaborates the case for solving the problem by 'intermediate technology'. Arguing that 'the primary consideration cannot be to maximise output per man, it must be to maximise work opportunities for the unemployed and underemployed',[8] Schumacher advocates a technology 'appropriate for labour surplus societies'.[9] Such a technology, he maintains, would need 'methods and equipment which are

- cheap enough so that they are accessible to virtually everyone;
- suitable for small-scale application; and
- compatible with man's need for creativity'.[10]

Accordingly, millions of small village workshops, with modest but well-made equipment, must be set up: they will make 'simple things – building materials, clothing, household goods, agricultural implements', and their production will be 'mainly from local materials and mainly for local use'.[11] Warming to the prospect of the honest industry thus created, Schumacher goes on, in words which would have done credit to Daniel Defoe when he surveyed the Yorkshire woollen industry in the early eighteenth century, to point out that 'even children would be allowed to make themselves useful, even old people. Everybody would be admitted to what is now the rarest privilege, the opportunity of working usefully, with his own hands and brains, in his own time and place, – and with excellent tools'.[12] He accepts, of course, that such work would be 'poorly paid and relatively unproductive'; but it is 'better than idleness', and 'it is only when they [the villagers] experience that their time and labour is of value that they can become interested in making it more valuable'.[13]

Schumacher justifies intermediate technology on the grounds that 'it does not imply simply a going-back in history to methods now outdated, although a systematic study of methods employed in the developed countries say, a hundred years ago, could yield highly suggestive results'.[14] But could it? Schumacher is never very specific about the tools and techniques he has in mind, but it must be assumed that, *inter alia*, the spinning wheel, handloom, sewing machine, small forge, and bench all come within the ambit of intermediate technology. Does the English experience of utilizing these tools in domestic workshops in the eighteenth and nineteenth centuries offer any encouragement to poor countries which might be tempted to follow Schumacher's advice and rely on them today?

The answer is, almost certainly not. Schumacher's ideal world is a world of self-employed craftsmen, rejoicing in healthy, wholesome labour around the familial hearth, exchanging their modest finished products for those of their near neighbours in the village community, and content to remain at a low standard of living. There never was such a world in the developed countries in the nineteenth century: intermediate technology, as then practised in the West, was part and parcel of unrestrained industrial capitalism and – from the worker's point of view – a disastrous and disagreeable part of it, too. One can see little 'honest independence', no communal exchange, and hardly any job satisfaction in most of the homework carried on at the behest of capitalists in nineteenth-century England: instead there is only hard work, insecurity, and low-paid drudgery in circumstances which contributed nothing to domestic comfort or personal happiness. In other words, intermediate technology will benefit the poor nations of today only if it is fitted into a very different institutional and ideological framework from that of nineteenth-century England. If it is merely a stage in the process of 'modernization' under private (or public) capitalism, it is likely to bring the poor very little in the way of either spiritual or material reward. If, on the other hand, it is to be part of a 'new moral world', dedicated to the goal of 'zero economic growth' and to the philosophy that 'small is beautiful' – in communities, work units, and material aspirations – it will only work in societies which have consciously and deliberately rejected the alternatives and have voluntarily welcomed the new philosophy in the full knowledge of its limitations. As a prescription forced on the starving and un-comprehending by sophisticated and well-fed outsiders, it seems doomed to create only frustration and disappointment.

Outwork, as it existed in the nineteenth century, was in fact one of the least acceptable of the many disagreeable aspects of private capitalism. The principle that 'labour' was a mere factor of production – one more item in an impersonal list of costs, to be acquired in the cheapest market without any regard for its human dimension – was perhaps put into practice more obviously in the outwork system than anywhere else. By the end of the nineteenth century as we have seen, the conditions apparently inseparable from homework had come to be regarded as an intolerable disgrace to a social democracy and, in so far as they still survived, they were judged ripe for radical legislation. Insecure, exploited, undefended, often unnoticed – left behind, indeed, in the Victorian 'march of progress' – the outworker certainly deserved sympathy; and it is depressing that it took so long for sympathy to be translated into effective public action. Advocates of a Utopia of spiritually fulfilled village craftsmen who have rejected material ambition and who do not abuse Nature's bounty should not confuse their optimistic ideal with the historical reality of the 'domestic system'. Outwork is rightly relegated to one of the darkest chapters of economic history; and now that it is virtually dead, none should regret its passing.

Notes

Introduction

1 For a recent reminder, see R. Samuel, 'The Workshop of the World: Steam Power and Hand Technology in Mid-Victorian Britain,' *History Workshop*, 1977, No. III, pp. 6-72.

2 S. Smiles, *Thrift*, 1888 edn., pp. 4-5, 7; C. Booth, *Life and Labour in London;* 1902 edn., 2nd Series: Industry, vol. 5, p. 293.

3 Smiles, op. cit., p. 14.

4 Booth, loc. cit.; Smiles, op. cit., p. 37.

5 Smiles, op. cit., p. 39.

6 F. Engels, *The Condition of the Working Class in England*, 1845, ed. and trs. W. O. Henderson and W. H. Chaloner, Oxford, 1958, p. 157.

7 E. P. Thompson and E. Yeo, eds., *The Unknown Mayhew*, 1971, p. 125.

8 C. Booth, *Life and Labour in London*, 1902 edn., 1st Series: Poverty, vol. 4, p. 342.

9 See Engels, op. cit., pp. 9-12.

10 See, for example, L. C. A. Knowles, *The Industrial and Commercial Revolutions in Great Britain during the Nineteenth Century*, 2nd edn., 1922, p. 82, where we read 'the fifth change [out of a list of six] was involved in the break-up of the home industry and its replacement by the factory'.

11 A. P. Usher, *An Introduction to the Industrial History of England*, 1921, p. 14.

12 J. H. Clapham, *The Early Railway Age* (*An Economic History of Modern Britain*, vol. 1), Cambridge, 1930, p. 178.

13 ibid., pp. 178-9.

14 Usher, op. cit., p. 15.

15 D. Defoe, *A Tour through the Whole Island of Great Britain*, Everyman's Library Edition, 1962, vol. I, p. 280.

16 Bamford's works have been reprinted as his *Autobiography*, ed. W. H. Chaloner, 2 vols., 1967; Gutteridge's autobiography has reappeared in *Master and Artisan in Victorian England*, ed. V. E. Chancellor, 1969.

17 Varley's diary is reprinted as an appendix in W. Bennett, *A History of Burnley*, Burnley, 1948, vol. 3; Lucy Luck's autobiography is included in J. Burnett, ed., *Useful Toil*, 1974.

18 For the 1834-5 inquiry, see D. Bythell, *The Handloom Weavers*, Cambridge, 1969, pp. 160-63.

19 He was prepared to argue, for instance, that immigrant Jewish workers in London's East End were willing to work 'in return for remuneration which . . . is not above that of an Indian coolie', and, on an average diet of three pieces of bread per day, plus tea and coffee, were nonetheless capable of a working day of between 18 and 20 hours! (P.P.* 1888 (361), vol. XX, QQ. 411–413).

20 For the Poor Law inquiry, see M. Blaug, 'The Myth of the Old Poor Law and the Making of the New', *Journal of Economic History*, 1963, vol. XXIII, and 'The Poor Law Report Re-examined', ibid., 1964, vol. XXIV.

21 P.P. 1845 (618), vol. XV, Q. 222.

22 P.P. 1837–8 (167), vol. XVIII, part I, Q. 2863.

PART ONE

Chapter 1

1 D. Defoe, *A Tour through the Whole Island of Great Britain*, Everyman's Library edition, 1962, vol. 2, p. 207. See also R. G. Wilson, 'The Supremacy of the Yorkshire Cloth Industry in the Eighteenth Century', in N.B. Harte and K. G. Ponting, eds., *Textile History and Economic History*, Manchester, 1973.

2 Defoe, op. cit., vol. 1, pp. 45 and 61.

3 T. W. Hanson, *The Story of Old Halifax*, Halifax, 1920, p. 204; C. Gulvin, *The Tweedmakers*, Newton Abbot, 1973, p. 36.

4 A. Young, *A Six Months Tour through the North of England*, 1770, vol. 3, p. 212; F. M. Eden, *The State of the Poor*, 1797, vol. 2, pp. 598, 84 and 169.

5 Young, op. cit., vol. 2, pp. 153 and 180.

6 E. L. Jones, 'The Agricultural Origins of Industry', *Past & Present*, 1968, no. 40, pp. 58–71.

7 ibid., p. 60. For a further discussion of the origins of outwork in the sixteenth and seventeenth centuries, see J. Thirsk, 'Industry in the Countryside' in F. J. Fisher, ed., *Essays in the Economic History of Tudor and Stuart England*, 1961.

8 Jones, op. cit., pp. 62–3.

9 For linen, see N.B. Harte, 'The Rise and Protection of the English Linen Trade, 1690–1790', in Harte and Ponting, op. cit.

10 C. Aspin and S. D. Chapman, *James Hargreaves and the Spinning Jenny*, Helmshore, 1964, p. 19.

11 ibid., pp. 46–60.

12 See W. G. Rimmer, *Marshalls of Leeds, Flax Spinners*, Cambridge, 1960, p. 9.

13 P.P. 1824 (420), vol. VI, pp. 391 and 399.

14 W. Cobbett, *Rural Rides*, Everyman's Library edition, 1924, vol. 2, p. 131.

15 F. M. Eden, *The State of the Poor*, 1797, vol. 2, pp. 177 and 478.

16 See E. L. Jones, 'The Agricultural Labour Market in England', *Economic History Review*, 1964–5, vol. XVII, pp. 323–5.

*Parliamentary Papers. This abbreviation is used throughout the Notes.

17   F. M. Eden, *The State of the Poor*, 1797, vol. 2, p. 530; R. A. Church, 'Messrs. Gotch & Sons and the Rise of the Kettering Footwear Industry', *Business History*, 1966, vol. VIII, pp. 140–49; H. A. Randall, 'The Kettering Worsted Industry of the Eighteenth Century', *Northamptonshire Past and Present*, 1970–1, vol. IV, pp. 313–20 and 349–56.

18   See M. Edwards, *The Growth of the British Cotton Trade, 1780–1815*, Manchester, 1967, esp. Chapters 3 and 4.

19   See P. Deane and W. A. Cole, *British Economic Growth 1689–1959*, Cambridge, 1962, pp. 52–3.

20   Eden, op. cit., vol. 2, p. 477.

21   P.P. 1840 (220), vol. XXIV, p. 627.

22   For a full description of the differences between the two branches of the wool-using textile industry, see H. Heaton, *The Yorkshire Woollen and Worsted Industries from Earliest Times up to the Industrial Revolution*, Oxford 1920, p. 260.

23   J. de L. Mann, *The Cloth Industry in the West of England from 1640 to 1880*, Oxford, 1971, p. 62. See also R. G. Wilson, 'The Supremacy of the Yorkshire Cloth Industry in the Eighteenth Century' in N.B. Harte and K. G. Ponting, eds., *Textile History and Economic History*, Manchester, 1973, pp. 225–46.

24   E. M. Sigsworth, *Black Dyke Mills*, Liverpool, 1958, p. 1.

25   J. G. Jenkins, *The Welsh Woollen Industry*, Cardiff, 1969, pp. 55–8.

26   Mann, op. cit., pp. 62, 123.

27   J. K. Edwards, 'The Decline of the Norwich Textiles Industry', *Yorkshire Bulletin*, 1964, vol. XVI, pp. 37–41.

28   See the evidence of James Ellis and Robert Cookson, master clothiers, in P.P. 1806 (268), vol. III, esp. pp. 603, 649, 661.

29   Sigsworth, op. cit., p. 142.

30   See Heaton, op. cit., pp. 418–35.

31   See W. B. Crump and G. Ghorbal, *History of the Huddersfield Woollen Industry*, Huddersfield, 1935, p. 66.

32   P.P. 1802–3 (71), vol. V, p. 307.

33   A. Plummer and R. E. Early, *The Blanket Makers*, 1969, p. 49.

34   Mann, op. cit., p. 161.

35   W. B. Crump, *The Leeds Woollen Industry 1780–1820*, Leeds, 1931, p. 6.

36   Mann, op. cit., p. 131.

37   Jenkins, op. cit., pp. 33–4.

38   P.P. 1806 (268), vol. III, pp. 899–901.

39   ibid., pp. 578–580.

40   Crump, op. cit., p. 25.

41   Jenkins, op. cit., p. 61.

42   P.P. 1840 (43), vol. XXIII, p. 373; Mann, op. cit., p. 194; Jenkins, op. cit., p. 138.

43   Factory returns, quoted Mann, op. cit., p. 220.

44   P.P. 1893–4 (c. 6894–XXIII), vol. XXXVII, part 1, p. 787.

45   Crump and Ghorbal, op. cit., p. 87.

46   Plummer and Early, op. cit., p. 125.

47   See F. Thompson, *Harris Tweed: The Story of a Hebridean Industry*, Newton Abbot, 1971, esp. pp. 58–66.

48   Sigsworth, op. cit., pp. 2–4.

49   Edwards, op. cit., pp. 31–6.

50   Sigsworth, op. cit., p. 10; P.P. 1840 (43) vol. XXIII, p. 402; J. H. Clapham, 'The Transference of the Worsted Industry from Norfolk to the West Riding', *Economic Journal*, 1910, vol. XX, p. 197.

51   G. A. Feather, 'A Pennine Worsted Community in the Mid-Nineteenth Century', *Textile History*, 1972, vol. III, p. 67.

52   Sigsworth, op. cit., p. 36.

53   This is the explanation for the lack of technical change in the Norwich industry given by Edwards, op. cit., p. 36.

54   See the report of H. S. Chapman in P.P. 1840 (43) vol. XXIII, p. 427. Women outnumbered men by 142 to 107 at Oxenhope in 1851 (Feather, op. cit., p. 71).

55   P.P. 1840 (43), vol. XXIII, p. 402.

56   ibid., pp. 171–3, 236.

57   Sigsworth, op. cit., pp. 9, 42.

58   The number of combers at Oxenhope increased by 40% between 1841 and 1851, during which period the number of weavers declined by roughly the same proportion (Feather, op. cit., p. 67).

59   P. Deane and W. A. Cole, *British Economic Growth 1688-1959*, Cambridge, 1962, pp. 204–6.

60   P.P. 1840 (43), vol. XXIII, p. 318.

61   ibid pp. 343, 324, and 329.

62   Deane and Cole, loc. cit.

63   P.P. 1865 (3548), vol. XX, p. 74.

64   J. H. Clapham, *An Economic History of Modern Britain*, vol. II: *Free Trade and Steel*, Cambridge, 1932, p. 28.

65   Deane and Cole, op. cit., p. 210.

66   C. Stella Davies, ed., *A History of Macclesfield*, Manchester, 1961, pp. 128–9.

67   P.P. 1840 (217), vol. XXIV, p. 21.

68   D. C. Coleman, "Growth and Decay during the Industrial Revolution: The Case of East Anglia', *Scandinavian Economic History Review*, 1962, vol. X, pp. 120–21.

69   P.P. 1856 (343), vol. XIII, Q. 1710.

70   P.P. 1840 (43), vol. XXIII, pp. 66–7, 73.

71   See D. J. Rowe, 'Chartism and the Spitalfields Silk Weavers', *Economic History Review*, 1967, vol. XX, pp. 482–93.

72   P.P. 1907 (290), vol. VI, Q. 1149.

73   Coleman, op. cit., pp. 122–7. See also D. C. Coleman, *Courtaulds: An Economic and Social History*, Oxford, 1969, vol. I, pp. 76–103.

74   J. H. Clapham, *An Economic History of Modern Britain*, vol. II: *Free Trade and Steel*, Cambridge, 1932, p. 87.

75   Davies, op. cit., p. 133.

76 Clapham, op. cit., p. 28.
77 A. P. Wadsworth and J. de L. Mann, *The Cotton Trade and Industrial Lancashire*, Manchester, 1931, pp. 347, 361, 369, and 256.
78 J. H. Clapham, *An Economic History of Modern Britain*, vol. I: *The Early Railway Age*, Cambridge, 1926; D. Bythell, *The Handloom Weavers*, Cambridge, 1969, pp. 260-61.
79 J. M. Prest, *The Industrial Revolution in Coventry*, Oxford, 1960, p. 47.
80 V. E. Chancellor, ed., *Master and Artisan in Victorian England*, 1969.
81 P.P. 1840 (217), vol. XXIV, p. 21.
82 ibid., p. 28.
83 ibid., pp. 50-51.
84 See Chancellor, op. cit., pp. 101-2.
85 P.P. 1840 (214), vol. XXIV, pp. 53-5.
86 ibid., pp. 55-7.
87 ibid., esp. pp. 244-5.
88 ibid., p. 65.
89 See Prest, op. cit., pp. 79-94.
90 For a full account of this remarkable development, see Prest, op. cit., pp. 94-112.
91 ibid., pp. 113-8.
92 P.P. 1866 (3678), vol. XXIV, p. 114.
93 Chancellor, op. cit., p. 178.

Chapter 2

1 For reminiscences of the clothing of the rural poor at the end of the nineteenth century, see Flora Thompson, *Lark Rise to Candleford*, Penguin Edition 1973, *passim*.
2 P.P. 1888 (361), vol. XX, Q. 1772.
3 P.P. 1864 (3414), vol. XXII, pp. 226-7.
4 P.P. 1887 (331), vol. LXXXIX, p. 15.
5 R. H. Tawney, *Studies in the Minimum Wage, No. 2*, 1915, pp. 16-17.
6 P.P. 1864 (3414), vol. XXII, p. 86; P.P. 1892 (c. 6795-ix), vol. XXXVI, part IV, p. 518.
7 P.P. 1876 (1443), vol. XXX, QQ. 10186-8; J. A. Schmiechen, 'State Reform and the Local Economy', *Economic History Review*, 2nd Series, 1975, vol. XXVII, pp. 413-28, has a general discussion of this problem.
8 Tawney, op. cit., p. 216.
9 P.P. 1856 (343), vol. XIII, QQ. 999-1001.
10 P.P. 1864 (3414), vol. XXII, pp. 66-67.
11 ibid., p. 69.
12 ibid., p. 163.
13 ibid., p. 227.
14 P.P. 1888 (361), vol. XX, QQ. 9427-30.
15 ibid., QQ. 9434-7.
16 P.P. 1893-4 (c. 6894-xxiii), vol. XXXVII, part 1, p. 582.
17 P.P. 1889 (331), vol. XIV, part 1, QQ. 26735-60.

18 P.P. 1889 (331), vol. XIV, part 1, QQ.26671-2, 28432. For a full account of the Leeds industry, see J. Thomas, *A History of the Leeds Clothing Industry (The Yorkshire Bulletin of Economic and Social Research,* Occasional Paper no. 1), 1955.
19 S.P. Dobbs, *The Clothing Workers of Great Britain,* 1928, p. 174.
20 P.P. 1843 (431), vol. XIV, pp. 833-4.
21 ibid., loc. cit.
22 P.P. 1864 (3414), vol. XXII, p. 230.
23 P.P. 1876 (1443), vol. XXX, Q. 17297.
24 P.P. 1864 (3414), vol. XXII, p. 68.
25 P.P. 1908 (246), vol. VIII, Q. 4082.
26 P.P. 1864 (3414), vol. XXII, p. 140.
27 ibid., p. 139.
28 ibid., p. 83.
29 ibid., loc. cit.
30 ibid., p. 241.
31 ibid., loc. cit.
32 G. Stedman Jones, *Outcast London,* Oxford, 1971, Appendix II, pp. 358-9.
33 P.P. 1864 (3414), vol. XXII, p. 46.
34 P.P. 1907 (290), vol. VI, QQ. 688, 691.
35 ibid., QQ. 1768-9.
36 Tawney, op. cit., pp. 12, 22.
37 *Census of England and Wales 1911,* vol. X, Table 26.
38 D. L. Munby, *Industry and Planning in Stepney,* 1951, pp. 54-5.
39 P.P. 1888 (361), vol. XX, Q. 1339.
40 ibid., Q. 1371.
41 Tawney, op. cit., pp. 192-3.
42 P.P. 1889 (331), vol. XIV, part 1, QQ. 30910-2. See also Thomas, op. cit., pp. 16-23.
43 P.P. 1888 (361), vol. XX, Q. 3340.
44 See the Report of John Burnett to the Board of Trade in P.P. 1887 (331), vol. LXXXIX, p. 6.
45 P.P. 1888 (361), vol. XX, Q. 3320.
46 See the account of the Rev. J. Munro of Bethnal Green in P.P. 1888 (361), vol. XX, Q. 1364.
47 P.P. 1889 (331), vol. XIV, part 1, Q. 26835.
48 P.P. 1907 (290), vol. VI, QQ. 456-60.
49 ibid., QQ. 501, 517.
50 P.P. 1893-4 (c. 6894-xxiii), vol. XXXVII, part 1, p. 640.
51 P.P. 1864 (3414), vol. XXII, p. lxix.
52 E. P. Thompson and Eileen Yeo, eds., *The Unknown Mayhew,* 1971, p. 116.
53 See especially C. Booth, *Life and Labour of the People in London,* 1889, *First Series: Poverty,* vol. 4: 'The Trades of East London Connected with Poverty', *passim.*
54 For further details of this industry, see M. Hartley and J. Ingilby, *The Old Hand-Knitters of the Dales,* 2nd edition Clapham, 1969.

55 See especially his *Nottinghamshire in the Eighteenth Century*, 1932.
56 W. Felkin, *History of the Machine-wrought Hosiery and Lace Manufactures*, 1867, pp. 72, 437.
57 A. Temple Patterson, *Radical Leicester 1780-1850*, 1954, pp. 49–54.
58 Felkin, op. cit., pp. 465-7.
59 P.P. 1845 (641), vol. LXV, p. 685.
60 P.P. 1854-5 (421), vol. XIV, Q. 379; P.P. 1864 (3414), vol. XXII, p. 34; Felkin, op. cit., p. 517.
61 P.P. 1819 (193), vol. V, p. 431; Felkin, op. cit., p. 517.
62 P.P. 1845 (641), vol. XV, Q. 2412.
63 P.P. 1863 (3170), vol. XVIII, p. 383.
64 P.P. 1854-5 (421), vol. XIV, Q. 7568.
65 ibid., QQ. 2923 and 2946.
66 P.P. 1854-5 (421), vol. XIV, QQ. 6502-3; P. P. 1845 (641), vol. XV, QQ. 4490-1, 4655.
67 ibid., Q. 4473.
68 P.P. 1854-5 (421), vol. XIV, QQ. 4286, 4333, 4407-11.
69 P.P. 1845 (609), vol. XV, p. 63.
70 ibid., p. 106.
71 ibid., p. 69; P.P. 1854-5 (421), vol. XIV, QQ. 6508-9.
72 P.P. 1845 (641), vol. XV, QQ. 5105-5108.
73 P.P. 1845 (609), vol. XV, p. 69.
74 ibid., p. 83.
75 P.P. 1819 (193) vol. V, p. 422; P.P. 1854-5 (421), vol. XIV, QQ. 349 and 605.
76 P.P. 1854-5 (421), vol. XIV, Q. 54.
77 P.P. 1845 (618), vol. XV, Q.3797.
78 P.P. 1854-5 (421), vol. XIV, QQ. 3061-85, 6975-9, 7325.
79 P.P. 1845 (641), vol. XV, Q. 1597.
80 P.P. 1812 (247), vol. II, pp. 218, and 220.
81 Felkin, op. cit., pp. 451-2. See also S. D. Chapman, 'Memoirs of Two Eighteenth Century Framework Knitters', *Textile History*, 1968, vol. I, p. 109 *et seq.*
82 P.P. 1854-5 (421), vol. XIV, Q.374.
83 P.P. 1845 (618), vol. XV, Q. 105.
84 ibid., QQ. 812-3.
85 P.P. 1854-5 (421), vol. XIV, QQ. 3108-9, 3961.
86 P.P. 1863 (3170), vol. XVIII, p. 363.
87 P.P. 1845 (609), vol. XV, pp. 103-4.
88 P.P. 1863 (3170), vol. XVIII, p. 367.
89 P.P. 1845 (618), vol. XV, Q. 882.
90 S. D. Chapman, 'Enterprise and Innovation in the British Hosiery Industry, 1750-1850', *Textile History*, 1974, vol. V, p. 32.
91 See Felkin, op. cit., pp. 434-5; P.P. 1812 (359), vol. II, pp. 271, 284.
92 P.P. 1819 (193), vol. V, pp. 408-11, 416, 420.
93 P.P. 1854-5 (421), vol. XIV, Q. 2157.
94 ibid., Q. 6400.
95 P.P. 1845 (609), vol. XV, p. 98.

96   P.P. 1819 (193), vol. V, p. 409; P.P. 1845 (618), vol. XV, Q. 3779.
97   P.P. 1845 (609), vol. XV, p. 99.
98   ibid., 49–50.
99   P.P. 1845 (618), vol. XV, Q. 856.
100 ibid., Q. 3090.
101 P.P. 1819 (193), vol. V, p. 418.
102 P.P. 1845 (641), vol. XV, Q. 1608.
103 P.P. 1845 (618), vol. XV, Q. 3058.
104 P.P. 1845 (609), vol. XV, pp. 52–3.
105 P.P. 1887 (c. 5172), vol. LXXXIX, p. 132; P.P. 1890 (c. 6161), vol. LXVIII, p. 40.
106 P.P. 1845 (618), vol. XV, QQ. 2884, 8039; P.P. 1845 (641), vol. XV, Q. 4471.
107 P.P 1845 (618), vol. XV, QQ. 3595, 917.
108 ibid., Q. 2525; P.P. 1845 (641), vol. XV, QQ. 4348, 4350, 4440.
109 P.P. 1845 (609), vol. XV, p. 67.
110 P.P. 1876 (1443), vol. XXX, QQ. 7556, 8103.
111 P.P. 1845 (609), vol. XV, pp. 86. 93.
112 P.P. 1845 (618), vol. XV, Q. 1343.
113 P.P. 1845 (641), vol. XV, Q. 4235.
114 P.P. 1845 (618), vol. XV, QQ. 7478–9.
115 ibid., QQ. 6761, 5622; P.P. 1845 (641), vol. XV, Q. 365.
116 P.P. 1854–5 (421), vol. XIV, Q. 2726.
117 P.P. 1845 (641), vol. XV, QQ. 3822, 4177.
118 P.P. 1845 (618), vol. XV, Q. 3620.
119 ibid., QQ. 7381, 7399, 7429, 7441.
120 See D. M. Smith, 'The Location of the British Hosiery Industry since the Middle of the Nineteenth Century', *East Midland Geographer*, (1970), vol. V, part 1, pp. 71–9.
121 P.P. 1845 (618), vol. XV, QQ. 6833, 7914.
122 P.P. 1845 (641), vol. XV, Q. 5039.
123 P.P. 1863 (3170), vol. XVIII, pp. 378–9.
124 P.P. 1892 (c. 6795-vi), vol. XXXVI, Part II, QQ. 13327, 13451.
125 P.P. 1908 (4423), vol. XXIV, Q. 1621.
126 W. Felkin, *History of the Machine-wrought Hosiery and Lace Manufactures*, 1867, p. 121.
127 ibid., pp. 133–8.
128 P.P. 1812 (247), vol. II, pp. 212–15.
129 See D. E. Varley, 'John Heathcoat, Founder of the Machine-Made Lace Industry', *Textile History*, 1968, vol. I, pp. 2–45.
130 Felkin, op. cit., p. 331.
131 P.P. 1863 (3170), vol. XVIII, p. 332.
132 R. A. Church, *Victorian Nottingham: Economic and Social Change in a Midland Town*, 1966, pp. 97–8.
133 ibid., pp. 285–6.
134 P.P. 1843 (431), vol. XIV, pp. 610–1.
135 Felkin, op. cit., pp. 398–9.
136 Church, op. cit., p. 82.

137 P.P. 1893-4 (c. 6894-xxiii), vol. XXXVII, Part 1, p. 709.
138 P.P. 1907 (290), vol. VI, Q. 990.
139 P.P. 1843 (431), vol. XIV, p. 605; P.P. 1863 (3170), vol. XVIII, p. 296.
140 P.P. 1908 (246), vol. VIII, Q. 1568.
141 P.P. 1863 (3170), vol. XVIII, pp. 298, 307.
142 P.P. 1843 (431), vol. XIV, p. 608.
143 F. B. Palliser, *The History of Lace*, 1902 edn., pp. 375-6.
144 F. M. Eden, *The State of the Poor*, 1797, vol. 2, pp. 8, 24, 548.
145 St John Priest, *A General View of the Agriculture of Buckinghamshire*, 1813, p. 81.
146 C. C. Channer and M. E. Roberts, *Lace-making in the Midlands*, 1900, p. 41.
147 Palliser, op cit., p. 413.
148 P.P. 1863 (3170), vol. XVIII, p. 353. For a recent account of the industry in the mid-nineteenth century, see G. R. F. Spenceley, 'The English Pillow-Lace Industry 1840-80', in *Business History*, 1977, vol. XIX, pp. 68-87.
149 P.P. 1863 (3170), vol. XVIII, pp. 342-3, 347-8.
150 P.P. 1843 (430), vol. XIII, p. 419
151 P.P. 1863 (3170), vol. XVIII, p. 355.
152 P.P. 1876 (1443) vol. XXIX, p. 173
153 Channer and Roberts, op.cit., pp. 31-7.
154 P.P. 1863 (3170) vol. XVIII, pp. 346-56.
155 P.P. 1888 (124), vol. LXXX, pp. 494-8.
156 ibid., p. 496
157 Channer and Roberts, op. cit., pp. 48-61. For a full account of this movement see G. Spenceley, 'The Lace Associations', *Victorian Studies*, 1973, vol. XVI, pp. 433-52.

Chapter 3

1 *Victoria County History of Northamptonshire*, vol. 2, p. 320.
2 ibid., p.324
3 See R. A. Church, 'Messrs. Gotch and Sons and the Rise of the Kettering Footwear Industry', *Business History*, 1966, vol. VIII, pp. 140-49
4 W. L. Sparks, *The Story of Shoemaking in Norwich*, 1949, p. 35; *Victoria County History of Staffordshire*, vol. 2, p. 231; P. R. Mounfield 'The Shoe Industry in Staffordshire, 1767-1951', *North Staffs Journal of Field Studies*, 1965, vol. V. p. 77.
5 *Victoria County History of Leicestershire*, vol. 4, p. 316.
6 ibid., p. 324; Sparks, op. cit., p. 68.
7 Church, op. cit., p. 141. See also P. R. Mounfield, 'The Footwear Industry of the East Midlands: (4) Leicestershire to 1911', in *East Midland Geographer*, 1966, vol. IV, part 1, pp. 11-16.
8 Sparks, op. cit., p. 33.
9 See T. Wright, *The Romance of the Shoe*, 1922, p. 172.

10 See R. A. Church, 'Labour Supply and Innovation 1800–1860: the Boot and Shoe Industry', in *Business History*, 1970, vol. XII, p. 39.

11 *Victoria County History of Leicestershire*, vol. 4, p. 315; Mounfield, 'Leicestershire', op. cit., pp. 10–11; R. A. Church, 'The Effect of the American Export Invasion on the British Boot and Shoe Industry', *Journal of Economic History*, 1968, vol. XXVIII, pp. 228–30.

12 P.P. 1864 (3414), vol. XXII, pp. 244–5, 253–4.

13 ibid., p. 247.

14 See V. A. Hatley, 'Monsters in Campbell Square: the Early History of Two Industrial Premises in Northampton', in *Northants Past and Present*, 1966–7, vol. IV, no. 1, pp. 51–9.

15 P.P. 1864 (3414) vol. XXII, p. 248.

16 P.P. 1876 (1443) vol. XXX, Q. 7140.

17 P.P. 1892 (c. 6795–vi) vol. XXXVI, Part II, QQ. 13950, 14484.

18 See P. Head, 'Boots and Shoes', in D. H. Aldcroft, ed., *The Development of British Industry and Foreign Competition 1875–1914*, 1968, pp. 159–83, and Church, 'American Export Invasion', pp. 223–54.

19 See E. Brunner, 'The Origins of Industrial Peace: the Case of the British Boot and Shoe Industry', *Oxford Economic Papers*, new series, 1949, vol. I, pp. 251–3.

20 See A. Fox, *History of the National Union of Boot and Shoe Operatives 1874–1957*, Oxford, 1958, esp. pp. 85 *et seq.*, 143 *et seq.*, and 202 *et seq.*, A. Head, op. cit., pp. 172–83; and R. A. Church, 'American Export Invasion', *passim*.

21 C. B. Hawkins, *Norwich: a Social Survey*, 1910, p. 31; Head, op. cit., p. 182.

22 See P.P. 1888 (361), vol. XX, Q. 1128 *et seq.*

23 See G. Stedman Jones, *Outcast London*, Oxford, 1971, Appendix 2, Tables 6 and 7.

24 *Census of England and Wales 1911*, vol. X, Intro., p. cix, and Tables 15 (a) and (b).

25 R. A. Church, 'Labour Supply and Innovation ....', loc. cit., p. 26.

26 *Census of England and Wales 1911*, vol. X, p. cix.

27 A. Fox, op. cit., pp. 16–17.

28 *Census of England and Wales, 1911*, vol. X, Table 15 (a) and (b).

29 See A. Fox, op. cit., pp. 85 and 202–3.

30 *Victoria County History of Leicestershire*, vol. 4, p. 318.

31 P.P. 1888 (361), vol. XX, Q. 582.

32 A. Head, op. cit., p. 183

33 P.P. 1887 (331), vol. LXXXIX, p. 18; P.P. 1888 (361), vol. XX, Q. 10054.

34 P.P. 1893–4 (c. 6894–ix), vol. XXXIV, Q. 33196.

35 *Census of England and Wales 1911*, vol. X, p. cix.

36 P.P. 1864 (3414), vol. XXII, p. 245.

37 P.P. 1888 (361), vol. XX, Q. 590.

38 P.P. 1876 (1443), vol. XXX, Q. 10944.

39 Hawkins, op. cit., pp. 23 and 33.

40 P.P. 1864 (3414), vol. XXII, p. 255.
41 ibid., p. 260.
42 P.P. 1843 (430), vol. XIII, p. 450; P.P. 1876 (1443), vol. XXIX, p. 108; P.P. 1907 (290), vol. VI, QQ. 620–1.
43 *Census of England and Wales 1911*, vol. X, p. cix.
44 F. M. Eden, *The State of the Poor*, 1797, vol. 2, p.2.
45 *Victoria Country History of Bedfordshire*, vol. 2, 1908, p. 120. For a full account of the origins of the two industries, see J. G. Dony, *A History of the Straw Hat Industry*, Luton, 1942, pp. 19–36.
46 P.P. 1864 (3414), vol. XXII, p. 279.
47 P.P. 1893–4 (c. 6894-xxiii), vol. XXXVII, part 1, p. 577.
48 Dony, op. cit., p. 73.
49 P.P. 1843 (431), vol, XIV, p. 65.
50 P.P. 1876 (1443), vol. XXX, QQ. 113, 3131; P.P. 1876 (1443), vol. XXIX, p. 188.
51 *Victoria County History of Bedfordshire*, vol. 2, p. 121.
52 P.P. 1893–4 (c. 6894-xxiii), vol. XXXVII, part 1, p. 577. See Dony, op. cit., pp. 88–92.
53 P.P. 1864 (3414), vol. XXII, pp. 288–9.
54 ibid., p. 287.
55 P.P. 1893–4 (c. 6894-xxiii), vol. XXXVII, part 1, p. 578. See Dony, op. cit., p. 128.
56 P.P. 1864 (3414), vol. XXII, p. 287.
57 ibid., p. 277.
58 Dony, op. cit., pp. 126 and 140.
59 P.P. 1892 (c6795-vi), vol. XXXVI, part 2, QQ. 15228 and 15244.
60 P.P. 1893–4 (c6894-xxiii), vol. XXXVII, part I, p. 30.
61 S. Timmins, ed., *The Resources, Products, and Industrial History of Birmingham and the Midland Hardware District*, 1866, p. 110.
62 ibid., p. 111.
63 See G. C. Allen, *The Industrial Development of Birmingham and the Black Country*, 1929, pp. 198–9.
64 Timmins, op. cit., p. 114; Allen, op. cit., p. 128.
65 Allen, op. cit., p. 76.
66 P.P. 1876 (1443), vol. XXIX, p. 76; Allen, op. cit., p. 184.
67 P.P. 1876 (1443), vol. XXX, Q. 5976; P.P. 1889 (165), vol. XIII, QQ. 20991–2.
68 P.P. 1876 (1443), vol. XXX, Q. 5976; P.P. 1889 (165), vol. XIII, Q. 20854.
69 P.P. 1889 (165), vol. XIII, QQ. 21038, 20885.
70 P.P. 1871 (c. 326), vol. XXXVI, pp. xxv–xxix; P.P. 1889 (165), vol. XIII, Q. 20225, *et. seq.*
71 P.P. 1892 (c. 6795-iv), vol. XXXVI, part I, Q. 17596.
72 R. H. Sherard, *The White Slaves of England*, 1897, pp. 86–94.
73 P.P. 1876 (1443), vol. XXX, Q. 6097; ibid., vol. XXIX, pp. 190–91.
74 P.P. 1889 (165), vol, XIII, QQ. 20247, 23010.
75 P.P. 1876 (1443), vol. XXX, Q. 6169 *et seq.*; ibid,. vol. XXIX, p. lxxx.

76 P.P. 1889 (165), vol. XIII, QQ. 19899-19901.
77 ibid., QQ. 21260, 21281, 21410.
78 P.P. 1893-4 (c. 6894-x), vol. XXXII, Q. 20043.
79 P.P. 1876 (1443), vol. XXX, Q. 6231.
80 Timmins, op. cit., p. 113.
81 P.P. 1889 (165), vol. XIII, Q. 19895.
82 P.P. 1892 (c. 6795-iv), vol. XXXVI, part I, QQ. 18436-18446.
83 P.P. 1893-4 (c. 6894-vii), vol. XXXII, Q. 20014.
84 Quoted in Allen, op. cit., pp. 184, 274.
85 P.P. 1889 (165), vol. XIII, QQ. 21409, 21520.
86 ibid., Q. 22913.
87 ibid., Q. 21539.
88 P.P. 1876 (1443), vol. XXIX, p. lxxxi.
89 Allen, op. cit., p. 94.
90 P.P. 1876 (1443), vol. XXX, Q. 6049 *et seq.*
91 P.P. 1892 (c. 6795-iv), vol. XXXVI, part I, QQ. 16925-7, 17275.
92 R. H. Tanwy, *Studies in the Minimum Wage, No. I,* 1914, pp. 4, 9, 11.
93 Tawney, op. cit., p. 10.
94 Allen, op. cit., p. 37.
95 Tawney, op. cit., p. 12.
96 ibid., p. 2.
97 ibid., pp. 11 - 12.
98 Allen, op. cit., pp. 184, 226.
99 P.P. 1889 (165), vol. XIII, QQ. 17616-17624; Sherard, op. cit., pp. 226-7.
100 P.P. 1889 (165), vol. XIII, QQ. 18173, 18688, 18783.
101 ibid., Q. 19041.
102 Allen, op. cit., p. 422.
103 Tawney, op. cit., p. 2.
104 P.P. 1876 (1443), vol. XXX, QQ. 5693-9.
105 P.P. 1889 (165), vol. XIII, Q. 18018.
106 ibid., Q. 19316.
107 ibid., Q. 22836.
108 ibid., Q. 21117.
109 Tawney, op. cit., pp. 16-21.
110 P.P. 1892 (c. 6795-iv), vol. XXXVI, part I, Q. 17247.
111 Tawney, op. cit., pp. 25-6.
112 Tawney, op. cit., p. 55.
113 ibid., pp. 106-10.
114 ibid., p. 36.
115 P.P. 1889 (165), vol. XIII, Appendix A, p. 681.
116 P.P. 1876 (1443), vol. XXX, QQ. 2915-9.
117 P.P. 1865 (3548), vol. XX, pp. 259-61.
118 P.P. 1907 (290), vol. VI, QQ. 627-8.
119 ibid., QQ. 544 and 554.

120 For examples of the range of these industries in the Birmingham area see E. Cadbury, M. C. Matheson and A. Shann, *Women's Work and Wages*, 1906, pp. 145-180.
121 P.P. 1907 (290), vol. VI, Q.630.
122 L. J. Mayes, *History of Chair Making in High Wycombe*, 1960, pp. 58 and 108.
123 'Economy and Society in late Victorian Britain', *Economic History Review*, 1965, vol. XVIII, pp. 183-98.
124 P.P. 1908 (246), vol. VIII, QQ. 2356-64, 2325, and 2294-9.
125 Some large manufacturing concerns, of course, had their own box-making departments on their own premises.
126 M. E. Bulkley, *Studies in the Minimum Wage, No. 3. Boxmaking*, 1915, pp. 1-6, 48.
127 C. Black, *Sweated Industry*, 1907, pp. 4-5.
128 Bulkley, op. cit., p. 71.
129 ibid., pp. 12-18, 68-71.
130 ibid., pp. 75-7.
131 ibid., p. xi.
132 P.P. 1907 (290), vol. VI, QQ. 1290-2, 1273, 1470, See also Cadbury *et al.*, loc. cit.
133 P.P. 1907 (290), vol. VI, QQ. 1293-7.

Conclusion to Part One

1 This line of argument is not incompatible with the general hypothesis recently advanced by Eric Richards that 'there was a substantial diminution of the economic role of women during the 19th century,' owing largely to the steady contraction of homework from 'about 1820', and that this was only reversed after the 1870s by the growth of new 'non-domestic' work opportunities in 'secondary' and 'tertiary' industry. But Richards fails to distinquish between full-time work on the one hand, and part-time or casual work on the other; and he does not sufficiently emphasize the regional differences in the timing of outwork's decline and disappearance. (E. Richards, 'Women in the British Economy since about 1700: an Interpretation', *History*, 1974, vol. LIX, pp. 337-57).
2 G. Stedman Jones, *Outcast London*, Oxford, 1971, p. 26.
3 E. H. Hunt, *Regional Wage Variations in Britain, 1850-1914*, Oxford, 1973, pp. 7 and 13.
4 J. A. Schmiechen, 'State Reform and the Local Economy', *Economic History Review*, 1975, vol. XXVIII, pp. 413-28.
5 Hunt, op. cit., chapters 1, 2, and 3, *passim*.
6 P.P. 1907 (290) vol. VI, appendix 3, p. 302.
7 *Annual Reports of the Medical Officers of Health*, P.P. 1909 (4633), vol. XXI, table 4, pp. 632-7.
8 Hunt, op. cit., p. 109.
9 See Richards, op. cit., pp. 351-2.

10 D. Sells, *The British Trade Boards System*, 1923, pp. 149-53.
11 For a discussion of some of the practical and conceptual difficulties involved in studying the changing real wages of the nineteenth century worker, see D. Bythell, 'The History of the Poor', *English Historical Review*, 1974, vol. LXXXIX, pp. 365-77.
12 C. F. G. Masterman, *The Condition of England*, 1909, p. 172.

PART TWO

Chapter 4

1 P.P. 1840 (43), vol. XXIII, p. 127.
2 P.P. 1840 (217), vol. XXIV, p. 205.
3 P.P. 1894 (c. 7421), vol. XXXV, p. 27, para. 39.
4 P.P. 1863 (3170), vol. XVIII, p. 307.
5 P.P. 1888 (361), vol. XX, Q. 801.
6 P.P. 1892 (c. 6708-vi), vol. XXXV, Q. 8373.
7 P.P. 1806 (268), vol. III, pp. 739, 623.
8 P.P. 1840 (43), vol. XXIII, p. 156.
9 D. Bythell, *The Handloom Weavers*, Cambridge, 1969, pp. 52-3.
10 P.P. 1802-3 (71), vol. V, p. 306.
11 P.P. 1812 (247), vol. II, p. 235.
12 P.P. 1840 (217), vol. XXIV, p. 50.
13 See C. Gulvin, *The Tweedmakers*, Newton Abbot, 1973, pp. 36, 55.
14 See J. Thirsk, 'Industry in the Countryside', in F. J. Fisher, ed, *Essays in the Economic History of Tudor and Stuart England*, 1961.
15 P.P. 1863 (3170), vol. XVIII, pp. 370-71.
16 See P. Boyaval, *La Lutte contre le 'Sweating System'*, Paris, 1911, p. 344; this is still much the fullest account of the long campaign against sweating. P.P. 1907 (290), vol. VI, QQ. 446-51.
17 P.P. 1908 (246), vol. VIII, QQ. 2706-7, 2713, and 2762.
18 P.P. 1843 (430), vol. XIII, p. 451.
19 P.P. 1907 (290), vol. VI, Q. 1401.
20 ibid., Q. 389.
21 P.P. 1889 (331), vol. XIV, part I, Q. 26282.
22 M. E. Bulkley, *Studies in the Minimum Wage, No. 3, Boxmaking*, 1915, p. 67.
23 P.P. 1889 (331), vol. XIV, part I, Q. 28795.
24 P.P. 1840 (217), vol. XXIV, p. 71.
25 J. D. Chambers, 'Three Essays on the Population and Economy of the Midlands', in D. V. Glass and D. E. C. Eversley, eds., *Population in History*, 1965, esp. pp. 332-4; D. Levine, 'The Demographic Implications of Rural Industrialisation: a Family Reconstitution Study of Shepshed, Leicestershire, 1600-1851', *Social History*, 1976, No. 2, p.185.

26 See E. A. Wrigley, 'Family Limitation in Pre-industrial England', in *Economic History Review*, 1966, second series, vol. XIX, pp. 82-109. Dr Wrigley's celebrated article makes no attempt to relate the changes in fertility which he demonstrates at Colyton to any developments which may have been taking place in the local economy.

27 H. J. Habakkuk, *Population Growth and Economic Development since 1750*, Leicester, 1971, p. 44; J. T. Krause, 'Some Aspects of Population Change 1690-1790', in E. L. Jones and G. E. Mingay, eds, *Land, Labour and Population in the Industrial Revolution*, 1967, p. 203.

28 For a summary in English of Professor Braun's work, see his essay 'The Impact of Cottage Industry on an Agricultural Population', in D. S. Landes, ed., *The Rise of Capitalism*, New York, 1966, pp. 53-64. For a general discussion of this problem in a broader European context, see W. Fischer, 'Rural Industrialisation and Population Change', *Comparative Studies in Society and History*, 1973, vol. XV, pp. 158-70, and Hans Medick, 'The Proto-Industrial Family Economy: the Structural Function of Household and Family during the Transition from Peasant Society to Industrial Captalism', *Social History*, 1976, No. 3, pp. 291-315.

29 P.P. 1840 (217), vol. XXIV, pp. 69, 74-5.

30 P.P. 1888 (124), vol. LXXX, p. 495.

31 P.P. 1843 (431), vol. XIV, p. 573.

32 See Bythell, op. cit., pp. 235-45.

33 See Bythell, op. cit., pp. 63-5.

34 P.P. 1887 (331), vol. LXXXIX, p. 7.

35 P.P. 1836 (40), vol. XXXIV, p. 583.

36 P.P. 1840 (43), vol. XXIII, p. 289.

37 P.P. 1845 (609), vol. XV, p. 113.

38 P.P. 1890 (169), vol. XVII, p. 299, para. 185.

39 P.P. 1840 (43), vol. XXIII, p. 307; P.P. 1836 (40), vol. XXXIV, p. 586.

40 P.P. 1876 (1443), vol. XXIX, p. lxxxi.

41 P.P. 1845 (641), vol. XV, Q. 1832.

42 P.P. 1893-4 (c. 6894-xxiii), vol. XXXVII, part I, p. 683.

43 P.P. 1907 (290), vol. VI, Q. 2701.

44 P.P. 1836 (40), vol. XXXIV, p. 454.

45 See Bythell, op. cit., pp. 76-80.

46 P.P. 1864 (3414), vol. XXII, p. 163.

47 P.P. 1864 (3414), vol. XXII, p. 86.

48 P.P. 1845 (618), vol. XV, Q. 929.

49 P.P. 1856 (343), vol. XIII, Q. 449, author's italics.

50 P.P. 1887 (331), vol. LXXXIX, p. 6.

51 See D. Bythell, op. cit., pp. 89-92.

52 For fragmentary evidence of the self-made man in cotton, see S. J. Chapman and F. J. Maquis, 'The Recruiting of the Employing Classes from the Ranks of Wage-Earners in the Cotton Industry', *Journal of the Royal Statistical Society*, 1912, vol. LXXV, pp. 293-306; for fuller evidence on hosiery, see C. K. Erickson, *British Industrialists: Steel and Hosiery*, Cambridge 1959, chapter 4, *passim*.

53 P.P. 1840 (43), vol. XXIII, p. 407.
54 P.P. 1893-4 (c. 6894-xxiii), vol. XXXVII, part I, p. 578.
55 P.P. 1888 (448), vol. XXI, Q. 12299 *et seq.*
56 P.P. 1863 (3170), vol. XVIII, p. 385.
57 For a discussion of this problem, see G. Stedman Jones, *Outcast London*, Oxford, 1971, chapter 2.
58 See the evidence of D. Sholto Douglas, a Shoreditch box-maker, to the Select Committee on homework, P.P. 1908 (246), vol. VIII, QQ. 189-90.
59 P.P. 1863 (3170), vol. XVIII, p. 314.
60 P.P. 1908 (246), vol. VIII, Q. 1568.
61 See C. Gulvin, *The Tweedmakers*, Newton Abbot, 1973, pp. 78 *et seq.*, 140 *et seq.*
62 P.P. 1845 (641), vol. XV, Q. 3921.
63 See G. H. Wood, 'Real Wages and the Standard of Comfort since 1850' *J.R.S.S.*, 1909, vol. LXXIII, reprinted in E. M. Carus-Wilson, ed., *Essays in Economic History*, vol. 3, 1962, pp. 132-43; and S. Pollard and D. W. Crossley, *The Wealth of Britan*, 1968, chapters 7 and 8.
64 P.P. 1889 (331), vol. XIV part I, Q. 28275.
65 For an overall view of the rise of the mass-market in Britain in the fourth quarter of the nineteenth century, see C. H. Wilson's important article 'Economy and Society in Late Victorian Britain', *Economic History Review*, 1965, vol. XVIII, pp. 183-98.
66 See for example R. H. Tawney, *Studies in the Minimum Wage. No. 2: Tailoring*, 1915, pp. 2-6.
67 See P. Head, 'The Boot and Shoe Industry', in D. H. Aldcroft, ed., *The Development of British Industry and Foreign Competition 1875-1914*, 1968, pp. 158-85.

PART THREE

Chapter 5

1   S. and B. Webb, *History of Trade Unionism*, 1911 ed., p. 35.
2   P.P. 1892 (c. 6795-VI), vol. XXXVI, part II, QQ. 15242-4; P.P. 1876 (1443), vol. XXX, Q. 7746 *et. seq;* P.P. 1907 (291), vol. VI, QQ. 416-9.
3   P.P. 1887 (331), vol. LXXXIX, p. 11; P.P. 1888 (361), vol. XX, QQ. 704, 933; P.P. 1889 (331), vol. XIV, part I, QQ. 30189-95.
4   P.P. 1840 (217), vol. XXIV, p. 251.
5   S. and B. Webb, op. cit., pp. 39-40.
6   A. Aspinall, *The Early English Trade Unions*, 1949.
7   See D. Bythell, *The Handloom Weavers*, Cambridge, 1969, chapter 8, *passim.*
8   See G. D. H. Cole, *Attempts at General Union*, 1953, Chapters 6 and 9.
9   P.P. 1840 (43), vol. XXIII, p. 177.
10 ibid., p. 178.

11 ibid., p. 236.
12 See the report of Joseph Fletcher to the handloom weavers' Royal Commission (P.P. 1840 (217), vol. XXIV), and also J. M. Prest, *The Industrial Revolution in Coventry*, Oxford, 1960, on which the following account is based.
13 P.P. 1840 (217), vol. XXIV, p. 257. Fletcher's italics.
14 For a full account, see Prest, op. cit., pp. 79-127.
15 P.P. 1840 (43), vol. XXIII, pp. 323-4.
16 C. Stella Davies, *History of Macclesfield*, Manchester, 1961, pp. 192-5.
17 P.P. 1892 (c. 6795-IV), vol. XXXVI, part I, QQ. 18434-5.
18 ibid., Q. 17654.
19 P.P. 1893-4 (c. 6894-VII), vol. XXXII, QQ. 20014, 20216-7.
20 For general accounts of trade unions in hosiery, see F. A. Wells, *The British Hosiery Trade: its History and Organisation*, 1935; A. T. Patterson, *Radical Leicester 1780-1850*, 1954; R. A. Church, *Economic and Social Change in a Midland Town*, 1966.
21 Church, op. cit., p. 51; for details of one such union in the Leicester glove trade, see the report of the Royal Commission on the framework knitters, especially the evidence of Joseph Biggs, Thomas Winters, Joseph Meadows and Francis Warner.
22 P.P. 1845 (618), vol. XV, Q. 3443.
23 On Mundella, see W. H. G. Armytage, *A. J. Mundella*, 1951; for an account of the working of the Nottingham Board, see Church, op. cit., pp. 270-77, on which the following paragraph is based.
24 See, for example, the memorandum submitted by Thomas Hunt, master of a small Leicester frame-shop (P.P. 1845 (618), vol. XV, p. 174).
25 Armytage, op. cit., p. 319.
26 P.P. 1843 (431), vol. XIV, p. 805.
27 See Lord's Select Committee on sweating, P.P. 1889 (331), vol. XIV, part I, QQ. 25654-8, 25800-8.
28 ibid., Q. 29918.
29 P.P. 1892 (c. 6795-VI), vol. XXXVI, part II, QQ. 14193, 14597-8.
30 P.P. 1889 (331), vol. XIV, part I, Q. 28878.
31 P.P. 1892 (c. 6795-VI), vol. XXXVI, part II, Q. 14193.
32 P.P. 1893-4 (c. 6894-IX), vol. XXXIV, Appendix 115, p. 683.
33 S. and B. Webb, op. cit., p. 423.
34 For a full account, see J. Ball, 'Account of Northampton Boot and Shoemakers Strike', in *Trade Societies and Strikes* (Papers presented to the Glasgow meeting of the National Association for the Promotion of Social Science), 1860: also V. A. Hatley, 'Monsters in Campbell Square', *Northants Past and Present*, 1966-7, vol. IV, No. I, pp. 51-9.
35 Quoted in Hatley, op. cit., p. 58.
36 H. A. Clegg, A. Fox, and A. F. Thompson, *History of British Trade Unions 1889-1910*, Oxford, 1964, p. 25.
37 For a full account of trade unionism in the boot and shoe trade in the late nineteenth century, see A. Fox, *History of the National Union of Boot and Shoe Operatives*, 1957, and E. Brunner, 'The Origins of

Industrial Peace', *Oxford Economic Papers*, 1949, New Series, vol. I, pp. 247-59.

38 See Fox, op. cit., pp. 143, 203.

39 See D. Jones, *Before Rebecca*, 1973, p. 18; and D. Williams, 'Chartism in Wales' in A. Briggs, ed., *Chartist Studies*, 1962, pp. 222-3, 229-32.

40 For different interpretations of Pentridge, see E. P. Thompson, op. cit., p. 660 and M. I. Thomis, *Politics and Society in Nottingham 1785-1835*, 1969, chapter 10.

41 For details, see Thomis, op. cit; R. A. Church, *Economic and Social Change in a Midland Town: Victorian Nottingham 1815-1900*, 1966; and A. T. Patterson, *Radical Leicester 1780-1850*,1954.

42 D. J. 'Chartism and the Spitalfields Silk-Weavers', *Economic History Review*, 1967, vol. XX, pp. 482-93.

43 J. M. Prest, *The Industrial Revolution on Coventry*, Oxford, 1960, p. 139.

44 H. Fearn, 'Chartism in Suffolk', in Briggs, ed., op. cit., p. 149.

45 For some contrasts between 'town' and 'country' support for parliamentary reform among the Lancashire handloom weavers in the 1830s and 1840s, see Bythell, op. cit., pp. 219-30.

46 R. B. Pugh, 'Chartism in Somerset and Wiltshire' and J. F. C. Harrison, 'Chartism in Leicester', in Briggs, ed., op. cit., pp. 216 and 100.

47 ibid., pp. 3, 7 and 9.

48 D. Thompson, ed., *The Early Chartists*, 1971, p. 12.

49 J. T. Ward, *Chartism*, 1973, esp. chapter 4.

50 For a general discussion of this problem, see J. Vincent, *The Formation of the Liberal Party*, 1966, and B. Harrison and P. Hollis, 'Chartism, Liberalism, and the Life of Robert Lowery', *English Historical Review*, 1972, vol. LXXXVII.

51 For details of Parliamentary elections in the years after 1885, see H. Pelling, *Social Geography of British Elections*, 1967.

52 E. J. Hobsbawm, 'The Machine Breakers', in *Labouring Men*, 1964, p. 7.

53 For differing interpretations of the general phenomenon of Luddism, see Thompson, op. cit., esp. chapter 14, and M. I. Thomis, *The Luddites*, 1970, *passim*.

54 For a contemporary account which demonstrates this mixture of motives, see W. Felkin, *History of the Machine-wrought Hosiery and Lace Manufactures*, 1867, pp. 230 *et. seq.*

55 ibid., pp. 237-42.

56 See Bythell, op. cit., pp. 197-204; for an eye-witness account of the Coventry riot of 1831, see Joseph Gutteridge's 'Autobiography' in V. E. Chancellor, ed., *Master and Artisan in Victorian England*, 1969, pp. 101-2.

57 For the west of England industry, see J. de. L. Mann, *The Cloth Industry in the West of England from 1640 to 1880*, Oxford, 1971, esp. chapters 5 and 6.

58 For a detailed study of the Christian Socialists and cooperation, see T. Christensen, *Origin and History of Christian Socialism 1848-1854*, Aarhus, Denmark, 1962, esp. chapters 4 and 6.

59 P. d'A. Jones, *The Christian Socialist Revival 1877-1914*, Princeton, New Jersey, 1968, p. 445.
60 P.P. 1888 (361), vol. XX, QQ. 1373-1416.
61 P.P. 1889 (331), *vol. XIV, part 1*, evidence of W. J. Walker, QQ. 31487-99.
62 P. Boyaval, *La Lutte contre le Sweating System*, Paris, 1911, pp. 145-6.
63 P.P. 1806 (268), vol. III, pp. 734-5.
64 ibid., p. 573.
65 ibid., p. 583.
66 P.P. 1809 (111), vol. III, p. 311. For a fuller account of the cotton weavers' Parliamentary efforts during the war years, see D. Bythell, *The Handloom Weavers*, Cambridge, 1969, pp. 148-55.
67 The reports of the two Committees are in P.P. 1812 (247), vol. II and P.P. 1819 (193), vol. V.
68 It should be noted, however, that the law was not immediately introduced in its full rigour, and that some of its most potentially harmful provisions - such as banning the supplementation of low earnings by various 'allowances' - were modified in practice: see Bythell, op. cit, chapter 10, *passim*, and M. E. Rose, 'The Allowance System under the New Poor Law', *Economic History Review*, 1966, vol. XIX, pp. 607-20.
69 See Bythell, op. cit., pp. 158-68.
70 The report and the appendixes of evidence are in P.P. 1845 (609), (618) and (641), vol. XV.
71 P.P. 1854-5 (421), vol. XIV.
72 P.P. 1871 (c. 326), vol. XXXVI.
73 See, for example, the indignant complaints of J. B. Maple, MP (of the furniture firm) about White's activities in P.P. 1888 (361), vol. XX, QQ. 5797, 5896; and the evidence of Walter Bassano, a Midlands magistrate and coal-owner, in P.P. 1889 (165), vol. XIII, Q. 22836.
74 P.P. 1890 (169), vol. XVII, p. 301, para, 204.
75 P. Boyaval, op. cit., p. 13.
76 P.P. 1893-4 (c. 7063-1), vol. XXXIX, part I, QQ. 3734 and 3805.
77 P.P. 1894 (c. 7421), vol. XXXV, pp. 116, 137.
78 C. Smith, *The Case for Wages Boards*, 1908, pp. 35-6.
79 Boyaval, op. cit., p. 365.
80 ibid., pp. 376-419.
81 For details, see published *Annual Reports of the National Anti-Sweating League*, Manchester, 1906 onwards. For a full account of the 1909 legislation, and of its subsequent extensions, see D. Sells, *The British Trade Boards System*, 1923.
82 P.P. 1876 (1443), vol. XXX, Q. 7737.
83 P.P. 1908 (246), vol. VIII, QQ. 2745-9.
84 ibid., QQ. 2729, 2733.
85 In fairness to the frequently maligned political economists of the early and mid-nineteenth century it should be pointed out that many of them *were* sympathetic to the general notion that the development of 'machinery' should in some sense be 'controlled' by the State: but they

rarely came up with any specific practical proposals. See D. P. O'Brien, *The Classical Economists*, Oxford, 1975, pp. 224-9, 279-80.
86 P.P. 1890 (169), vol. XVII, p. 299, para. 182.
87 P.P. 1854-5 (421), vol. XIV, QQ. 2844-6.
88 The standard history is still B. L. Hutchins and B. A. Harrison, *A History of Factory Legislation*, 2nd edn., 1911, from which the following paragraphs are derived. For a recent interpretation of the effects of the law on the place of homeworking, especially in London at the very end of the nineteenth century, see J. A. Schmiechen, 'State Reform and the Local Economy' in *Economic History Review*, 1975, 2nd series, vol. XXVIII, pp. 413-28, where, however, undue emphasis appears to be put on the role of legislation in keeping homeworking alive, to the exclusion of the relevant economic factors.
89 See Schmiechen, op. cit., pp. 421-6.
90 P.P. 1890 (169), vol. XVII, p. 300, para. 186.
91 See Boyaval, op. cit., pp. 159-62.
92 C. Black, *Sweated Industry*, 1907, pp. 21-2.
93 P.P. 1888 (445), vol. XXI, QQ. 10959 and 11009 *et seq.*
94 P.P. 1888 (361), vol. XX, Q. 1330; P.P. 1890 vol. XVII, p. 295, para. 149.
95 Boyaval, op. cit., pp. 350-51.
96 P.P. 1908 (4422), vol XXXIV, para. 13.
97 See Boyaval, op. cit., pp. 260-300.
98 P.P. 1908 (246), vol. VIII, QQ. 3676, 3817.
99 P.P. 1907 (290), vol. VI, Q. 3937 *et seq.*, 882.
100 P.P. 1908 (4423), vol. XXXIV, Q. 6092.
101 P.P. 1908 (246), vol. VIII, p. 14, para. 38.
102 P.P. 1907 (290), vol. VI, Q. 4436.
103 ibid., Q. 4535.
104 ibid., Q. 4563.
105 See especially the League's *5th and 6th Reports*, Manchester, 1911 and 1912.
106 R. H. Tawney, *Studies in the Minimum Wage, No. 2: Tailoring*, 1915, p. 4.
107 ibid., pp. 24-38.
108 ibid., p. 35.

Conclusion

1 See, *inter alia*, C. and R. Tilly, 'Agenda for European Economic History in the 1970s', *Journal of Economic History*, 1971, vol. XXXI, pp. 184-198; F. F. Mendels, 'Protoindustrialisation: The First Phase of the Industrialisation Process', *Journal of Economic History*, 1972, vol. XXXII, pp. 241-61; W. Fischer, 'Rural Industrialisation and Population Change', *Comparative Studies in Society and History*, 1973, vol. XV, pp. 158-70.

2 Tilly, op. cit., p. 187.
3 Mendels, op. cit., p. 242.
4 Fischer, op. cit., pp. 160–1.
5 Mendels, op. cit., p. 244.
6 ibid., p. 245.
7 ibid, p. 246
8 E. F. Schumacher, *Small is Beautiful*, 1974, p. 145.
9 ibid., p. 156.
10 ibid., p. 27.
11 ibid., pp. 155, 147.
12 ibid., pp. 126–7.
13 ibid., p. 145.
14 ibid., p. 156.

List of Principal Government Publications Consulted

The publications are listed in chronological order

Abbreviations: P.P. Parliamentary Papers
R.C.   Royal Commission
S.C.   Select Committee
(H.L.)   House of Lords. All Select Committees are Committees of the House of Commons, unless otherwise indicated.

P.P. 1802-3 (30) and (71), vol. V; P.P. 1803-4 (66), vol. V; P.P. 1805 (105), vol. III; P.P. 1806 (268), vol. III. Reports of the S.C.s on the woollen manufacture of England.

P.P. 1808 (177), vol. II; P.P. 1809 (111), vol. III; P. P. 1810-11 (232), vol. II. Reports of the S.C.s on the petitions of cotton manufacturers and weavers.

P.P 1812 (247) and (349), vol. II; P.P. 1819 (193), vol. V. Reports of the S.C.s on the framework knitters' petitions.

P.P. 1824 (420), vol. VI. Report of the S.C. on poor rate returns.

P.P 1826 (404), vol. IV; P.P. 1826-7 (88), (237) and (550), vol. V. Reports of the S.C. on emigration from the United Kingdom.

P.P. 1834 (44), vol. XXVII et seq. Report of the R.C. on the Poor Laws.

P.P. 1834 (556), vol. X; P.P. 1835 (341), vol. XIII. Reports of the S.C. on handloom weavers' petitions.

P.P. 1836 (40), vol. XXXIV. Report of the R.C. on the condition of the poorer classes in Ireland.

P.P. 1837-8 (681), vol. XVIII. Report of the S.C. on the administration of the Poor Law Amendment Act.

P.P. 1839 (159), vol. XLII; P.P. 1840 (43), vol. XXIII; P.P. 1840 (217), (220), and (636), vol. XXIV; P.P. 1841 (296), vol. X. Reports of the R.C. on the handloom weavers.

P.P. 1843 (430), vol. XIII; P.P. 1843 (431), vol. XIV; P.P. 1843 (432), vol. XV. Reports of the R.C. on children's employment in trades and manufactures.

P.P. 1845 (609), (618) and (641), vol. XV. Reports of the R.C. on the condition of the framework knitters.

P.P. 1856 (343), vol. XIII. Report of the S.C. on masters and operatives (equitable councils of conciliation).

P.P. 1860 (307), vol. XXII. Report of the S.C. on the best means of settling disputes between masters and operatives.

P.P. 1863 (3170), vol. XVIII; P.P. 1864 (3414), vol. XXII; P.P. 1865 (3548), vol. XX; P.P. 1866 (3678), vol. XXIV; P.P. 1867 (3796), vol. XVI. Reports of the R.C. on children's employment.

P.P. 1871 (c. 326), vol. XXXVI. Report of the R.C. on the truck system.

P.P. 1876 (1443), vols. XXIX and XXX. Reports of the R.C. on the working of the Factory and workshop acts.

P.P. 1887 (331), vol. LXXXIX; P.P. 1888 (c. 5513) vol. LXXXVI. Reports from the labour correspondent of the Board of Trade on the sweating system (London and Leeds).

P.P. 1888 (142), vol. LXXX. Report of the Commissioner on the Honiton lace industry.

P.P. 1888 (361), vol. XX; P.P. 1888 (448), vol. XXI; P.P. 1889 (165), vol. XIII; P.P. 1889 (331), vol. XIV; P.P. 1890 (169), vol. XVII. Reports of the S.C. (H.L.) on the sweating system.

P.P. 1892 (c. 6708), vols. XXIV and XXXV; P.P. 1892 (c. 6795), vol. XXXVI; P.P. 1893-4 (c. 6894), vols. XXXII, XXXIV and XXXVII; P.P. 1893-4 (c. 7063), vol. XXXIX; P.P. 1894 (c. 7421), vol. XXXV. Reports of the R.C. on labour.

P.P. 1907 (290), vol. VI; P.P. 1908 (246), vol. VIII. Reports of the S.C. on homework.

P.P. 1908 (4422) and (4423), vol. XXXIV. Reports of the S.C. on the working of the fair wages resolution.

P.P. 1909 (4633), vol. XXI. Annual Reports of the Medical Officers of Health for 1907.

Index

279